"Christians . . . have been uncharacteristically diffident about the meaning of the 9/11 attacks, except to say that it's not this and it's not that, and to venture generally that we should hate evil and love good. . . . [They] have imposed on themselves a kind of gag rule, apparently counting it the better part of humility. To be sure, there has been plenty of pulpiteering . . .—preachers in the line of Zedekiah son of Kenaanah (1 Kings 22:11) who bravely take positions that everybody agrees with already. Others . . . are so careful not to 'darken counsel' that they do not shed much light at all on this befuddled country. Their selected texts are the ones that best illustrate that, when all is said and done, we cannot know what God is doing and why. . . . Rather than theology by negation (i.e., 'we can't say this, we can't say that'), why not a more helpful theology of fullness of truth (i.e., 'this is there, and that is there too'). Let us not tender the world an empty tin cup. . . . Ours is a Spirit of boldness, not timidity, that compels us to speak something—not nothing—into a world that, since September 11, 2001, still picks through the ashes of despondency and stumbles at noon as in the dark."

ANDREE SEU, OCTOBER 20, 2001

"He is sifting out the hearts of men before His judgment seat:
Oh! Be swift my soul, to answer Him!"

JULIA WARD HOWE,
"THE BATTLE HYMN OF THE REPUBLIC," 1862

GOD'S JUDGMENTS

Interpreting History and the Christian Faith

Steven J. Keillor

IVP Academic

An imprint of InterVarsity Press
Downers Grove, Illinois

To Jeremy

InterVarsity Press
P.O. Box 1400, Downers Grove, IL 60515-1426
World Wide Web: www.ivpress.com
E-mail: email@ivpress.com

InterVarsity Press® is the book-publishing division of InterVarsity Christian Fellowship/USA®, a student movement active on campus at hundreds of universities, colleges and schools of nursing in the United States of America, and a member movement of the International Fellowship of Evangelical Students. For information about local and regional activities, write Public Relations Dept., InterVarsity Christian Fellowship/USA, 6400 Schroeder Rd., P.O. Box 7895, Madison, WI 53707-7895, or visit the IVCF website at <www.intervarsity.org>.

Design: Cindy Kiple
Images: Battle of Bunker Hill: Snark/Art Resource, NY
    Battle of Fair Oaks: Art Resource, NY
    Lincoln by tent: Getty Images
    civil war: Art Resource, NY
    underground railroad: Art Resource, NY
    twin towers: David Allocca/Getty Images
    Lincoln: Vladimir Ivanov/istockphoto
    white crosses: Fred de Groot/istockphoto
    cross beams: Lowell Gordon/istockphoto
    aftermath of hurricane: Scott Leigh/istock photo

ISBN-13: 978-0-8308-2565-3

Printed in the United States of America ∞

Library of Congress Cataloging-in-Publication Data

Keillor, Steven J. (Steven James).
  God's judgments: interpreting history and the Christian faith/Steven J. Keillor.
    p. cm.
  Includes bibliographical references and index.
  ISBN-13: 978-0-8308-2565-3 (pbk.: alk. paper)
  ISBN-10: 0-8308-2565-7 (pbk.: alk. paper)
  1. Judgment of God. 2. History—Religious aspects—Christianity. 3. United States—History—Religious aspects—Christianity. I. Title.
BT180.J8K45 2006
231.7'6—dc22
                                           2006030493

P	19	18	17	16	15	14	13	12	11	10	9	8	7	6	5	4	3	2	1
Y	22	21	20	19	18	17	16	15	14	13	12	11	10	09	08	07			

Contents

Foreword

As he demonstrated with an earlier book from InterVarsity Press (*This Rebellious House: American History and the Truths of Christianity* [1996]), Steven Keillor is nothing if not an engaged and wise Christian historian. He is engaged because he uses a combination of historical expertise and Christian faith to say something specific about the contemporary state of the world. He is Christian in boldly using his faith to interpret current events. He is wise in putting both historical expertise and Christian reasoning to use carefully, judiciously and transparently. And he is a historian who does his homework thoroughly on the records of the past and important interpretations of the past, before he advances his own conclusions.

In *God's Judgments* Keillor wants to interpret events as a Christian not just by expecting Scripture and classical theology to provide moral standards for evaluating historical events but by actually seeking in those sources the means of saying, with some definiteness, what God is accomplishing in history. Of course, many others have been doing the same, and for a very long time—but these other efforts are usually made by people shooting from the hip theologically, running roughshod over serious historical labor, and appealing only to those who already share their own angle of vision.

Keillor's books are different because he knows his history, he knows theology, and he knows how important it is to argue logically and clearly. Yet he is attempting what few other academic Christian historians, who are all too aware of the pitfalls of such attempts, have been willing to take on.

In his earlier book, Keillor offered an explicitly theological interpretation of the entire history of the United States. With this one, he ponders the judgment of nations and, in particular, the work of God as it may have been connected with the events of September 11, 2001. Even more than in the former volume, this book brings clearly to the surface his Christian framework of interpretation.

In a word, *God's Judgments* argues that events like 9/11 can and should be identified as judgments of God against nations. The argument is unusually well thought out. It breaks down into something like the following steps:

1. Snap Christian judgments about God's purposes for 9/11 were inadequate for how they were stated—especially by Pat Robertson and Jerry Falwell, who treated the event as divine punishment for the United States' toleration of abortion on demand and out-of-control sexuality. But it was not wrong, in principle, to make such judgments.

2. Attempts to interpret the history of the United States on the basis of a special divine covenant with this particular nation are misguided, since God's concern is for a people from every tribe and nation.

3. In the Old Testament, God's judgment of the nations was a very important theme (e.g., in book of Daniel, or the judgment of Tyre for rejoicing in Jerusalem's fall, which is Keillor's interpretation of Ezek 26 and Zech 9:4).

4. While the New Testament does not specifically identify God's judgments against the nations, neither does it deny that they have ended.

5. Moreover, sound theological reasoning based in the New Testament demands the conclusion that God's judgments of the nation continue in this age and that believers can identify them. This conclusion comes from what Keillor describes as a proper understanding of Christ as the Son of Man who descended from glory to become the humblest of humans ("even to death on a cross"), who was raised from death, who ascended, and who will come again at the End of the Age to bring all things to a God-glorifying conclusion. Responsible Christian believers not only can but must employ these truths in order to be faithful in responding to the saving work of the Son of Man (i.e., the authority of Christ extends to the nations now as an anticipation of what will come more fully at the end).

6. Worldview reasoning, such as evangelical academics often apply to public policy, is inadequate. It amounts to an acceptance of faulty Enlightenment standards and detracts from the edification that judgment-thinking could supply for the contemporary church. Worldview reasoning depends upon a large measure of procedural Enlightenment rationality and so moves toward a functional Deism.

◆ ◆ ◆

When Keillor moves from stating general principles to interpreting historical cases, things become very interesting, especially for those who have independent knowledge of the cases or who have pondered the general complexity found in all historical situations.

7. In Keillor's view, a historically informed Christian believer could hold that the destruction of Washington, D.C., by the British during the War of 1812 was an act of divine judgment on the leadership, but not the people, of the United States. Leaders like Presidents Jefferson and Madison were gentlemen infidels whose policies (like the Embargo of 1807ff.) represented a fallacious utopian misapplication of the power that God had ordained for governments to use. The people at large, however, were in the process of turning to God (the Sec-

ond Great Awakening) and so were spared. (Questions for Keillor arising from comparisons make things more interesting at this point: the Mexican War was a more egregious violation of divine standards than Jefferson's embargo, and yet in it the United States was successful.)

8. The Civil War presents the strongest case for seeing divine judgment falling on the United States. It represented God's retribution for the sins of slavery that extended back to the seventeenth century, that were enshrined in the Constitution by the Deist Founding Fathers, and that were continually reaffirmed by white believers in the decades between the nation's founding and 1860. (Again, a further questions arises: why did God's judgment not fall on the nation after the end of Reconstruction in 1876 when once again a sinful subjugation of African Americans took place and with the full compliance of the American government and most American churches?)

9. Conventional analyses of 9/11 fall far short:

   - The Right wants to defend a free market in goods and services, but not in ideas, morals and culture.

   - The Left wants to defend a free market in ideas, morals and culture, but not in goods and services.

   - The Center wants to regulate both (moderately) but on pragmatic grounds rather than with principles.

   - Pat Robertson and Jerry Falwell merely transferred their personal ideologies into snap, unfounded judgments.

10. A better way is to look seriously at the reasons radical Muslims gave for why they attacked the U.S.

   a. Because of U.S. support for Israel.

   b. Because of U.S. sanctions against Iraq.

   c. Because of U.S. troops in Saudi Arabia, who were there in order to protect the flow of Saudi oil to the U.S., which was required because of the West's insatiable demand for petroleum.

   d. Because of U.S. support of globalization and globalized free trade that (in the view of Islamists) enriched the West and impoverished less developed nations. (This is the sphere that the American conservative Right treats as amoral market self-regulation.)

   e. Because of decadent Western culture, exemplified by Hollywood's export of sexually explicit entertainment.

   f. Because of Western decadence more generally, which presents the fruits of a Christian heritage.

    g. Because of U.S. responsibility for creating the *mujahideen* in Afghanistan in order to fight the Soviets, a process that led to the U.S. equipping the very ones who had cause for wanting to attack the U.S.

11. Keillor argues that reasons (a) and (b) do not lead to the conclusion that God was judging the United States, but that several of the others might. For example,

- (e) A holy God must be angered by a nation benefiting from businesses that aim to seduce others for profit.

- (f) If the West has enjoyed gospel preaching for centuries and has then turned against the gospel, is it not a fitting irony that Muslims are used to remind Westerners of the gospel's high moral standards? In other words, apostasy in Scripture is a communal as well as personal problem, and the West, in Christian terms, looks apostate.

- (g) Scripture teaches that governments wield the sword by the will of God, but also that governments are responsible to God for how they use the sword. If the U.S. used military might unwisely in the Cold War, it is no surprise if it reaps the evil fruit of that use (and the same might be said for the former Soviet Union as well).

◆ ◆ ◆

Finally, Keillor reasons that cautious yet biblically based reasoning can led to the conclusion that September 11, 2001, represented God's judgment on the United States for stimulating economic greed, for promoting immorality in other parts of the world and for misusing the nation's military might. In his view, if such conclusions manage to offend the Right (which doesn't regard economic greed as a sin), the Left (which doesn't treat immoral cultural exports as sin), the Center (which armed the *mujahideen* in Afghanistan because any means was justified in checking the Soviet Union), and evangelicals (who employ worldview reasoning and who take refuge in agnosticism about what God is accomplishing now), so much the better for stimulating straightforward Christian thinking.

    The clarity of Steven Keillor's theological reasoning as well as the boldness of his historical conclusions demand very serious attention. As myself an evangelical who is partial to worldview reasoning, I am not sure he has entirely convinced me. But I know he has made me think, and think hard.

Mark A. Noll
Francis A. McAnaney Professor of History
University of Notre Dame

Acknowledgments

Space does not permit acknowledgment of my innumerable debts to others for Christian teaching and fellowship and for training and encouragement in historical scholarship. Yet I must thank my wife, Margaret, for her support for my research and writing over many years.

The endnotes and bibliography list my many specific debts to other writers. For more personal input, my thanks to George Marsden for his comments on my paper on testimony, judgment and Lincoln's second inaugural address, to Mark Noll for his insightful comments on an earlier draft, and to the other (anonymous) reader of it. Rick Kennedy's work on testimony has aided me. I am not just indulging in the usual cliché of academic acknowledgements when I add that responsibility for this work rests with me alone. No other historian has expressed eagerness to apply the idea of divine judgment to specific historical events—nor have the above-mentioned historians, who cannot be held responsible for this book. Thus, odd as it may sound, my exploration of that idea began during my independent campaign for Minnesota's State Senate, in 2002, as I observed the shortcomings of public commemorations of the one-year anniversary of September 11. As in the captivity stories of Daniel Boone's day, the only way to freedom may be to run the gauntlet and get whacked at from both sides. That explicitly Christian but independent campaign was a liberating experience (and a friendly, relatively painless one), made possible by many fine Christian people who helped me—the Gollys, the Malones, the Pritchards, the Teichroews and others. Thanks go to several pastors who encouraged my campaign and, more importantly, discussed the idea of divine judgment with me during it: Kevin Carr, Doug Green, Ivan Fiske and Jeff Touchinski. I owe a special debt to Pastor Carr for years of fine expository preaching; he is not responsible for my exact theological views, however. My thanks also go to Gary Deddo, IVP editor, for guiding this work through the process and into print.

Introduction

In essence, this book began as an attempt to answer Andree Seu's call for a "theology of fullness of truth" about the tragedy of September 11, 2001, rather than the "kind of gag rule" by which evangelicals, especially, were restricted to saying "we cannot know what God is doing and why." Specifically, God's judgments were the subtext: we cannot know that God is judging the nation. Yet September 11 is only the starting point. This book continues on, and ends, as an attempt to respond to Os Guinness's call, in *Prophetic Untimeliness,* for "[a] rediscovery of the hard and the unpopular themes of the gospel"—here, God's judgments—that can "be such a rediscovery of the whole gospel that the result may lead to reformation and revival."[1] The inadequacy of our thinking about September 11 can point the way to a return to old Christian themes that decades of peace and prosperity seemed to have rendered obsolete, until that tragedy exposed the holes in our peace, prosperity and security.

Talk of revival overstates my case, for I am a historian and not a theologian or a pastor. Given my calling and use of September 11 as a starting point, this book focuses on God's judgments on the nations in history, not on his judgment of individuals in history or at the Last Judgment—topics more closely associated with revival. I do not deny or minimize the latter judgments but argue from the lesser and the obscure to the greater and more obvious: if God judges nations, and one like the U.S. not mentioned in Scripture, then how much more does he judge individuals, as clearly stated in Scripture. I stress Christ's reign over the nations more than the substitutionary atonement he offers to individuals, but safeguarding the latter doctrine is very much one of my purposes. If divine judgment against sin fell on the innocent Son, then how much more is judgment on sinful nations and individuals a valid gospel theme, albeit "hard and unpopular"? Judgment and salvation are two sides of the one coin of God's righteous activity

---

[1]Andree Seu, "True Perspectives," *World,* October 20, 2001, p. 41; Os Guinness, *Prophetic Untimeliness: A Challenge to the Idol of Relevance* (Grand Rapids: Baker, 2003), p. 100; see also p. 20.

in history. By no means is this book meant as doom and gloom. At any time, the reader may mentally flip the coin and see the salvation offered through Christ's atoning work—albeit one partly defined by being a salvation from judgment rather than one left free for us to define as what Guinness calls "therapeutic self-concern" or as some other answer to our felt needs.[2]

This book argues for a partial reversal of the prevalent notion that Christianity is a worldview. As a dominant concept in evangelical circles, worldview thinking must share the blame for what Seu identified as an inadequate "theology by negation" after September 11. Worldview thought has been a useful corrective to past errors, but it needs to be challenged, and its diffidence about the tragedy demonstrates that. It is better suited to the predictable regularities of science or to our intentional choices than to unique, unpredictable events. The "knowing self" seated in its armchair develops a worldview and ignores its location in history's flight path. Grounded in philosophy, worldview thought seems unable to explain unique historical events or our ongoing vulnerability to them. In the West and in the United States, we imagine that our technology, our military might and our economic clout reduce uncontrollable events to a minimum. New Testament Christianity addresses this vulnerability in history more than it presents a comprehensive worldview. Worldview ideas admirably begin Paul's Mars Hill apologetic, with its appeal to a universal creation order, but they tend never to arrive at Paul's conclusion: "He has set a day when he will judge the world with justice by the man he has appointed. He has given proof of this to all men by raising him from the dead" (Acts 17:31). We will make it to the end of Paul's sermon.

I offer this critique of worldview thinking in a friendly spirit that acknowledges its many past contributions. One painful reality of our fragmented, politically polarized society is that we are most likely to discuss and argue with our friends, those closest to our position. Secularists of the left, center and right are very unlikely to read this book, so I must address my likely readers, evangelicals, many of whom subscribe to worldview thinking—now so predominant that I must take it as my debating partner. My argument (that inherent defects in worldview thinking prevent it from adequately addressing divine judgment in history) cannot prove a negative (that it can never do so). While I make my case as strong as possible to argue for a more historical approach, my critique of worldview must be understood with the qualifiers "so far," "seemingly" and "as far as I know." Already, David F. Wells's recent *Above All Earthly Pow'rs: Christ in a Postmodern World* goes a long way toward using judgment-in-history

---

[2]Guinness, *Prophetic Untimeliness,* pp. 54, 100.

against postmodern thought and seeker-sensitive church strategies, while still retaining "worldview" as a term.[3]

Some problems with worldview are not logical but sociological: people who use it often occupy niches in our society—generational, professional, political—and their special concerns shape its use. Boomers with unresolved issues about "growing up fundamentalist" may rely on worldview to disavow parents' warnings of God's wrath, when we should come to terms with that biblical concept by discarding distortions of it and embracing what remains. The rise to social influence of an evangelical professional knowledge class has had great benefits, but that class's use of worldview to gain professional status and a hearing in the public square (see chapter 11) can boomerang by influencing the church more than the world. This class, too, must be encouraged to press on to the risky end of Paul's sermon; the status and the hearing must be risked for the gospel's sake. I am a Boomer in the knowledge class, so I am preaching to myself, too. Finally, worldview thinking has been utilized to make so many different (and opposed) political arguments that they indicate that the New Testament does not present one comprehensive worldview covering matters of politics, economics and international relations.

One version of worldview thinking criticizes postmodernism, and so does this book. My case is emphatically not a postmodern one. Postmodernism shares certain features of philosophy. We think more clearly when we acknowledge that we are in history's flight path rather than when we imagine ourselves safe and snug in philosophy's armchair. Stressing texts and their readings, postmodernism is very much in the reader's armchair, even if several armchairs are circled round to create a reading community. This is a book about events that do not have multiple readings. God's judgments in historical events fall on all sorts of people, not only the faith community, and they cannot be read as acts of deliverance. Christ's return cannot be read as his defeat.

This book argues that Christianity is an interpretation of history (not an alternative reading of it but an old-fashioned metanarrative interpretation) far more than it is a worldview or philosophy. Thus, we must start with some comments on history and the historian. We historians usually balk at writing anything about recent events, for the final outcome is unknown and might come back to haunt us later. We like events that are safely past, and most or all of the consequences have already occurred. We like to be the last to bid during the card game, so to speak, after all other bids are known and final—and after we know the cards in

---

[3]David F. Wells, *Above All Earthly Pow'rs: Christ in a Postmodern World* (Grand Rapids: Eerdmans, 2005).

the other players' hands—and then we speak. Sometimes the usual rules do not work and will not suffice. This cautious approach might leave our readers with the false and dangerous illusion that history is safely past for them, too, and that they are as safe from the unpredictable as the historian who writes about the Pilgrims.

"Americans' holiday from history is over," wrote columnist George F. Will after the tragic attacks on September 11. His comment intrigued me then and still does today. Our cultural mindset hinders us from seeing ourselves as vulnerable human beings caught up in a stream of events over which we have little or no control. So pervasive is this mindset that it is highly unlikely even a major event like September 11 can reawaken in us a sense of our vulnerability and end our self-proclaimed "holiday from history." By the word *history,* Will did not mean "past events," for September 11 did not awaken us to the importance of the Treaty of Westphalia (1648). I believe that he meant by it what I mean by it: the human condition of having our lives caught up in a stream of events—past, present and future—that can crash in on our lives from the outside, as it were, without our ability to initiate, prevent or control them. We know that past persons such as Christopher Columbus or George Washington were caught in this vulnerable condition, but we dismiss our own vulnerability (as we do our own mortality) from our minds. Our culture makes this mental dismissal relatively easy.

History has two primary meanings: the sum total of past events, or some part of them; a written account of past events.[4] Yet it also has a third, an all-encompassing meaning, as the one stream of events from the distant past to the unknown future: past events continue to affect the present, as present ones will the future, in one ongoing stream. That may seem academic when we are calmly navigating the stream, but when we realize we have lost control and are bobbing up and down in it, then our vulnerability becomes the chief fact of our existence.

We must not slide over that little word *event* either. It basically means "something that happens"; however, it implies that this something is unusual or unpredictable and outside our control. We might not dignify the sunrise or our breakfast with the title of "events." Often, the things that happen are governed by nature's regularities or by our own choices. Then we lose sight of how happenings can be unwanted and unexpected but insistent intruders in our lives. Such times of normality are misleading, and September 11 awakened us to the true state of affairs.

---

[4]See, for example, Robert Eric Frykenberg, *History and Belief: The Foundations of Historical Understanding* (Grand Rapids: Eerdmans, 1996), pp. 19-22, 25-37.

Christianity is an interpretation of history. That is too impersonal a description, for Christianity is faith in a person, Jesus Christ. This book focuses on his title (his favorite self-designation), Son of Man, which points to him as the meaning of human history (in the third sense) and the only rescue from its calamities and its corrosive, destructive ebbs and flows that are forms of divine judgment. The Son of Man descended to the cross to bear divine judgment for us and ascended to heaven from whence he can rescue us from history's calamities and its erasing of our transitory lives. The salvation he offers is a deliverance from judgment, not a comprehensive worldview that delivers the self from ignorance or incomprehension or intellectual problems.

Yet, we must define what we mean by *judgment,* and this book focuses intently on the meaning of the Hebrew word *mishpat*—especially the one meaning of a "sifting out." Thus, judgment is not only a final, curtain-dropping event but also a lengthy process with God as an active investigator testing people's hearts, giving the wicked a chance to repent and the righteous to fall away. This meaning helps to bridge the gap between judgment as a scriptural doctrine that most believers do not question and specific events they might be reluctant to identify as judgments. We cannot hear God's verdict, "Guilty," but in some cases we can discern a process whereby public ambiguity gives way to a clearer separation of those who seek to do good from those who seek to do evil. We do not achieve perfect discernment, but we have enough insight to avoid the agnostic view that events are so confusing we must take judgment off the table as an unknowable concept. We cannot do so, for the final curtain-dropping event remains, and this book does not minimize that reality.

September 11 raised the question: was God judging the nation? Reverends Pat Robertson and Jerry Falwell hastily tried to answer that question on a television talk show two days later. They soon apologized, at least in part. Yet readers of Scripture realized that it talks of divine judgment, that the issue could not be so easily or hurriedly decided or dismissed. This book tries to address the issue in a thoughtful way. As an American and a student of this nation's history, I focus on the American experience. These ideas are not limited or especially applicable to the United States. God judges all nations. But here the event (September 11), the author and the focus are American.

This book is not an attempt to exploit the tragedy, which is only the starting point for its questions and answers, nor is it a rapid response to cash in on a tragedy. The passage of time has allowed for valid responses: comfort for the bereaved, debate over the war on terrorism, measures to increase homeland security and debate between liberals and conservatives over what domestic and foreign policies might best address the issues raised by the tragedy. All are valid, but they are incomplete. As long as we sidestep divine judgment, we will not learn the all-encompassing lessons of September 11. And, since the sifting out is ongoing, September 11 may be a test of our present and future response to God. I survey a broad group of commentators on the tragedy; however, my quotes from certain writers or journals should not be misconstrued as approval of their viewpoints on September 11 or of their ideological stance. Erroneous views can be instructive. Thus, the basic idea of this book—that we must return (cautiously and accurately) to the concept of God's judging activity in history as central to Christianity—emerges partly out of the inadequacy of other ideas.

To send this interpretation into a polarized society is risky. It is almost to court misunderstanding and distortion by left, right or center. Let me try to avoid that. Since most evangelicals vote Republican, any independent evangelical case may be seen as automatically subversive, an attempt to lure them from their allegiance with an argument that departs from widely held conservative views and that claims the divine *mishpat* falls on Republicans as well as Democrats. A personal note: I am a rural, pro-life independent, a long-time board member for a Christian school and no Jim Wallis. Yet I write here as a historian who feels it is his Christian calling to be nonpartisan but even more to try to analyze events and not to add one more bit of political speech to our confusing debates. Real events continue to occur despite the partisan spin that is applied to them. To analyze God's judgments as falling on both political parties is not to equate them or to measure their respective failings (which only God can do) or to set oneself up as a mediator between them—it is to argue that the fear of the Lord ought to fall on them both and on us all. This is not meant as a moralizing judgment on both sides but as an attempt to discern the workings of God in history, however difficult that task certainly is. Yet it is necessary, lest the idea of God's sovereignty lose its force and become a cliché. Partisans on both sides, so to speak, hit the "Reduce" button on the copy machine and come up with a version of Christ that is only 77 percent or 93 percent of actual size, to fit him in to their broad coalition. My hope is that people on both sides might see that the chief benefit of rising above partisan battle smoke is to gain a clearer view of the glories of Christ, and so chapter 6 is the key section of this book.

The ultimate justification for this book is that you, the reader, see Christ's glory more clearly by means of it. The ultimate protection against its distortion can only be a prayer that the Lord will defend whatever truth it contains. Its ultimate goal is that you may know him, "whom to know is life eternal."

1

If September 11 Was a Message, Then What Did It Mean?

O ur thinking about September 11 now must begin where it did that day—with the enormous loss of individual human lives. We must never lose sight of them, these human beings created in God's image, each having immeasurable worth. Nearly three thousand people were killed that day, at the World Trade Center, at the Pentagon and in that field in Pennsylvania.[1] For weeks, the *New York Times* ran profiles of the dead, describing their individual careers, families and personalities. Millions of Americans grieved with their loved ones, and mourning is certainly the first and fundamental response to September 11.

Some say that our thinking about September 11 should stop here, that we should not attempt to find meaning, that enormous calamities like the Holocaust and September 11—the list could be expanded—render obscene any notion that history has a meaning.[2] Let the victims' suffering stand alone. A search for meaning trivializes their suffering. This view unintentionally grants to Hitler, Osama bin Laden and Mohammed Atta the power to render history meaningless. It cannot undo the damage, bring back a single victim or grant more honor to a single victim. In fact, the press was full of thoughts about September 11, very few political or social perspectives were silent on it, and a Christian assessment of all these comments is not out of order. We must go beyond these pragmatic, realist reasons for rejecting the call to silence. It is erroneous. Scripture teaches that God directs the course of events so as to give meaning to history, however difficult it often is for us to discern that meaning. No terrorist or tyrant

---

[1]According to one website (www.september11victims.com), there were 2,996 deaths as of August 8, 2004: 24 persons were reported dead, 24 were reported missing, and the remaining 2,948 were confirmed dead.

[2]William Stacy Johnson expresses a version of this view in "Probing the 'Meaning' of September 11, 2001," *Princeton Seminary Bulletin* 23, no. 1 (new series: 2002): 41.

can render history meaningless by committing so great a criminal, abhorrent act that the course of events henceforth is so tainted by it as to lose all possibility of meaning.

A Brief Sampling of Opinions Expressed in Mass-Circulation Magazines

Writing in *Newsweek* days after the disaster, columnist Anna Quindlen focused on one family of victims, the Hansons of Massachusetts. "Anything can happen when human beings allow ideology to trump their humanity, when they elevate an idea above the lives of individuals." Nineteen hijackers committed their evil act of sending "those planes like fiery torpedoes into public buildings" because they were willing "to see themselves, as well as their passengers, as merely incidental cargo in the service of some heinous greater good."[3] True, individuals cannot morally be used as combustible cargo to be rammed into tall buildings. Yet we might balk at the conclusion that no idea whatsoever can be "elevate[d] . . . above the lives of individuals," for that might deny to the Hansons any higher meaning to their lives: nothing to live or die for. That might demean the heroic actions of police and firefighters who raced toward flames and climbed up stairwells that survivors were descending. They elevated duty and a love for the victims above their individual lives. We commend them for it. "Greater love has no one than this, that he lay down his life for his friends" (John 15:13).

To be fair, we note that Quindlen specified that ideology should not trump individual lives. No impersonal, grandiose, abstract Cause justifies taking innocent life. True enough. Yet exalting the individual leaves one prone to consumerism, apt to sink into the sofa of self-indulgence, if nothing is worth the sacrifice of one's life. A month after the catastrophe, columnist David Brooks critiqued our "individualistic society" and our "building little private paradises for ourselves. We've renovated our kitchens, refurbished our home entertainment systems," but we have "withdr[awn] from public life, often not even bothering to vote."[4] Observers like Brooks saw September 11 as a chance for Americans "to think like a nation" again, to repeat our ancestors' self-sacrificing courage after Pearl Harbor.

Fareed Zakaria and others argued that September 11 disproved Francis Fukuyama's thesis that the end of a Cold War of rival ideologies signaled the "End of History." Fukuyama claimed that free-market democracy won because this individual-friendly ideology did not "trump" individual humanity but best satisfied individuals' desires for equality, comfort and recognition. No ideology was

---

[3]Anna Quindlen, "Imagining the Hanson Family," *Newsweek,* September 24, 2001, p. 96.
[4]David Brooks, "Facing Up to Our Fears," *Newsweek,* October 22, 2001, p. 69.

left to compete against it. No more Pearl Harbors would occur. History—the battle of ideologies—had ended. Not so, Zakaria asserted. "This is surely the End of the End of History." Radical Islam ended history's end; it did not offer individuals more, but it was angry that Western capitalism did. "It turns out that it takes only one side to restart History." For his part, Fukuyama insisted that radical Islam could only delay the triumph of democratic capitalism; September 11 only postponed the End of History.[5]

Fukuyama miscast democratic capitalism in the starring role as the Omega point of history, a role belonging to Christ alone. We will examine that issue later. For now, we note that not everyone agrees with his definition of history as a struggle of ideologies. Other commentators defined September 11 as history, a public event coming from the outside to invade the consumer cocoon in which we felt secure and able to ignore foreign affairs. Brooks noted, "A country that has basically ignored foreign affairs since the cold war ended has discovered that foreign affairs has not ignored it." By 2001, television coverage of foreign news had dropped to one-third of the 1989 coverage. Yet bedrock reality cannot be turned off by the remote or by postmodernists' talk of socially constructed signifiers. "The planes that plowed into the World Trade Center and the Pentagon were real," essayist Roger Rosenblatt intoned in *Time*. "The flames, smoke, sirens—real. The chalky landscape, the silence of the streets—real."[6]

History as reality invaded the United States against our democratic wishes, despite a majority denying that it could happen here. Democracies are not immune to tragic history. They can grant rights to individuals but sometimes cannot defend individuals. In *Casey* v. *Planned Parenthood,* the Supreme Court ruled, "At the heart of liberty is the right to define one's own concept of existence, of meaning, of the universe, and of the mystery of human life." We can define our concept of existence but sometimes cannot defend our very existence. History is bigger than democracy. Yet, as the saying goes, to a hammer every problem is a nail. In a democracy, every problem tends to be seen as a cause and a call for greater citizen involvement in public affairs. But even a 100-percent voter turnout in the 2000 election would have contributed nothing toward preventing September 11. Commentators observed that, after a decade when we focused on the private entrepreneur, the attacks highlighted anew the

[5]Fareed Zakaria, "The End of the End of History," *Newsweek,* September 24, 2001, p. 70; Francis Fukuyama, *The End of History and the Last Man* (New York: Avon, 1993). For a summary of Fukuyama's post-September 11 statements, see Stanley Kurtz, "The Future of 'History,'" *Policy Review* June and July 2002, p. 47.

[6]David Gates, "Living a New Normal," *Newsweek,* October 8, 2001, p. 59; Brooks, "Facing Up," p. 67; Roger Rosenblatt, "The Age of Irony Comes to an End," *Time,* September 24, 2001, p. 79.

indispensable role of government, which alone can screen travelers and baggage, send firefighters into burning buildings, and dispatch F-16s to patrol the skies.[7] True, and we have no choice but to rely on government, but September 11 dramatically showed its limitations. The world's most powerful government could not protect its own citizens on its own soil.

Deep-seated individualism almost insured that the hopes of political scientist Robert Putnam (Bowling Alone) for revived "community involvement" would be dashed. We Americans had the right to define or deny the tragedy as we saw fit. At first, we threw ourselves into the national disaster and its foreign causes. "We are all intelligence officers now," Time noted. "Two hundred people showed up for 'Middle East 101' at Christ Community Church in Idaho Falls, Idaho. Books on biological warfare, the Taliban and terrorism are selling out; so is the Koran, and maps of Afghanistan." It did not last. By Thanksgiving 2001, observers noted a renewed retreat into the consumer cocoon; fear of public places and travel increased our "nesting instinct"; we spent more to pad private paradises as refuges from public dangers.[8]

Nesting after the fact did not erase the trauma from television images of people jumping from the Twin Towers. We needed psychologists' advice: fear, unlike grief, does not come in stages; reactions to terrorism vary from person to person; a "daylight, rational part of the brain is full of reassurance, but the deeper, instinctual part is not so sure"; Israelis' use of regular rules to reduce randomness makes sense in combating fear.[9] Clergy gave reassurances. The archbishop of Canterbury, Rowan Williams, imagined God saying to troubled souls, "Don't be afraid, nothing will stop me welcoming you"; "Be afraid only of your own deep longing to control me."[10] The next Sunday, a pastor north of New York gave "a nuanced argument for moving away from rage" only to realize people wanted reassurance, not closely reasoned arguments. "This Sunday," Time reported, "he will ask people sitting in the pews to split into small groups of three or four and share with one another small signs of God's goodness."[11]

Understandable in the days following a catastrophe, these responses will not

[7]See, for example, Bill Moyers, "This Isn't the Speech I Expected . . . ," in New YorkSeptember-ElevenTwoThousandOne, ed. Giorgio Baravalle and Cari Modine (New York: Design Method of Operation, 2001).

[8]Geoffrey Cowley, "Sowing Seeds of Redemption," Newsweek, November 26, 2001, p. 74; Time, October 8, 2001, 24; Cathleen McGuigan, "Nesting Instincts," Newsweek, November 26, 2001, p. 72.

[9]Brooks, "Facing Up," pp. 67-68.

[10]Rowan Williams, "End of War," 28, in Dissent from the Homeland: Essays After September 11, ed. Stanley Hauerwas and Frank Lentricchia (Durham, N.C.: Duke University Press, 2003).

[11]"A Crisis of Faith," Time, October 1, 2001, p. 97.

prove sufficient for the years following it, when we may be ready for and may require more searching answers. Commending President George W. Bush's immediate call for military action against the "evil" of terrorism as necessary, George Will recognized that it was insufficient in the long run: "There will be time enough to reflect on the deeper meanings of September 11, including the resilience, indeed the permanence, of evil."[12] That time has come.

A Brief Survey of Opinion in Leftist, Centrist and Right-Wing Journals

Intellectual, specialized journals often display an elitist disdain for popular culture. Why pay more to subscribe to *The Nation* if *Newsweek* contains all the important ideas? The definite article "the" proclaims a definite sense of superiority. Left-wing journals disdain right-wing ones, and centrist ones may disdain both. All sides tended to think September 11 proved they had been right all along. We sample the debate in a broad spectrum of the intellectual press, where commentators made more hard-hitting arguments and critiqued each other more harshly. Mass-circulation magazines may moderate opinions to maximize sales, and we do not want our search to be thus limited. Our sample starts with the leftists.

An oft-cited, oft-criticized piece dismissive of the government's messages to its popular audience was Susan Sontag's statement in *The New Yorker*. "The disconnect between last Tuesday's monstrous dose of reality and the self-righteous drivel and outright deceptions being peddled by public figures and TV commentators is startling, depressing." Public figures "seem to have joined together in a campaign to infantilize the public" with simplistic kindergarten stories that cowardly bad men had attacked an innocent "free world." No, she insisted, the hijackers might be evil, but they were not cowards. Nor was a U.S. government that bombed Iraqi civilians innocent. Officials substituted "psychotherapy" for policy debates essential to democracy. "Let's by all means grieve together. But let's not be stupid together."[13]

Leftist writers condemned the attack but argued it was a predictable consequence of—almost a judgment for—American misdeeds they had long opposed: the superpower's economic dominance overseas, its support for Israel's oppression of the Palestinians, its sanctions that hurt Iraqi civilians, its funding of bin Laden and the war of the *mujahideen* against Soviet troops in Afghanistan, and its hubris in ahistorically portraying itself in 2001 as the Pearl Harbor-

---

[12]George F. Will, "On the Health of the State," *Newsweek*, October 1, 2001, p. 70.
[13]Susan Sontag, "The Disconnect . . . ," in "The Talk of the Town" section, *The New Yorker*, September 24, 2001, p. 32.

era, innocent victim going out to save the world.[14] Leftists charged that the U.S. government had committed immoral and unjust acts; September 11 somehow resulted from those acts; this terrible payback was not totally unjust or surprising, even if it was marred by its own immoralities. They did not cite God as a personal agent bringing justice on an arrogant superpower. Impersonal mechanisms did. "Our broken promises . . . led inevitably to this tragedy" (Robert Fisk); the attacks "might be the consequence of the recent Israeli rampages in the occupied territories" (Alexander Cockburn); they were "blowback" from American foreign policy (Noam Chomsky); "the singularities (species, individuals and cultures)" ended by a globalization "governed by a single power are taking their revenge today" (Jean Baudrillard). They did not excuse terrorists, but impersonal mechanisms enabled them to suggest the payback was understandable and reasonable even if the hijackers were not.[15]

Taken from Chalmers Johnson's book by that name, "blowback" was a new word for unintended, deserved consequences that sounded like a term from physics or chemistry. "Blowback," Louis Menand explained in *The New Yorker,* "as the term is used in the literature on September 11th, is intended to carry moral weight: if you insist on tramping through other people's flower gardens, you can't complain when you get stung is the general idea."[16]

Centrists were angered by leftists blaming the victim. In *The Atlantic Monthly,* Christopher Hitchens criticized Sontag's "disdainful geopolitical analysis" and Chomsky's view "that the September 11 crime is a mere bagatelle when set beside the offenses of the [U.S.] Empire." Such views he likened to those of "the religious dogmatists [Falwell and Robertson?] who regard September 11 in the light of a divine judgment on a sinful society." To equate U.S. foreign policy actions with a terrorist network's plots was to take "shelter in half-baked moral equivalence" and to join all critics of the U.S. government. "If the enemy of your enemy is your friend," concluded Jonathan Rauch, in the centrist *Atlantic Monthly,* "then it is not so surprising that postmodern

---

[14]This summary is based on the following pieces: Liza Featherstone, "A Peaceful Justice?" *The Nation,* October 22, 2001, p. 18; Alexander Cockburn, "Faceless Cowards?" *The Nation,* October 1, 2001, p. 8; Robert Fisk, "Terror in America," *The Nation,* October 1, 2001, p. 7; Lewis H. Lapham, "Drums Along the Potomac: New War, Old Music," *Harper's Magazine,* November 2001, pp. 35-41; and Louis Menand, "Faith, Hope and Clarity: September 11th and the American Soul," *The New Yorker,* September 16, 2002, pp. 98-104. Menand summarizes and critiques leftist views.

[15]Fisk, "Terror," p. 7; Cockburn, "Cowards?" p. 8; Menand, "Clarity," pp. 100, 101 (quoting Baudrillard).

[16]Menand, "Clarity," p. 100; Chalmers A. Johnson, *Blowback: The Costs and Consequences of American Empire* (New York: Henry Holt, 2000).

Marxists should make common cause with radical mullahs."[17]

Centrists offered hard-headed pragmatism, not leftist talk about justice. Richard A. Posner charged leftist academics with "writing precipitately about matters outside their area of professional specialization." September 11 raised issues of "policing, intelligence, military strategy and tactics, and foreign affairs," of which leftist intellectuals knew little. *The New Republic* rebutted Fisk's charges in *The Nation* by arguing that the United States had pressured Israel to give Palestinians a state; that Saddam Hussein's military expenses, not sanctions, caused civilian deaths; and that bin Laden supported ethnic or religious cleansing.[18]

Centrists focused on what to do next and denied broader themes (e.g., divine judgment). The attack came because the nation had neglected to do what was on centrists' "to-do" list. *The New Republic* categorized calamities as impersonal acts of nature to be accepted or enemies' personal acts of aggression to be fought. September 11 was the latter. "What happened in New York and Washington was not a tragedy that should leave us feeling philosophical; it was an aggression that should leave us feeling historical"—not feeling vulnerable to events but duty-bound to be actors in history, not helpless mourners. "The only solace is strategy. . . . We must throw ourselves into the world in a storm of engagement." Yet actors can be partly helpless. This false choice excluded a divine Actor whose doings had to be pondered eventually, even if defeating aggression was the immediate, practical, necessary response.[19]

Conservatives agreed on decisive military action and on the error of leftists' talk of U.S. misdeeds and of terrorists as criminals best left to international courts. Talk-show host Sean Hannity saw a war between "Judeo-Christian values" and "the violent nihilism of radical Islam." In Pearl-Harbor-era terms, he accused liberals of being "ideologically inclined toward appeasement." Liberals' response to the attacks proved conservatives' charge that they were "moral relativists" who aided the enemy by "engag[ing] in a dangerous and destructive effort to morally disarm our children."[20] The Clinton gloves should be taken off, Islamic terrorists annihilated and the United States returned to its World War II

---

[17]Christopher Hitchens, "Stranger in a Strange Land," *The Atlantic Monthly,* December 2001, pp. 32-34; Jonathan Rauch, "The Mullahs and Postmodernists," *The Atlantic Monthly,* January 2002, pp. 21-22.

[18]Richard A. Posner, "The Professors Profess," *The Atlantic Monthly,* February 2002, p. 28; Peter Beinart, "Fault Lines," *The New Republic,* October 1, 2001, p. 8.

[19]"Mourning and Strategy," *The New Republic,* October 1, 2001, p. 9.

[20]Sean Hannity, *Let Freedom Ring: Winning the War of Liberty over Liberalism* (New York: HarperCollins, 2002), pp. 6, 8; see pp. 6-8, 11, 115-16, and *Deliver Us from Evil: Defeating Terrorism, Despotism and Liberalism* (New York: HarperCollins, 2004), pp. 2-3, 4-5; see also pp. 7-9, 15, 25-53, 166.

policy of unconditional surrender. What the left saw as U.S. misdeeds the right saw as virtues. *The National Review*'s columnists rejected the left's "tendency to self-blame and [its] taste for complex causal explanations . . . made still more complex by social science jargon." Falwell and Robertson were "[e]arly entrants in the creep sweepstakes" for claiming divine judgment.[21]

In "Why West Is Best," Paul Johnson praised Western civilization for its Greco-Roman law, constitutionalism and capitalism, not its Christian faith. God's judgment on the West was unnecessary: "capitalism is based on human nature, not dogma," and "is self-correcting." It was "the protean ability of Western civilization to be self-critical and self-correcting—not only in producing wealth but over the whole range of human activities—that constitutes its most decisive superiority over any of its rivals."[22] Divine judgment was superfluous, it seemed: God would be unjust to correct a self-correcting civilization. In *The National Review*, Richard Brookhiser quoted at length from Revelation 18, the account of Babylon's fall. New York, like Babylon, "drew the envy and excited the resentment of rubes and poets everywhere." The archaic words from the King James Version were mere literary adornments for him. Babylon's trade might be wicked; New York merchants' trade was mainly "just, cleansed by their honest effort." The apostle John had "a vision of the human heart in eternity"; immigrants to New York had "a vision of tomorrow, a little better than the day before."[23] The ancient text could not possibly apply to New York.

Nonmoral Social Scientific Analysis and a Moral, Initial Hunch

Some academics wrote for ideological journals, but others approached September 11 with an attempt to be nonideological. Social scientists attempted a scientific analysis; some had a political bias or a postmodern view that one's "analytic perspective" depended on "the position one occupies in the world"; all shared secular assumptions.[24] Social sciences analyze humans and their societies using assumptions and methods of the natural sciences, as much as possible, partly to

[21]Paul Johnson, "Relentlessly and Thoroughly," *National Review*, October 15, 2001, pp. 20-21; David Gelernter, "Eight Thoughts on Mass Murder," *National Review*, October 1, 2001, p. 10; Daniel Pipes, "War, Not 'Crimes,' " *National Review*, October 1, 2001, p. 12; Victor Davis Hanson, "What Are We Made Of?" *National Review*, October 1, 2001, p. 14; John O'Sullivan, "Their Amerika," *National Review*, October 15, 2001, p. 28; "Hall of Shame," *National Review*, October 15, 2001, p. 15.
[22]Paul Johnson, "Why West Is Best," *National Review*, December 3, 2001, pp. 18, 20.
[23]Richard Brookhiser, "Our Day of Infamy," *National Review*, October 1, 2001, p. 17.
[24]Craig Calhoun, Paul Price and Ashley Timmers, eds., *Understanding September 11* (New York: The New Press, 2002); Eric Hershberg and Kevin W. Moore, eds., *Critical Views of September 11: Analyses from Around the World* (New York: The New Press, 2002). The quote is from Hershberg and Moore, "Introduction," p. 4.

develop expertise that a democracy's citizens and leaders can use to formulate policies.[25] Common sense alerts us that such an "analytic perspective" is not as neutral or objective as it might appear and that a nonmoral perspective will find it very difficult to analyze accurately such an explosion of evil as September 11.

The first puzzle was how to define terrorism. Suspicious of its "negative connotations," political scientist Robert Keohane defined it as "deliberately targeted surprise attacks on arbitrarily chosen civilians, designed to frighten other people." None of those words had to mean something immoral. To avoid moral terms further, he employed a geometrical one: asymmetrical (power is *"asymmetrical interdependence"*). Achin Vanaik, a scholar from India, also sought "a morally neutral definition," in which civilians were not innocent per se nor terrorists guilty: the targets were "physically defenseless," and the actors had a duty to use means proportional to their ends. Thus, a government's disproportionate use of violence could be terrorism. Focusing on Islamic terrorism, political scientists James Der Derian and Seyla Benhabib described it in philosophical terms as "apocalyptic nihilism."[26]

That description is very inadequate. Radical Islamists are hardly nihilists who deny that humans can know what is true or what is moral or what is life's meaning. They are all too confident that they know all these things, which social scientists think they cannot know. Social scientists leave us with impossible questions: what is morally equivalent, what is proportional, how many civilian victims constitute an atrocity, how are rights and wrongs on two competing sides to be balanced or weighed. As limited human beings, we cannot answer these questions. Social scientists' exclusion of the supernatural and their treatment of religion as a human invention rob us of clarifying ideas: government's God-given sword (Romans 13:1-7); civilians' lack of a legitimate equal sword but (thus) their right to freedom from attacks by other civilians; governments' provisional right to judge individuals but lack of ultimate rights to annihilate a people or end history; God's right to hold governments accountable. Absent these ideas, any "evaluatively neutral way" of thinking

---

[25]Dorothy Ross, "Social Science," in *A Companion to American Thought*, ed. Richard Wightman Fox and James T. Kloppenberg (Malden, Mass.: Blackwell Publishers, 1998), pp. 634-36.

[26]Robert O. Keohane, "The Globalization of Informal Violence, Theories of World Politics and the 'Liberalism of Fear,' " in *Understanding September 11*, ed. Craig Calhoun, Paul Price and Ashley Timmers (New York: The New Press, 2002), pp. 77-78, 81, 82; Achin Vanaik, "The Ethics and Efficacy of Political Terrorism," in *Critical Views of September 11: Analyses from Around the World*, ed. Eric Hershberg and Kevin W. Moore (New York: The New Press, 2002), pp. 24, 26-28, 32; James Der Derian, "9/11: Before, After and In Between," in *Understanding September 11*, ed. Craig Calhoun, Paul Price and Ashley Timmers (New York: The New Press, 2002), p. 178; Seyla Benhabib, "Unholy War: Reclaiming Democratic Virtues After September 11," in *Understanding September 11*, ed. Craig Calhoun, Paul Price and Ashley Timmers (New York: The New Press, 2002), p. 245 ("The new jihad is not only apocalyptic; it is nihilistic").

about the act of flying passenger aircraft into buildings will prove inadequate, even immoral itself, in the end.[27]

Partly, social scientists avoid moralizing, religious talk lest such ideas divide a democracy. That may leave democratic politics as the highest value. Political sociologist Peter Alexander Meyers "argue[d] that the acts of September 11 were an assault on politics itself and that a citizen's most important response . . . is to defend politics"[28] or to attend Middle East 101 and pore over the map of Afghanistan—worthwhile and necessary acts but hardly sufficient ones for us who are creatures facing our Creator as well as citizens writing our senator. The focus on what the United States should do next revealed a proud assumption that we were the actors, when, in fact, we may have been mostly acted on at that point in history.

Social scientists admit that their failure to take religion seriously hinders their analysis. They developed the theory of secularization (as societies modernize, they are secularized). No wonder they were surprised when the first major war of the twenty-first century involves "of all things, religion—secularism's old, long-banished foe." Sociologist Mark Juergensmeyer used "religionization" as a now-necessary opposite of secularization.[29] He took religion more seriously; his was perhaps the most helpful analysis. He saw al-Qaeda as a "religious assault on the secular state" that tries to limit and perhaps destroy religion. In retaliation, Al Qaeda and other Islamic terrorists put themselves "on a par with the leaders of governments that they target" by staging "a public performance of violence" replayed on television sets and computer screens around the world, in order to bring "the rest of the world into their world view" of a global religious war.[30]

Revising his view by taking the Christian faith seriously, we arrive at an initial hunch about September 11. Vigilantes acting on an unimaginable scale, religious zealots took for themselves God's right to judge (ultimately) and governments' right to wield the sword (presently), in their apocalyptic-style, highly visible attack on their unsuspecting foe. Given their limited power, they chose targets of high symbolic value, lacked any capacity to institute a new governmental order, produced a temporary chaos and anarchy instead and dared not

---

[27]The phrase "evaluatively neutral way" is Vanaik's, in "Ethics and Efficacy," p. 24.
[28]Peter Alexander Meyer, "Terrorism and the Assault on Politics," in *Understanding September 11*, ed. Craig Calhoun, Paul Price and Ashley Timmers (New York: The New Press, 2002), p. 255.
[29]Mark Juergensmeyer, "Religious Terror and Global War," in *Understanding September 11*, ed. Craig Calhoun, Paul Price and Ashley Timmers (New York: The New Press, 2002), pp. 28-29.
[30]Ibid., pp. 27-28, 30-31, 33.

attack military forces (the Pentagon was an office building, not a fort) but killed civilians. They thought they enacted justice on guilty foes. This is no morally neutral hunch; theirs was a monstrous act of iniquity. They took what was God's: the civilians bore his image; the government that sought to protect civilians did so by his sanction; the judgment they thought they enacted was his alone to determine; the course of events they sought decisively to change was fundamentally his to continue or change.

That is only a preliminary conclusion. Before we turn to religious reflections, we can summarize using Menand's piece in *The New Yorker,* a survey of writings on the tragedy. Writing not from left or right but from far above, as if from a lofty peak, Menand wittily skewered the ideas of left, right and center. "The most surprising thing about most of the published reflections on September 11th is how devoid of surprise they are." Leftists, centrists and conservatives saw the attack as confirmation: "It just proves what I've always said." The cataclysm changed no one's mind. Menand dismissed the idea it might have been a "wake-up call" that might change one's beliefs: after car accidents, survivors "sometimes react by reassessing their entire lives—as though the accident were a judgment. It wasn't; it was an accident. . . . The meaning of their whole way of life was not at stake."[31] That is too flippant. An event can be both an accident and a judgment. What is sound advice for an individual after a car accident might not be for a nation after an attack. "Entire lives" exaggerates: perhaps only the recent past needs to be reassessed.

A Brief Sampling of Opinions Expressed in Religious (Christian) Books and Journals

Religious thinking was not isolated from the political thinking. Mainline journals such as *The Christian Century* reflect left or center arguments; evangelical journals like *Christianity Today,* center or right ones. We examine religious opinion, starting from the left again.

The Christian Century confessed, "We want a word from God." Not a word from Falwell and Robertson, or radical Islam, or patriots' "calls for vengeance" on terrorists, or Jeremiah's prophecies of judgment, but his positive statement (Jeremiah 9:24): "I am the LORD, who exercises kindness, / justice and righteousness on earth." The editors did not condone the atrocity—"We are angry beyond words, and justifiably so"—but they hoped it would lead to love, justice and integrity, not to "hatred and vengeance." It should lead to an international effort "to bring criminals to justice" and to negotiate an end to the Israeli-Palestin-

---

[31]Menand, "Clarity," pp. 98, 100, 101, 103.

ian conflict.[32] They reprinted Jon Gunnerman's sermon (September 13); the lectionary text for the coming Sunday (Jeremiah 4:11-12, 22-28) *was* Jeremiah's prophecy that God would judge a foolish people. "Dare we use this text for our circumstances?" he asked. "The roar of the wind of jets putting cities to ruin, laying waste fields in Pennsylvania—dare we call this the angry spirit of God?" No, Gunnerman said, "It's bad exegesis, isn't it, the way televangelists use biblical texts? . . . Doesn't it imply a callous disregard for the deaths and suffering of innocents? And surely it is sacrilegious to suggest that God in some way willed this as punishment." His question marks did not eliminate such a view. "No, we cannot use the text this way, but we also cannot put it aside," he hesitated. "Let us concede that Jeremiah was more confident in his reading of God's acts in history than we are, or at least than I am." To call September 11 "the judgment or will of God commits us to similar judgments about all human misfortune," thus "trivializing human suffering and rendering God capricious."[33] Yet, if some events were judgments, that did not mean all were. Did accountability to God trivialize suffering more than did a sheer randomness in tragic events?

In *Word & World,* a Lutheran professor, Walter Sundberg, was less sure that judgment could be excluded. A theology of judgment is today "often neglected, rejected, dismissed, and derided all across the church. Why should this be? Because this theology has been misused? It certainly has! But every theology across the centuries has been misused. Why single out this one?" In his second inaugural address, Lincoln interpreted the Civil War as God's judgment on the nation for slavery. Today a therapeutic mindset rules our culture. "It is in the air we breathe. It runs the show. And so we accommodate it. Under its spell, the theological ideas that inspired Lincoln are alien to us, impossible for us to employ." Sundberg seemingly left them there, as impossibilities.[34]

Christian thinkers on the left did not hesitate to point out "criminal facts of American history" (Frank Lentricchia's words) that might anger God, even if he did not judge them directly. Christian pacifist Stanley Hauerwas and Lentricchia edited a book of essays sharply accusing the U.S. government of acts of injustice. Hauerwas warned, "God's blessing incurs God's judgment" but did not cite September 11. For Lentricchia, "the largest obscenity of all is the howl of American self-pity in the wake of September 11." He could hardly have made himself more controversial by saying it was God's judgment. Yet the Muslim, Jewish,

---

[32]*The Christian Century* 118, no. 26 (September 26-October 3, 2001): 3-4.
[33]Jon Gunnerman, "Naming the Terror," *Christian Century* 118, no. 26 (September 26-October 3, 2001): 4-5.
[34]Walter Sundberg, "'Evil' After 9/11: The Alien Work of God," *Word & World* (spring 2004): 204-7.

Catholic and Protestant contributors could not have agreed on the exact identity of the God who might be doing the judging.[35]

The editors of *First Things*, a center-right journal, argued that a government must "protect its citizens," but it was subject to just war theory as it did so. *First Things* disdained leftists as a "morally debilitated professoriat" and "inveterate complexifiers, offering detailed analyses of the seven sides of four-sided questions while declaring their achingly superior sensitivities that make them too sensitive for decent company." Social scientists' secular focus and leftists' stress on religious tolerance were inadequate. This was "inescapably a war of religion," for the terrorists "hate us because we are the infidel who has . . . humiliated the chosen people of God." *First Things* writer J. Bottum thought the Chomsky versus Hitchens debate somewhat empty, for both used "the categories of contemporary political discourse"—not religion—and so could not explain "both the blood spilled and the essential wrongness of its spilling." *First Things* offered pragmatic advice to policymakers, whom it did not offend by printing talk of divine judgment.[36]

Christianity Today took a cautious center-right approach, applauding patriotism but warning against "God-and-country Christianity," gently reproving Falwell but balancing that with criticism of Oprah Winfrey's view "that each victim of the terror strikes instantly became an angel" (*CT*'s words), running stories on Todd Beamer, on President Bush's September 20 meeting with religious leaders and on overseas Christians' experiences with Islamic militants. Its managing editor's piece cited social scientists' analyses of Islamic terrorism to advise leaders and citizens on what to do next. Here, Christians were ordinary citizens, not believers in a faith that had a view of history every bit as eschatological as Islam's. Social science and history were cited more than Scripture. Apart from a different audience, the piece resembled *Newsweek*'s.[37]

For evangelicals, a key text was Luke 13:1-5, Jesus' comment on the fallen

---

[35]Stanley Hauerwas and Frank Lentricchia, "Introductory Notes from the Editors," *Dissent from the Homeland: Essays After September 11*, ed. Stanley Hauerwas and Frank Lentricchia (Durham, N.C.: Duke University Press, 2003), pp. 5, 8.

[36]"In a Time of War," *First Things*, December 2001, pp. 11, 12-13, 16; Stanley Hauerwas's letter to the editors, *First Things*, February 2002, p. 3 (the editors' response is on pp. 14-15); J. Bottum, "What Violence Is For," *First Things*, December 2001, p. 33; James Neuchterlein, "Hard Thoughts in Wartime," *First Things*, January 2002, pp. 13-14.

[37]"Todd Beamer: Sunday-School Teacher, Hero of Fatal Flight," *Christianity Today [CT]*, October 22, 2001, p. 18; Tony Carnes, "Day of Terror, Day of Grace," *CT*, October 22, 2001, pp. 16-22; "The Hard-Won Lessons of Terror and Persecution," *CT*, October 22, 2001, pp. 20-21; Mark Galli, "Now What?" *CT*, October 22, 2001, pp. 24-27; "Rally Round the Flag" and "Blame Game," *CT*, November 12, 2001, pp. 36-37; Tony Carnes, "Bush's Defining Moment," *CT*, November 12, 2001, pp. 38-42.

tower in Siloam. *CT* saw such "reminders of our mortality" as "ideal times" to turn to God in repentance for our sins, not to point at others. The pressing task of comforting the bereaved and helping the shell-shocked fully on him, Tim Keller of Manhattan's Redeemer Presbyterian Church understandably softened the text's message. "Jesus was asked if a massacre and (ironically) a falling tower were signs of God's judgment on those killed. His answer was an unequivocal 'no,' but he added cryptically 'you yourselves should repent.'" In *CT*, Charles Colson was less comforting: "Jesus gave no soothing explanations. Instead, he reminded them of others killed by a falling tower and said, 'Repent or you, too, will perish.'"[38] (What did that ominous "too" mean? Had the victims died because they had not repented?)

Colson's "Wake-up Call" suggested September 11 might be God's judgment. "For years, many of us have only half-jokingly said that if God doesn't bring judgment on America soon, he'll have to apologize to Sodom and Gomorrah." And yet, he trod "gingerly": "this is not a time for angry finger-pointing" at others. "Judgment always begins with God's people." The church must repent of its idolatry. That was scripturally sound and diverted talk of judgment from the nation's foreign policy and global economic dominance (the left's target) and from evangelicals' secularist enemies in the culture wars (Falwell's and Robertson's targets) and aimed it at the church.[39] However, the particulars of September 11 did not fit his idea, for the terrorists' targets were not linked to the church but to the nation's financial and military institutions.

More direct was Frederica Mathewes-Green, writing in the broadly orthodox *Touchstone*. On September 12, she had attended her church near Washington, D.C. Her pastor asked her, "Why do you think that happened yesterday?" She pled ignorance. "It was the punishment of God." She had "just finished an intensive study of the fall of Jerusalem in A.D. 70" but had not applied that to her own nation. She cited Jesus' words in Luke 13:5 but now applied them to the nation. "National suffering should bring about repentance." Repent of abortion, "sexual promiscuity and materialism, the contempt of God, the spreading infection of American culture." Don't "spray on some superficial piety" by singing "God Bless America." Don't ask God to bless the sinful status quo. "A friend of mine says the local strip club has changed its sign to read 'God Bless America,' which just about sums up the problem." She feared Americans would be too

---

[38]"Blame Game," *CT*, November 12, 2001, p. 37; Pastor Tim Keller, "Questions on Everyone's Mind," posted September 14, 2001, on <www.redeemer2.com/news/index> (accessed on May 8, 2002); Charles Colson, "Wake-up Call," *CT*, November 12, 2001, p. 112.
[39]Colson, "Wake-up Call," p. 112.

proud to repent but would only "focus on how much we have been wronged, and smite our adversaries by our own considerable earthly power."[40]

A reader demanded that she apologize: judgment was an Old Testament idea for theocratic Israel, not a New Testament idea for a pluralistic, free, open society. Matthewes-Green admitted the United States is not ancient Israel, but God "punished and blessed other nations as well" and could still intervene in history even though "a single event will affect a wide range of people, believers and non-believers, 'guilty' and 'innocent,' as the rain falls on the just and unjust alike." She did not apologize. Warnings of judgment were meant for good, and those who warned were not misanthropic. "If history is any guide, a nation that doesn't get the message the first time is given another opportunity to learn it, and I think we'd all rather avoid that."[41]

---

[40]Frederica Mathewes-Green, "Why Did This Happen?" *Touchstone: A Journal of Mere Christianity* 14, no. 9 (November 2001): 13-14.

[41]*Touchstone*, January-February 2002, p. 9.

2

Why September 11 Couldn't Be God's Judgment (Or Could It?)

These reflections do not relate to the nearly three thousand victims of September 11, as individuals, as families, as co-workers in an office. At this individual level—who was at work in the World Trade Center that morning and who just missed the subway, who worked on a lower floor and who on an upper floor, who made it down the stairs and who didn't—the seeming randomness is akin to a tornado twisting across the landscape. We humans are unable to explain why the Hansons were in that plane and perished but John McLane was not in his World Trade Center office and lived. To try would be folly similar to Job's supposed friends interpreting his suffering for him. Nor do these reflections relate to the entire group. Their killers did not know them or aim at them because of who *they* were. Why this group and not another is a question we cannot answer. What we might be able to answer is why this nation's symbols were hit and not another nation's.

Some observers would insist that we not look beyond the individual or group levels, that Christians especially not look beyond: they would insist religion exists only to comfort afflicted individuals or groups. Yet that will hardly do. Human agents with clear intentions, not random-seeming natural forces, clearly aimed at symbols of U.S. financial and military power, and this was correctly perceived as an attack on the nation itself. Secular observers of all political persuasions searched for broader meanings, and so must Christians. Tragically, the survivors and those whose loved ones did not survive September 11 will also have to endure hearing that event discussed innumerable times in future decades. In that respect, September 11 resembles Pearl Harbor. An epochal public event will be analyzed in public, and Christians will see it from the perspective that their faith provides.

The Christian faith is an interpretation of history—that is why it can comfort the afflicted. If such an interpretation is clueless about major events in history, its comfort seems less credible. Yet the meanings we seek do not relate specifically to the victims. We ask why the nation was attacked, not why certain individuals happened to be in its symbols when they were hit.

The Necessity of a Christian Look at Broader Meanings of September 11

It is foolish to claim everything changed with September 11, but naive to think nothing did. Coming years and decades will separate temporary from permanent changes. Initial signs point to a significant shift in attitudes toward religion. Evangelicals ignore these changes at our peril.

A week after Thankgsiving 2001, Joseph Stowell, president of Moody Bible Institute, attended the Chicago Leadership prayer breakfast and was alarmed at a marked change in its tone. Inclusion of all religions and exclusion of Jesus Christ's truth claims were noticeable. The master of ceremonies began "by reading an excerpt from Diane Eck's bestseller, *A New Religious America: How a 'Christian Country' Has Become the World's Most Religiously Diverse Nation.*" The MC stressed the need for "a new paradigm . . . a fresh wind of cooperation and tolerance" in religion. An Islamic leader prayed to Allah. "A woman rabbi, a Catholic priest, and a minister" from a liberal Protestant church led "a coordinated sequence of prayers and then finished by praying in unison." Stowell "kept waiting to hear it, but Jesus' name was not mentioned once." "The rector of Trinity Church, Wall Street, New York City," the main speaker, told "stories of tragedy and triumph at Ground Zero."[1]

Stowell found these stories moving, but they proved to be the texts for a sermon on religious diversity. "Theology is the name of the game after 9/11!" the speaker proclaimed, but exclusivist theologies would have to die so that Theology could live. Stowell summarized: "But, he noted, given the broad diversity of religions in America, we now need to give up the 'traditions' that divide those of us who believe in 'God.' . . . He was telling us in no uncertain terms that an 'Only-Way-Jesus' didn't fit in the new religious order." Stowell heard other calls for a new order. *New York Times* columnist Thomas Friedman asked Christians and Jews to go "back to their sacred texts to reinterpret their traditions to embrace modernity and pluralism, and to create space for secularism and alternative faiths." For him, September 11 meant war against "religious totalitarianism," against all exclusive truth claims for one faith.[2]

---

[1]Joseph M. Stowell, *The Trouble with Jesus* (Chicago: Moody Press, 2003), pp. 13-15.
[2]Ibid., pp. 15-16; Thomas L. Friedman, *Longitudes and Attitudes: Exploring the World After September 11* (New York: Farrar Straus Giroux, 2002), p. 113. Stowell quotes Friedman's newspaper column, while I quote the revised version ("The Real War," pp. 112-14) in Friedman's book.

When a tragedy is employed in an argument to compel us to "reinterpret" our "traditions," then we are justified in asking whether we ought not first to interpret the tragedy. Rather than weasel out of the dilemma Friedman and the rector set for us by claiming that our exclusivist faith is exclusive only in the depth and range of its love and toleration, we start with the interpretation that seems hardest for our exclusivist "tradition" to defend: the idea proposed by Mathewes-Green and others that September 11 was God's judgment on the nation.

The idea of judgment implies several questions. What is justice? What is injustice? Who determines which acts or conditions are unjust? How can justice be restored after unjust acts? Who restores justice? Justice or injustice can exist in various dimensions: private or public; social or individual; different spheres of life—family, society, economy, politics; within a nation or between nations; among and between human beings or between humanity and God. That last question will prove especially controversial. Can human acts toward God be considered unjust? How might that relate to what Stowell identifies as Jesus' exclusive truth claims?

Whole volumes have been written on these issues. This is not a book (much less a bookshelf) defining justice. We focus on ideas about justice revealed in the responses to September 11, especially on objections from right, center and left to the idea that September 11 was God's judgment on the nation.[3] All three political views are children of the eighteenth-century Enlightenment—itself a reaction against seventeenth-century religious intolerance and warfare and a call, like Friedman's, for religion to be confined to a private sphere of values and the home, in order to provide space for secularism and science to reign in a public sphere of facts and politics.[4] Thus, none of the three are likely to accept a literal, biblical God stepping into the public sphere to judge nations. And all are prone to support the Enlightenment's utopian projects. We must go beyond the specific stance on September 11 taken by the three political views and examine their general stance on justice and judgment.

---

[3]For the following, I am indebted in a general way to Seymour Martin Lipset's comparison of U.S. to European politics in *American Exceptionalism: A Double-Edged Sword* (New York: Norton, 1996); to Russell L. Hanson's history of "democracy" as a concept in *The Democratic Imagination in America: Conversations with Our Past* (Princeton, N.J.: Princeton University Press, 1985); and to James W. Skillen's survey of Christian political positions in *The Scattered Voice: Christians at Odds in the Public Square* (Grand Rapids: Zondervan, 1990).
[4]For the public sphere/private sphere, I am greatly indebted to Lesslie Newbigin, *Foolishness to the Greeks: The Gospel and Western Culture* (Grand Rapids: Eerdmans, 1986).

Conservative Ideas of Justice and Why September 11 Could Not Be God's Judgment

Conservatives quickly criticized Falwell's and Robertson's remarks. On the surface, that may surprise us. Falwell's listed enemies—the ACLU, People for the American Way, feminists, gays, pro-choice activists—are conservatives' enemies, too. After the left attacked the two reverends and, like Friedman, portrayed the new war as one against Christian *and* Islamic fundamentalism, the *National Review* softened its criticism of the two: "conservative Christian leaders are not bringing down buildings."[5] Yet conservatives did criticize the idea of judgment. President Bush's spokesman announced, "The president believes that terrorists are responsible for those acts. He . . . believes those remarks are inappropriate."[6] Preachers' talk of judgment endangered their political allies, who distanced themselves from such talk. In a democracy, it is impolitic to threaten voters with talk of divine judgment against them. Yet many secular conservatives genuinely disagree, on principle, with such talk.

The secular right sees Christian faith as a political and social ally: promoting private morality, family stability, good work habits and respect for law so that a free-market democratic society can function. Free markets and free elections do not guarantee morality and order, for competitors' self-interest may cause them to act immorally or disorderly. Christian teaching helps to keep employees moral and citizens law-abiding. Geoffrey Hodgson calls this the "impurity principle": "every socio-economic system must rely on one structurally dissimilar subsystem to function."[7] Free-market democracy uses a dissimilar Christian subsystem run neither on market nor democratic principles to help the main system function. "God talk" is a means to human ends of peace, order and prosperity. To use it against the society it is to help is to pervert it, in this conservative view, and Christian pastors who preach judgment commit a kind of social treason against the social order they are there to facilitate.

On a global scale, conservatives see a United States more moral and devout than other industrialized nations as the best guarantor of some semblance of global peace, prosperity and order. American free-market democracy proved a vital

---

[5]"Transcript of Pat Robertson's Interview with Jerry Falwell Broadcast on the 700 Club, September 13, 2001," Appendix D, in Bruce Lincoln, *Holy Terrors: Thinking About Religion After September 11* (Chicago: University of Chicago Press, 2003), pp. 104-7; Ramesh Ponnuru, "What We're Not Fighting For," *National Review*, November 5, 2001, pp. 20, 22. Bruce Lincoln gives a wide-ranging analysis of Falwell's and Robertson's interview; however, my citing it does not indicate my agreement with his views.

[6]Lincoln, *Holy Terrors*, p. 36.

[7]Geoffrey M. Hodgson, *Economics and Utopia: Why the Learning Economy Is Not the End of History* (London: Routledge, 1999), p. 126.

ally for Christianity against communism in the Cold War—and against Islamic fundamentalism recently. For the Christian God to judge his American ally now seems counterproductive. If the present war, as Sean Hannity claims, is "between the Judeo-Christian values . . . and the violent nihilism of radical Islam," then how can a Judeo-Christian God give even a temporary victory to radical Islam?[8] How can he turn on the nation that gives him the freest platform for his views?

Free-market ideas tend to negate the idea of judgment. They come from the Enlightenment: Bernard Mandeville's claim in *Fable of the Bees* that private vices turn into public benefits and Adam Smith's in *Wealth of Nations* that an Invisible Hand turns an individual's self-interested behavior into a public benefit. That idea undercuts the notion of God's judgment. If a selfish vice promotes others' good, then why should God judge it? Or so the argument goes. This Invisible Hand does work in setting prices by pitting sellers' self-interest against buyers' self-interest; in adjusting the supply of goods by this price mechanism; in allocating resources to those economic activities of highest demand. Yet it cannot purify intangible, nonquantifiable aspects of vice, for example, immoral aspects and harmful results of pornography, although sales receipts increase the nation's gross national product (GNP) and sales clerks decrease its unemployment rate.[9] Harmful results are "externalized"; they are off the selling corporation's profit-and-loss statement. They are not absent from the divine accounting. The Invisible Hand cannot launder evil to avoid judgment.

To be fair to conservatives, we must add that they correctly see markets as disciplining tools by which a people's lack of a work ethic, for example, can result in competitors' seizing their former customers. God can use markets to discipline or judge peoples or individuals in this way. The conservative resurgence, since the mid-1970s, was partly caused by the right turning to competitive markets as disciplining forces—after the antinomianism of the 1960s counterculture had rejected prior disciplining forces, such as tradition, religion, the rule of law and patriotism. All we need establish here is that, while God can use markets to judge, they cannot successfully be used against him to hide evil or to transform it into a public good that cannot be judged.

Conservatives stress individuals' rights to property acquired in the marketplace. If I got it in the market, I earned it, and it's mine. Partly, this idea is biblical: I should work for a living, get paid for it and not have my property stolen.

---

[8]Sean Hannity, *Let Freedom Ring: Winning the War of Liberty over Liberalism* (New York: HarperCollins, 2002), p. 6.
[9]In "What We're Not Fighting For," Ramesh Ponnuru did oppose liberals' claim that we were fighting for the right to enjoy sexual freedom and pornography (*National Review*, November 5, 2001).

Yet this idea may be invalid when used against God or the governments he ordained, to whom I owe tithes and taxes respectively. Conservatives cite property
rights to oppose government's attempts to tax, regulate or confiscate property.
That might imply a case against judgment. Can God take away what is mine or
judge me for misusing it? Writ large: the United States earned its prosperity fairly;
God would be unfair to judge us for it or to take it away. By contrast, a concept
of Christian stewardship accepts the possibility of a judgment on misuse of
property or a divine taking of it.

Conservatives deny that a grossly unequal division of wealth is an unjust condition. Brookhiser sees John wrongly envying Babylon's prosperity (not attacking its evils) and the world envying New York's.[10] A movie star makes millions
corrupting people; a dairy farmer works eighty-hour weeks feeding people and
earns very little; that is the market's decree; it is just by definition. Many Americans can afford $250,000 homes; Third-World peoples live in tarpaper shacks;
that is global markets' just decree. How can God judge when no injustice has
been committed?

A market in ideas exists, too. Conservatives are slower to say that whatever
proves popular in it must be true, good and just. That reasoning, they see, leads
to relativism, immorality and disorder. They see Friedman's call for Christians to
allow pluralism, secularism and alternative faiths as misguided political correctness. The Christian faith cannot be an effective moral agent unless its adherents
believe its message is true. Stowell and Falwell must be allowed to preach that
Jesus Christ is the only way. Yet consumers of ideas make choices and determine an idea's market share. For preachers to claim God judged people for not
choosing Christ would violate the market's rules. Preachers may threaten (in
words that consumers can believe or disbelieve), but God may not actually
judge (in deeds apart from consumer choice). If preaching God's judgment of
individuals makes them good employees or law-abiding citizens, that is acceptable. Preaching his judgment on a nation is not acceptable, in this view of
things.

Conservatives also exalt tough use of military force. Repenting after God's
judgment sounds like weakness before the enemy. Appropriately angered at
television images of "dancing in the streets of Middle Eastern cities," *National
Review* called for "retaliatory strikes" that "may involve clearing some of those
streets" and did not stop to ask what just-war theory says about wholesale kill-
ing of civilians[11] or whether God might judge us for such an act. They forgot

---

[10]Richard Brookhiser, "Our Day of Infamy," *National Review*, October 1, 2001, p. 17.
[11]"At War," *National Review*, October 1, 2001, p. 6 (editorial).

that Osama bin Laden was a CIA tool against the Soviets in the 1980s. That God gives states the sword does not mean he will fail to hold them accountable for how they use it. The left erroneously but frequently holds states to a church's standards; however, just because God does not expect a government hit hard on September 11 to turn the other cheek and not retaliate does not mean that he will excuse any and all forms of retaliation.

Conservatives see markets and the military as means to the patriotic end of defending the United States. Patriotic sacrifice, such as military service, is a legitimate way for the individual to offer—and the government to demand—an individual's time. An unquestioning patriotism that supports "my country right or wrong" does undercut the idea of God's judgment. The patriot sees prophetic cries of judgment as unpatriotic. Recall the outcry against Jeremiah. Yet markets, the military and the nation they serve are not exempt from the God who directs history.

Centrist Ideas of Justice and Why September 11 Could Not Be God's Judgment

After September 11, centrists agreed with conservatives that this was war, not a manhunt, and it must be waged with patriotic toughness. (Our look at centrists may include leftists whom tragedy temporarily drove to the center.) Centrists tend not to say that "West is best" in a superlative absolute sense, as Paul Johnson did, but that Western free-market democracy works better than the alternatives. Justice is downsized in this pragmatism. Justice means statutes passed by elected legislatures and enforced by courts. Centrists disdain grand, cosmic ideas of justice from left or right. Christopher Hitchins disdained Noam Chomsky's opinion that September 11 was a just reprisal for America's imperial misdeeds and the "world view" of "the religious dogmatists" who saw it as "a divine judgment on a sinful society."[12]

Centrists stress democracy more than free markets. Markets work in practical ways; we have no better mechanism; but they do not create absolute property rights. Democracies may regulate them so that no one earns too little to be an effective citizen, and no one earns so much that he or she controls other citizens and the democratic process. Practical policy wonks will decide the details, not moralizing prophets condemning injustice. Decisions arise out of a democratic "conversation" in our civil society. Conversation in the international community and its institutions constitutes a global civil society with a

---

[12]Christopher Hitchens, "Stranger in a Strange Land," *The Atlantic Monthly*, December 2001, p. 32.

public opinion that can aid failed states and limit rogue ones. For centrists, talk about justice is absolutist and uncompromising; it makes demands and truth claims the democratic conversation cannot handle. They agree with fellow centrist, Friedman, that exclusivist religions endanger peace. Talk of God judging evil tends to silence the "conversation" about pragmatic next steps toward limited goals.

Yet problems arise. Absent absolutes that can relativize it, centrists' democracy balloons into a cosmic idea. The best available means for fixing sales tax rates or highway routes is blown up into the only means for deciding when life begins or if humans should be cloned. Individuals take the political rights democracy gives them and apply these to culture, lifestyle, sexuality, worldview, the cosmos. The Supreme Court rules that liberty involves "the right to define one's own concept of existence, of meaning, of the universe, and of the mystery of human life."[13] From governing a township to defining the universe is one giant leap for democracy.

Given freedom and funds for enjoying private life, ordinary citizens play there and try to avoid the public conversation. Policy wonks and political strategists who do converse then assume grand, cosmic roles of finding history's meaning, fixing its "end," strategizing about a new world order, discussing the fate of nations.[14] Presuming to take on topics that are God's to decide, they presume to charge preachers like Falwell, who announce God's judgment on the nation, with being presumptuous. For them, the international community has a theoretical moral right to define injustice, but its divisions leave the sole superpower as, practically, the one judge who can restore a pragmatic justice after September 11. In the pages of the policy journals, the policy community sits as the judge of what the superpower should do.

To be fair, centrist policy wonks perform functions that are essential and necessary—but not sufficient. Democracy is only one of our systems and citizen only one of our roles. As created beings cast into a history we do not control, we must also consider the God who does control the stream of events. To single-mindedly confine all informed analysis of September 11 to foreign policy and intelligence gathering and to exclude informed thought about God in history as out of bounds and presumptuous is to privilege one role so as to forget another.

---

[13]Quoted from *Casey* v. *Planned Parenthood,* by Ponnuru, "What We're Not Fighting For," p. 20.
[14]See, e.g., the fall 2001 issue of *New Perspectives Quarterly.*

Leftist Ideas of Justice and Why September 11 Could Not Be Judgment

After September 11, centrists lambasted the left for "show[ing] contempt—preferring to shock and insult mainstream America than to participate in democratic politics as loyal and responsible members of the national community."[15] Leftists' strong sense of injustice tended to shock other Americans. The left issues prophetic critiques against corporations that manipulate markets, the rich who exploit the poor, rich donors who improperly influence campaigns, the U.S. government that maintains hegemony over the world, bankers who control international financial institutions. It calls on the democratic majority to restore justice at home; the international community, to restore it abroad. The left takes unpopular stands in warning Americans against the dangers of national arrogance and exclusive trust in military power.

The left's moral sense of justice seems on the surface to fit Old Testament prophets' call for social justice for the poor and Jesus' call for peacemaking, nonresistance to evil and charity for the poor. That is its ancient source, but the stream is now far from its source. A century ago, the left largely accepted evolution and higher criticism and thus dropped a literal interpretation of Scripture (identified with its conservative opponents). It saw an end to economic injustice and to war as primary moral issues, and personal morality as secondary. Leftists settled on a human-centered concept of justice, without a literal God as Judge to enforce it, with Jesus as a means to the ends of aiding the poor and bringing peace—not an exclusive means, for Buddha or Muhammed or any revered religious symbol might help achieve the ends, too. Placing humans as ends and displacing God meant placing the burden on humans to bring justice to history. When history seemed to be moving inexorably leftward, that task seemed doable. The idea of evolution undercut the idea of God as Judge in history. Justice became a generalization lacking the exclusive, personal God who acted and whom grateful, holy people then worshiped.

During the recent conservative resurgence, the left has agonized in doubt over where history as evolution is headed. Its prophetic critiques sound like rants, as if Elijah had called in vain for divine fire to come down, then descended from Carmel and prophesied against Ahab and Jezebel anyway, in despairing anger. In its version of the Enlightenment utopian project, the left seeks a people, idea or force to bring justice to history: the proletariat, socialism, science, revolution, diversity, multiculturalism. Many have noted how Marxism is Christian eschatology remade: the party is the church; the proletariat, the Messiah; and the withering away of the state, the millennium. When the proletariat

---

[15]Peter Beinart, "Sidelines," *The New Republic,* September 24, 2001, p. 8.

votes conservative or the revolution is frozen in bureaucracy, the left wonders how history can be made to turn out properly.

Leftists find recent history discouraging: Marxism all but dead; the people mired in consumer "false consciousness"; socialism retreating; religion reviving; science co-opted for corporate profit; multinationals ruling economies; the U.S. "hegemon" dominant; the international community ignored by the United States or subservient to it. Fire has come down for Baal's prophets but not for them. They seek a judge to end this injustice: their reason favors the international community or, if that fails, impersonal mechanisms like blowback; their anger sounds willing to let Islamists or the Arab street wreak justice as revenge. They do not seek the biblical God as the Judge. That concept they regard as premodern, too Western for a multicultural world, too supernatural for an age of evolutionary science, too absolute for a postmodern era. Yet how can mere humans presume to know where history is headed? Evolutionary theory was itself the product of an historical moment, the nineteenth-century faith in progress, and it does not transcend history or give history meaning. The fundamental leftist error is to imagine that the supernatural Judge could be dead or ineffectual but that justice would go on living.

The 1990s: Age of Democratic, Free-Market, Internet Relativism and Consumerism

Most Americans—while bemoaning political divisions—may not greatly object to a stalemate between "red" and "blue" America. Our right, center and left originated in nineteenth-century liberalism, a stress on individual liberty and free markets in ideas, goods and services. The right advocated retaining free markets in goods and services but not always in ideas, in culture. The left sought to regulate markets for goods and services but not ideas. The practical center would regulate both but not for ideological reasons. When Americans split power among the three groups and entrust it wholly to none, they retain maximum freedom in economic and cultural realms. They prevent any consensus definition of justice and confine its meaning to individual rights: my right to use my wealth, my mind and my body in any way I see fit. This assertion excludes a divine Judge. If I can "define [my] own concept of existence, of meaning, of the universe, and of the mystery of human life," then I can define a divine Judge as nonexistent.

The 1990s were the heyday of individualistic, technology-empowered consumerism, driven by information technology (IT) and the Internet, which the free-market right kept largely unregulated and partly for-profit, the pragmatic center and President Clinton (the policy wonk) promoted as the democratic economic-growth technology, and the free-thought left supported as an uncensored, anti-authoritarian, global forum that offered free services to peoples around the globe. The Internet represented a kind of synergy of all political viewpoints and offered chat rooms and websites for all of them. The IT-driven prosperity of the 1990s demonstrated that these viewpoints had similarities and might converge. Belief in free markets, democratic pragmatism, global capitalism, individual consumerism and evolution might be means to the same end. As the Enlightenment's children, they could join in a human-centered utopian project, rational and scientific in methods, global and cosmopolitan in scope— even if they could not agree on its exact blueprint.

A flamboyant expression of 1990s New-Economy utopian hopes appeared in the October 1999 "Big Issue" of *Forbes ASAP*, on Teilhard de Chardin's idea that "everything that rises must converge." A paleontologist and Jesuit priest, de Chardin (1881-1955) theorized that evolution was shaping humanity into a near-divinity and prophesied that computers would form one globe-spanning "nervous system for humanity" accelerating that process. For *ASAP*, noted authors, pundits, CEOs and celebrities wrote essays on convergence. The few naysayers did not oppose the idea because humans were not divine and God would judge them before they got near that goal. They feared that it might conflict with personal privacy, leisure time or tradition.

From many political perspectives, the many yeasayers stressed that high-tech innovation and the Web gave humans a kind of omniscience, omnipresence and omnipotence. For free-market guru George Gilder, the Web was the market writ global at the speed of light, "the creative interplay of limit and infinite, the flesh and the divine." Sociobiologist Edmund O. Wilson ("Hardwired for God") claimed science answered ultimate questions: "The origin of existence, the essence of life, the nature of mind, the meaning of human life, the wellsprings of ethics and religious faith." Science would prove the "biological origin" of our idea of God. No one wrote, "Humanity is becoming the only divinity," but they came close. Chardin's Omega Point of convergence, novelist Mark Helprin noted, "by any name is God."[16]

Converging were conservatives' faith in free markets, centrists' pragmatic opinion that free markets and democratic individualism worked best to stimulate technological innovation and economic growth, a center-right advocacy of

---

[16]George Gilder, "The Brightest Star," pp. 29-34 (quote from p. 34); Edward O. Wilson, "Hardwired for God," p. 132, see also pp. 133-34; Mark Helprin, "Contrivance: A Theory of Everything Signifying Nothing," p. 246, see pp. 244-50; Tom Wolfe, "Digibabble, Fairy Dust and the Human Anthill," pp. 213-27, all in *Forbes ASAP*, Big Issue 4 (October 1999).

globalization, and leftists' confidence that advancing science and technology united peoples and encouraged multicultural pluralism. None of these ideologies took literally and seriously claims that God reigned and humans must obey; none defined human infringement on God's rights as injustice that would meet its Judge one day; therefore, none saw the Omega Point as a sign this path was blasphemous and must be abandoned. Excluding the divine Judge had consequences; it enabled diverse groups to work toward the same utopian project because, in the Internet that no one governed, an agreed-on advance blueprint was unnecessary.

In a striking piece at the end of this issue of *ASAP*, Helprin gave one of the strongest secular prophecies that this 1990s hubris was bound to end in some catastrophe such as September 11, just as turn-of-the-century overconfidence ended in World War I. He quoted Thomas Hardy's poem on the shipbuilders' indestructible *Titanic* and its end, "The Convergence of the Twain: Lines on the Loss of the *Titanic*": "And as the smart ship grew / In stature, grace, and hue, / In shadowy silent distance grew the Iceberg too." Iceberg and ship seemed too distant to have any link to each other, "Till the Spinner of the Years / Said 'Now!' And each one hears, / And consummation comes, and jars two hemispheres." Helprin drew this moral: "throughout history grandiose expectations are almost always confounded and overturned in tragedy." Hardy attributed the overturning to God ("the Spinner of the Years"). Helprin did not do so explicitly but merely warned, that is the way things happen in history.[17]

There is a poetic sense of justice in this near-prophetic piece, but it does not exactly work in interpreting September 11. The Spinner of the Years might not jar two hemispheres because of one issue of one magazine. Nor was the 1990s New Economy the only factor that put the West "in the face" of radical Islam. We must seek a more explicitly Christian and a more nuanced view if we are to interpret that tragedy. More broadly, Helprin's literary critique only created a short critical distance from this utopian project. We must go beyond or behind the Enlightenment in order to recover a proper sense of justice and judgment, and especially to include an active God in both concepts. Ultimately, we must go to the Scriptures and their prophets, and not rest content with literary writers who perform distant echoes of the prophets' roles. But first, we must find a way beyond the dominant idea of Christianity as worldview, which is the Enlightenment's child also.

---

[17]Helprin, "Contrivance," p. 250.

3

Why Is Worldview Thinking Agnostic on God's Judgments in History?

Why could not an evangelical writer warn that the Spinner of the Years was set to judge human arrogance or had done so in an event like September 11? Why is it permissible to raise such issues with a poem from the literary canon but not with a text from the scriptural canon? In this chapter we look at how a dominant worldview apologetics hinders discussion of judgment. We consider how a historical view of the faith might interpret September 11 as God's judgment on the nation. To arrive at a more historical view of our faith, we must get past a major barrier—the more philosophical one known as worldview thinking. To speak figuratively, like a protective lens, it blocks out the rays of specific historical events (as ones we cannot interpret) and lets through the generalized light of philosophical principles. If we are to introduce a new view (really, the recovery of an ancient one), we must get past the one that presently prevails. That does not mean shoving it aside in an unfriendly way that disregards its many contributions.

It is impossible to prove a negative: that no worldview thinker warned of judgment or identified it after the fact. But my survey of some Christian worldview writers did not find such cases, and worldview thought works against such warnings. The idea of a "worldview" (translated from the German *Weltanschauung*) comes out of the Enlightenment, to which broad outlook evangelical worldview thinking has adapted. To argue against secular aspects of this outlook, to be heard in academic and other circles ruled by this outlook, evangelical apologists accept some of its ground rules for reasoning and arguing. In our look at worldview, we will be greatly aided by David Naugle's excellent book, *Worldview: The History of a Concept.*[1]

---

[1]David Naugle, *Worldview: The History of a Concept* (Grand Rapids: Eerdmans, 2002). See also James W. Sire's insightful response to Naugle, *Naming the Elephant: Worldview as a Concept* (Downers Grove, Ill.: InterVarsity Press, 2004).

Naugle accurately describes how "the last several decades have witnessed an explosion of interest in worldview in certain circles of the evangelical church." The idea of Christianity as a worldview has "come to the rescue" of a church besieged, since the Enlightenment, by "secularizing forces" that have exiled "theistic perspectives" from "public life" and confined faith "to matters of personal piety." To engage the culture, believers have employed "the explanatory power, intellectual coherence, and pragmatic effectiveness of the Christian worldview."[2]

This concept has been set forth by so many fine Christian writers, possessing such love for the Lord and zeal to win souls for Christ and employing such sophisticated arguments—all in greater quantity and quality than I possess—that I am reluctant to critique it. Yet worldview thinking seems to have a blind spot regarding God's judgments in historical events. It seems not to define the Christian faith as salvation from judgment, as an interpretation of history. It tends to praise Paul's opening but never to arrive at his concluding remarks on Mars Hill. Were these matters not so vital to biblical faith, we should let the prevailing apologetic battle its intellectual enemies and pray for its success. But they are vital, and we do need to interpret September 11.

An "Agnostic" Worldview: Who Can Know If September 11 Was Judgment?

Here we revisit Andree Seu's lament about Christians being "diffident" about September 11 "except to say that it's not this and it's not that, and to venture generally that we should hate evil and love good." Agnostics on judgment, they chose biblical texts showing that "we cannot know what God is doing and why." A concept as influential as the one Naugle describes must share responsibility for this "gag rule," this "theology of negation."[3] For example, the Breakpoint webpage gave an agnostic response to the question, "Why did God allow this? . . . The specific answer: we don't know." To support this answer, it cited Deuteronomy 29:29 ("The secret things belong to the LORD our God").[4] And yet, Deuteronomy 29:18-28 predict that even the surrounding heathen nations will see and understand that the calamities that come on Israel in Canaan are God's judgment upon its fall into idolatry. So the calamitous judgments are not secret things.

---

[2]Naugle, *Worldview*, pp. xv, 4-5, 31-32.
[3]Andree Seu, "True Perspectives," *World*, October 20, 2001, p. 41.
[4]"Making Biblical Sense of This National Tragedy," <www.breakpoint.org> or <www.pfm.org>; downloaded by author on May 8, 2002, and still archived there. It is unclear what that passage means by the "secret things," but certainly the Lord's law that Israel is to obey and the calamities that will result from disobedience are not considered secrets.

Christianity Today avoided the question of judgment and implied that we don't know, so we won't even discuss it, and it might be dangerous to do so. In "Rally Round the Flag," *CT* spoke on behalf of evangelicals as citizens with a worldview, one that, thankfully, did not place itself above the nation-state but left them as loyal citizens helping the nation achieve justice, not proclaiming that God would achieve it. Before September 11, evangelicals believed "they could pursue justice" by mouthing words critical of injustice "from the safety of the pulpit (or with the scathing editorial)." September 11 revealed the inadequacy of a verbal, worldview-informed opinion on human justice. Yet *CT* did not turn to proclaiming a God who judges injustice. Instead, governments would do so, aided by worldview-informed evangelical citizens.[5]

That omitted God's actions and his other tools besides governments. Believers must act as citizens according to biblical commands; however, we have other roles. One role is to be Christ's ambassadors (2 Corinthians 5:20). While under house arrest in Rome, Paul preached to Caesar's palace guard (Philippians 1:13) as "an ambassador in chains" (Ephesians 6:20) for the gospel. An ambassador proclaims the policy of the government that sent him or her. To do so is not presumption. For an ambassador to disregard instructions and act as a mere private citizen, mowing the lawn and shopping and expressing private views at birthday parties, is presumptuous behavior. It is to defy orders. We need not decide the controversy about whether, on July 25, 1989, Ambassador April Glaspie clearly proclaimed to Saddam Hussein the U.S. government's views regarding his threats against Kuwait. We need only observe that, if she had not done so but had pretended to be a private citizen (she did go on vacation right after this meeting), then thousands of lives and billions of dollars may have been wasted as a result.[6] We do our contemporaries no favors by denying our ambassadorial role, pretending we have just a personal worldview and omitting divine judgment.

Agnostic evangelical avoidance appears in the frequent post-9/11 comment that now we see that evil is real.[7] Yes, but that is misleadingly terse. It is not a "theology of fullness of truth." To talk about evil without mentioning the divine Judge is like giving a talk on crime as a philosophical concept without mention-

---

[5]"Rally Round the Flag," *Christianity Today,* November 12, 2001, pp. 36-37.

[6]M. J. Akbar, *The Shade of Swords: Jihad and the Conflict Between Islam and Christianity* (London: Routledge, 2003), p. 261. Akbar absolves Glaspie of direct responsibility: "She solemnly parroted the State Department line that America had no opinion on Arab conflicts." David Wells discusses this ambassadorial role in *Above All Earthly Pow'rs: Christ in a Postmodern World* (Grand Rapids: Eerdmans, 2005), p. 10.

[7]Charles Colson, "Terrorism, War and Evil," 1 of 2, and Jim Tonkowich, "Ten Things We Should Have Learned since September 11, 2001," 2 of 4, both on the Breakpoint website, <www.pfm.org/AM>, downloaded by the author on January 29, 2005.

ing laws, sheriffs, district attorneys, courts and sentences. One web page stated, "Christianity has a theology of evil that explains events like 9/11 and gives the solution for it" but did not give that theology or that solution.[8]

An agnostic "gag rule" about God's judgments arises partly from the intellectual dominance of worldview thinking within evangelicalism, when compared with somewhat primitive, somewhat fundamentalist "judgment talk" such as Falwell's on Robertson's *700 Club*. Fearful lest talk of judgment arouse primeval passions and hasty opinions in evangelical churches, the shapers of evangelical opinion impose the "gag rule" and privilege worldview thinking to keep evangelicals less controversial and enable us to make a stronger, more reasoned appeal to the world. They are often right in so doing. Yet this is a false dichotomy. This book aims to present a fuller analysis, so that worldview thinkers do not have only talk-show hosts and their guests to compete against.

Arguments are partly shaped, in a sociological manner almost, by their normal audiences. Aimed mainly at educated audiences and produced by academic writers to persuade them, worldview thinking is fine-tuned in the process; aimed at a mass-market evangelical audience and produced by mass-market preachers and writers and media experts, "judgment" thinking is simplified and popularized. Worldview thinking acquires more intellectual and spiritual weight than its arguments warrant—and ideas of judgment, less weight than warranted. This look at God's judgments in history is intended to help correct this imbalance. In light of Scripture and the history of Christian theology, ideas of God's judgment are by no means simplistic. In their zeal to give a Christian interpretation of current events, writers for popular audiences have woefully exaggerated the rate of historical change, made wildly erroneous guesses as to the identity of the antichrist and made unwarranted predictions of the time of Christ's return. Yet, as Sundberg argued, "every theology across the centuries has been misused. Why single this one out?"[9]

Worldview thinking is not totally erroneous or always unhelpful. Yet not every problem is a nail this hammer can solve. Well-suited for the mid-twentieth-century campus of genuinely inquiring students confronting secular modernism, worldview apologetics may not fare so well in a very different twenty-first century. I recall an on-campus lecture on apologetics that ended after making a case for the-

---

[8]Tonkowich, "Ten Things," p. 2. Tonkowich's article did attempt a broad worldview-informed assessment of September 11 but, as Louis Menand said of other such attempts, it largely concluded that worldview thinkers had been right all along. One of his ten lessons was "We must develop a Christian worldview in order to survive" (1 of 4).
[9]Walter Sundberg, "'Evil' After 9/11: The Alien Work of God," *Word & World* (spring 2004): pp. 204-7.

istic perspectives in academia. That may not be adequate when monotheists are slamming jet planes into tall buildings. Radical Islamists seem even less open to rational dialogue than were secular Marxists. And, mere monotheism never saved anyone. Can philosophical reasoning arrive at Christ's specific, historical substitutionary atonement that can save? Worldview is tied to the Enlightenment's philosophical categories and so has trouble battling anti-Enlightenment postmodernism. Worldview apologetics often just argues that relativism itself claims to be an absolute truth, that postmodernist rejection of meta-narratives is itself a meta-narrative. We can do better than a logic of negation, of opponents' self-contradiction. We can point to a history that positively confirms our faith.[10]

Worldview thinking, needing and using definitions, tends to perceive concepts or systems like free-market capitalism as relatively fixed and unchanging. Some would argue that free-market capitalism is part of a Christian worldview. What then do we make of the utopian, New-Economy, high-tech global-capitalism-as-Omega-Point in *Forbes ASAP?* This is not your grandfather's capitalism. Because it privileges fixed philosophical categories over historical change, Christianity as worldview is vulnerable to transforming events like the rise of radical Islam or the emergence of a high-tech, postmodern, utopian capitalism. To be fair, some thinkers merely use *worldview* to mean that everyone starts with presuppositions—they may not identify *one* Christian worldview. Presuppositions are a psychological reality but must be tested by Scripture, and popularizers do identify one Christian worldview.

Why Worldview Philosophy Seems Unable to Come to Grips with Tragic History

Naugle's excellent book helps us to see why the concept of worldview does not come to grips with God's judgments in history and, thus, with the essence of the human predicament. German philosopher Immanuel Kant coined the term *Weltanschauung* in his *Critique of Judgment* (1790; discussing human discernment, not divine judgment). "Kant's Copernican revolution in philosophy, with its emphasis on the knowing and willing self as the cognitive and moral center of the universe, created the conceptual space" for this idea, Naugle notes. It played a minor role in Kant's argument but was emphasized by his followers,

---

[10]See, e.g., Millard J. Erickson, *The Postmodern World: Discerning the Times and the Spirit of Our Age* (Wheaton, Ill.: Crossway, 2002), pp. 101-3. The best ad hoc argument against postmodernism I have heard came during the question-and-answer time after a session at the 1994 Wheaton Theology Conference, when someone asked the postmodern presenter whether Christ's Return ("the *eschaton*") would be witnessed by everyone on earth or only by the "faith community." He had no real answer.

"mostly in the German idealist and romantic traditions." The term comes to us marked by the notion of Kant's knowing self at the universe's center. It is the self that needs a worldview and the self that constructs one out of the available materials. This subjective and relativistic connotation has grown more pronounced over the past two centuries, Naugle concludes.[11]

Naugle does a thorough job of radical surgery, grounding worldview in the biblical concept of the "heart," grafting on to the idea the reality of sin's harmful effects, injecting a strong dose of objectivity, adjusting for spiritual warfare and setting it in the context of salvation history.[12] Commendably, he honestly discusses shortcomings of an idea he used in campus ministry. Also commendably, James W. Sire rethinks worldview in light of Naugle's book. To his prior philosophical analysis, Sire adds a "master" narrative: "Would it be better to consider a worldview as the *story* we live by?" Yes. "Most of the Bible is story . . . a history, a story of events that really happened (not just-so stories, or likely stories, or myths)."[13] Yet this surgery does not remake a worldview into something other than an answer to questions the knowing self poses about *other things* besides its own guilt. The concept is still plagued with philosophical conundrums: whether the self should start with reality (ontology), how it knows reality (epistemology), how words relate to reality (semiotics), how it interprets words (hermeneutics).[14]

The knowing self is central. Perversely, the inquiring self that questions to gain knowledge of God morphs into a supposedly innocent self that questions if this God meets its high standards. The classroom becomes a courtroom. C. S. Lewis noted, "The ancient man approached God . . . as the accused person approaches his judge. For the modern man the roles are reversed. He is the judge; God is in the dock." God's existence is doubted. The knowing self looks to the evidence to see if God exists, how she can know that, how "God" might be interpreted and if the Christian interpretation is credible. The knowing self presumes to judge whether God is innocent or guilty. A modern person "is quite a kindly judge; if God should have a reasonable defence for being the god who permits war, poverty, and disease, he is ready to listen to it. The trial may even end in God's acquittal." The key fact "is that man is on the Bench and God is in the Dock."[15]

This supposed trial runs counter to Scripture. Yet, to gain the ear of modern

---

[11]Naugle, *Worldview*, pp. 58-59; see also pp. 256-58.
[12]Ibid., 260-90.
[13]Ibid., pp. xx-xxi; James W. Sire, *Naming the Elephant: Worldview as a Concept* (Downers Grove, Ill.: InterVarsity Press, 2004), pp. 100-102.
[14]These concerns are raised in Sire, *Naming the Elephant*, pp. 48-49, 52-63; and Naugle, *Worldview*, pp. 291-96, 305-6.
[15]C. S. Lewis, "God in the Dock," *Essay Collections* (New York: HarperCollins, 2000), p. 36.

audiences, Christian apologists often play by its rules. (Postmodern thinking conducts the trial differently, but God is still in the dock.) Worldview's knowing self no more wants to consider an infinitely holy, judging God than the district attorney wants to interrupt a trial to file charges against himself.

In *Above All Earthly Pow'rs,* David Wells refuses to play by those rules and critiques the seeker-sensitive, consumer-oriented, early-twenty-first-century evangelical church that "rearranges itself around human needs and desires." Here, Scripture's history of salvation is "irrelevant because for any valid, compelling story to emerge it must begin, not with God, but within the consumer." To counter this view, Wells turns to the doctrine of judgment and warns that our "way of life . . . lies under the judgment of God." However, Wells continues to use the term *worldview* as an unproblematic one and to rely on the self-contradiction of relativism being presented as (absolute) truth. He refers briefly to Naugle's book but not to Naugle's critique of worldview as a term. He does not explain how consumer and knowing self are related or how judgment relates to Christian worldview. History and philosophy just sit side by side.[16]

The self's centrality also is a major reason why worldview thinking has trouble successfully opposing utopian projects that exalt the self. *ASAP*'s issue on the human-as-god Omega Point reflects scientific advances—cyborg technology, human cloning, embryonic stem cell research, manipulations of the genetic code—that promise healing and new capabilities for the human self (see chapter 11). Avoiding a controversial argument from Scripture, stressing possible dangers to humanity or the self and pointing to a fixed creation order, worldview thinking risks losing its case. Science may remove the present dangers of any technique. The knowing self will welcome scientific enhancements to itself, if not dangerous to itself. The created universe may not have been designed by God such that human assumption of godlike powers automatically causes the system to crash apart from his personal intervention. The unpopular warning that the Creator God will not be demeaned may be the only argument against enhancing humans in the long run.

Believing Testimony, Not a Worldview, About Judgment and Salvation in History

As we shall see in the next three chapters, Scripture's testimony is that guilty

---

[16]Wells, *Above All Earthly Pow'rs,* pp. 229, 304; see also pp. 74-90, 198, 200-201, 302. Wells sees Naugle's autonomous self as mainly a postmodern phenomenon and thus not related to the modernist concept of a worldview, but Naugle links the concept of worldview to the autonomous self.

humanity has been, is being and will be tried and judged in a stream of events it cannot control, end or avoid. Human mortality, the toil for survival, the transitory nature of human achievements and the threat of catastrophe from natural forces or human enemies—all are events in history that, as general categories, represent God's judgment on human sin. (Our vulnerability to catastrophe is a judgment, although a specific catastrophe may not be one.) And, a painful eternity apart from God awaits the guilty soul after history ends. The question confronting the self is how to escape God's judgment, not whether a tree exists in reality or in the mind, or how the self can know if a tree exists or whether the word *tree* represents the reality.

Before turning to Scripture, we consider what sort of knowledge is there represented, if it is not a worldview. This message comes as testimony: ancient texts claiming to be (or to be based on) eyewitness accounts of historical events and to give authoritative interpretations of those events as well as prophecies of future ones (2 Peter 1:16-21, Luke 1:1-4). This testimony may run counter to appearances (e.g., Christ's reign) or to assumptions about what can occur (e.g., Christ's resurrection). One definition of faith is a belief in God's promises and his testimony, appearances to the contrary notwithstanding. Worldview thinking stresses the knowing self that believes because it perceives the intellectual coherence of the Christian faith. A more biblical view is that the guilty self, helpless in a stream of events threatening imminent divine judgment, is thrown a lifesaving testimony to believe despite misleading appearances and other hindrances to belief. Belief is warranted due to the trustworthy character of the Testifier not because the testimony is so clearly true, even self-evident, as to form the conclusion to a syllogism.

Historian Rick Kennedy describes testimony's role in the "history of reasonableness." "Early Christian apologetics was founded on appeals to the authority of history and eyewitness testimony"; apologists "recogniz[ed] that the reasonableness of Christianity fundamentally required trusting testifiers rather than one's own intuition or experience." The faith is grounded in historical events: the birth, life, teachings, crucifixion, resurrection and ascension of Jesus of Nazareth, a real historical figure. Postapostolic generations had to believe testimony about events they could not witness. They could not put their hands into his wounded side ("blessed are those who have not seen and yet have believed," John 20:29). Gradually, some apologists "embraced rationalism," believing "the probabilities and uncertainties of apologetics based on testimony could be superseded by the certainties of scientific logic." Kennedy argues, "The general tendency of the Christian intellectual elite throughout history has been to seek a stronger and more certain faith than that offered by a dialectic rooted in trusting human and divine testimony."[17] Worldview thinking is surely only the latest product of that search. We will examine the role of this elite, this knowledge class, in later chapters.

No surprise that the main philosopher who minimized testimony as a means to knowledge was Kant, who coined *Weltanschauung*. Kant sought "to counteract the hubris of people who say they know the mind of God or have access to unwarranted certainty of historical events," Kennedy asserts. So he "encourage[d] a self-absorbed insistence that reasonable people trust themselves, not others."[18] Yet an irreducible core of Christian faith is testimony about past events.

No surprise that the Enlightenment minimized history and that this baggage accompanies worldview thinking. In Sire's list of "seven prime questions" that a worldview answers, the last question is "What is the meaning of human history?" To be fair, he has recently added the master narrative of salvation history as another component, and he quotes Lesslie Newbigin: "The Bible is universal history." Nevertheless, he defines a worldview as "a commitment, a fundamental orientation of the heart," which could "be expressed" *either* "as a story or in a set of propositions . . . which we hold . . . about the basic constitution of reality, and that provides the foundation on which we live and move and have our being."[19] His commendable surgery on the term grafts history in more than it cuts philosophy out.

No surprise either that this Enlightenment-derived concept leaves Christians susceptible to being co-opted by the Enlightenment-derived political ideologies of left, center and right.

The Christian faith is a history of salvation from judgment. The self believes this testimony. Salvation history is external to the self, not a product of the self's reasoning about reality, history or private life. Whatever its "fundamental orientation," the self must latch on to this testimony to escape God's judgment in its own personal history. This gospel is a train leaving a station; to escape disaster, the self must jump on board—though it has kept no model trains, read no railroading magazines, had no engineer father, never seen a train before, never read a train schedule, finds no word for train in its language and dislikes a rail rescue. The train runs on its tracks, on its schedule, not by the self's chosen route and timing.

---

[17]Rick Kennedy, *A History of Reasonableness: Testimony and Authority in the Art of Thinking* (Rochester, N.Y.: University of Rochester Press, 2004), pp. 43-46. For testimony as a valid means of knowing, I am also greatly indebted to C. A. J. Coady, *Testimony: A Philosophical Study* (Oxford: Oxford University Press, 1992).

[18]Kennedy, *History of Reasonableness*, p. 229.

[19]Sire, *Naming the Elephant*, pp. 101, 102, 104-5, 161.

This salvation history is a tangent touching the unbeliever's self-centered circle at only one point, but that point must become central, and the self-center must become peripheral. The tangent does not wrap itself around the self's circle. The self-circle must follow the tangent.

The Christian faith is not the knowing self's worldview. It is God's view of the helpless, guilty self, his coming down into human history to save that self and his testimony as to what he has done. Appearances to the contrary notwithstanding, the self must believe that testimony in order to escape judgment. At many points, appearances might fit more neatly into a worldview than does the gospel history. A worldview generated by a guilty self will never save it from its guilt.

Worldview may be defined so broadly that its defenders would say that this more historical perspective is itself a worldview. That is philosophers' ancient method of shoehorning us back into the age-old conundrums of ontology, epistemology, semiotics and hermeneutics. But this perspective is a history of divine promises external to the self but believed despite seeming impossibility or seeming incoherence until they are fulfilled in events. Its concept of truth is not ontological (do we know the "really real") but historical (did God do what he promised to do). To dispute relativism, this perspective points out that Jesus predicted the Herodian temple's destruction (Mark 13:2), and it was destroyed, and that event cannot be interpreted as a vindication of the high priest and a repudiation of Jesus' words. The event that fulfills promises and prophecies is what ultimately disproves postmodernism. More recent events also confirm the truth of the gospel: its worldwide proclamation in the nineteenth and twentieth centuries fulfills Christ's promise (Mark 13:10; Matthew 24:14); the survival of the Jewish people in exile despite pressures for assimilation; the return of Jews to set up a state of Israel after some eighteen hundred years (we need not approve of the policies of that state). The individual also finds confirmation of God's truth and faithfulness in his personal history, and that deepens his love for the Testifier. True testimony, unlike syllogisms or axioms or systems of thought, creates a personal relationship.

A Tentative Interpretation of September 11 (Not a Reinterpretation of Christian Faith)

We explore in later chapters this scriptural history of judgment and salvation, as two sides of one coin of God's righteous activity, centered first in one nation, Israel, and then in one individual, the Son of Man, Jesus of Nazareth. For now, we take up the challenge we began with—to see how a more historical view of the Christian faith might interpret September 11 as God's judgment on the nation. We focus on that event, not because it is central to our history of judgment and salvation but because it poses a tough challenge to any such historical view that cannot be evaded. It is not an unsolvable problem. Rather than reinterpret our faith in light of the tragedy, we would reinterpret the tragedy in light of our faith.

One mistake of Falwell and Robertson was to blame the judgment on sins that concerned them the most. A more objective, cautious approach is to identify major actions or features of the United States and the West that anger radical Islamists the most and then to see if any might also anger a holy God. (Some direct causal factors, that are not causes of Islamic anger, might also represent God's judgment.) We do that not to limit God to Islamic grievances or to suggest that he condones Islamic terrorists' acts of vengeance but to limit ourselves and our propensity for partisan, biased reasoning. We limit our list of judged sins to acts or conditions that clearly played a causal role.

Habakkuk questioned God's use of the wicked, cruel Babylonians to judge Israel: "O LORD, you have appointed them to execute judgment" (Habakkuk 1:12). The Lord warned Babylon that he would judge it too: "The cup from the LORD's right hand is coming around to you, / and disgrace will cover your glory!" (Habakkuk 2:16). How can God use wicked tools to judge sinners and yet not partake in their wickedness? It is simply stated in Scripture, and we accept that testimony.

Not all Islamic grievances will Christians see as also offensive to God. The presence of American troops in Saudi Arabia, site of the Muslim holy places of Mecca and Medina, angered Osama bin Laden and other Islamists; however, Christians cannot see the God of Israel and the Father of Jesus as angered by this fact alone (unless the troops commit unjust acts while there).

In a recent book, Peter G. Riddell and Peter Cotterell list "the most frequently stated causes" of the resentment of "the Muslim masses" against the West that Islamic radicals use to recruit support. We will go through these, one by one, to see if any might be causes of divine judgment. One is U.S. support for Israel in its battle against the Palestinians. While God undoubtedly holds the Israeli government responsible for its actions, and some portion of Israel's problem with Palestinian violence is "blowback" from those actions, we get into serious complications if we try to trace a divine judgment against the United States. Israel often does not inform the U.S. government in advance of its actions, and the United States often condemns them after the fact. How much behind-the-scenes collusion exists is hard to determine. As Riddell and Cotterell point out, the Muslim masses want "Israel to disappear as a state"; Christians can hardly say God's judgment rests on the United States for acting to prevent that desired extinction of Israel.[20]

The second is United Nations sanctions against Saddam Hussein's Iraq (since lifted, along with Hussein). Given Hussein's brutal deeds, we will not see God's anger aroused by these sanctions per se. A third is the presence of American troops in Saudi Arabia, which were clearly sent to "protect Saudi Arabia's oil reserves," and our security interests as the chief consumer of that nation's oil.[21] Our troops in Saudi Arabia result from our dependence on that region's oil supplies. Arab resentment partly results from our insatiable desire for oil. Their fourth cause is the globalization that enriches the West and impoverishes less-developed nations, in Islamists' view.[22] Their third and fourth causes can be considered together. Our oil imports and economic dominance occur in the marketplace, and conservatives say self-interested economic behavior in the market is not immoral. That is an Enlightenment view, not a scriptural one. We must take seriously this cause of Muslim anger as a possible judgment on our economic greed. To say that is not to accept leftist anger at America or to claim to be able to sort out what percent of our consumption is somehow excessive. It is to refuse to exempt from judgment all our acts in the market, as if the market scrubbed them clean, and it is to claim that an omniscient God can sort it all out. A God who cannot look behind market transactions is no God at all. It is not purchasing oil that is the issue but our rampant materialism—the sense that our goods are our gods—of which oil consumption is just a symptom and an approximate indicator. God might be angry at a materialistic people.

Riddell and Cotterell dismiss the fifth cause with a pejorative term "Westophobia," a "perception among Muslims of Western culture being decadent and debased" partly "fueled by statements in the Muslim media . . . that reflect and often exaggerate moral decay in Western societies." They admit Hollywood's "worldwide distribution of films including sexually explicit material," but they claim the West is a victim of "negative stereotyping" that exaggerates its immorality.[23] Yet the global impact of Western media is undeniable, and these products offend devout Muslims. To what degree Muslims exaggerate Western moral decay is an academic question. The term "Westophobia" conveniently blames those offended by Western media for the offense. Here, we can say that a holy God is angered by this enterprise of seducing others for profit.

---

[20]Peter G. Riddell and Peter Cotterell, *Islam in Context: Past, Present and Future* (Grand Rapids: Baker Academic, 2003), pp. 153-54.
[21]Ibid., pp. 154-56; M. J. Akbar, *Shade of Swords: Jihad and the Conflict Between Islam and Christianity* (London: Routledge, 2003), p. 208.
[22]Riddell and Cotterell, *Islam in Context*, pp. 154-56, 157-58.
[23]Ibid., pp. 159-60.

The offense is compounded because, Bernard Lewis argues, Muslims tend not to see Western secularism as a rejection of Christianity but as a form of Christianity.[24] Hollywood's output is seen as Christian material, and the Christian God is despised in Islam accordingly. This refusal to take Western secularism at face value, although misinformed, is a divine judgment: the secular West cannot escape responsibility for its religious heritage. Judgment falls on its apostasy. The West has enjoyed the preaching of the gospel for centuries, has turned against it but is still held to the gospel's high moral standards, ironically, by angry Islamists.

We can go to the most direct cause, the terrorists who committed the atrocity. Osama bin Ladin and the *mujahideen,* the original core of al-Qaeda, are indirect creations of the Central Intelligence Agency (CIA) in its 1980s war by proxy against the Soviets in Afghanistan. After the Soviet army seized Afghanistan, the United States sought to trap the U.S.S.R. in its own Vietnam by working through the Pakistani government to fund and arm *mujahideen* who fought the Soviets. During the 1980s, 1.5 million Afghans and thousands of Soviet troops died in an American-financed *jihad* that included terroristic dirty tricks and tactics that could not meet any just-war standard. At the start of this guerrilla war, "In a famous remark Zbigniew Brzezinski, national security adviser to Jimmy Carter, asked whether a few stirred up Muslims were more important than the defeat of the Soviet Union and the liberation of eastern Europe."[25] We can hear the other shoe about to drop. God gives governments the sword, but he holds them accountable for their use of it. He uses one of our Cold War tools against us and has undoubtedly judged Russia similarly. This is not impersonal "blowback," as leftist critics argue, but the act of a personal God who punishes our error of acting as if anti-communist ends justify any and all war-making tactics.

We arrive at this cautious, cause-restricted interpretation of September 11 as possibly God's judgment on us for our materialism, our cultural exports seducing others into immorality and our use of terroristic guerrilla units against the Soviets. It is no more implausible than many partisan views—in fact, it may fit a scriptural view of God. This list will offend the right, which denies that materialism is a sin to be judged; the left, which denies that immoral cultural exports are sins; and the center, which balks at God judging pragmatic strategizers like Brzezinski. It may offend evangelicals of left, center or right and worldview evangelicals, agnostic on judgment.

---

[24]Bernard Lewis, "Secularism and the Civil Society," *What Went Wrong? Western Impact and Middle Eastern Response* (New York: Oxford University Press, 2002), pp. 96-116.
[25]Akbar, *Shade of Swords,* p. 159. See also pp. 158, 161, 206-8, 216.

We cannot be certain, but that is true of many historical interpretations, yet we do not stop interpreting the past. We must beware of presumption in claiming to know the mind of God. But the pendulum has swung to the opposite extreme, where the inability to know for sure morphs into a refusal to ask questions that cannot be answered with certainty and then into a dismissal of the category of divine judgment. This tentative interpretation is meant to restore that category to our minds, and with it the scriptural view, rather than the knowing self's worldview of God. We cannot take God's judgments in history off the table for this generation—a move that Scripture does not authorize us to make. It is to the Scriptures that we now turn, first to the Old Testament, to see if this view squares with God's acts in historical events B.C., as prophesied and recorded in the Old Testament. We turn to God's revealed testimony about his judging role in history.

4

What Does the Old Testament Say About God's Judgments?

$\mathbf{O}$bjections more fundamental than left-center-right ones will be raised against this tentative interpretation. Isn't it self-righteous to talk of God's judgments on others? Don't those who do so presume to know God's mind? Aren't other interpretations possible? If God was angry at these evils, then why didn't he control events so that only those directly responsible were judged? Why the innocent victims? How can he use fanatical killers for his purposes without being himself contaminated by their horrible evil? To try to answer all these questions would be to attempt a theodicy, an argument for God's justice in allowing evil to exist. That is beyond the scope of this book. It is also a branch of philosophy, which we seek to avoid. Scripture gives us a history of God's dealings with humanity. We turn to the Old Testament and then the New Testament to trace his dealings so that we can find *some* answers, if not a worldview answering everything.

The very idea of turning to the Old Testament to find answers about God's judgments in history would be anathema to Enlightenment thought, which was sometimes anti-Semitic and always cosmopolitan and universal. Enlightenment philosophers disdained this ancient testimony that God had a chosen people through whom he worked his will in specific historical events.[1] Such a unique, arbitrary choice seemed unfair to Gentiles, and it left philosophers with no general principle or axiom on which to base their deductive reasoning.

Postconservative evangelicals also tend to reject Old Testament testimony on judgment. They argue that a New Testament ethic of nonviolence and forgiveness of enemies renders Old Testament holy wars anathema, mistakes that God

---

[1]See, e.g., Peter Gay, *The Enlightenment: An Interpretation*, vol. 1, *The Rise of Modern Paganism* (New York: Knopf, 1967).

never intended. In a book of rival views on the conquest of Canaan, C. S. Cowles argues, "Amid the hopes, dreams, and lives shattered" on September 11 "was evangelicalism's easy accommodation with Old Testament genocidal 'texts of terror' " that ordered Israel to wage holy war ("Yahweh war") against its enemies. Falwell and Robertson, he contends, were caught "on the horns of a dilemma" facing Christians interpreting the Old Testament: "How do we harmonize the warrior God of Israel with the God of love incarnate in Jesus?" They got caught, he argues, diagnosing Old Testament judgment that the New Testament made obsolete.[2]

Cowles argues for a "Christological hermeneutic" for interpreting the Old Testament: any Old Testament texts that present a God other than the one we see in the loving, forgiving, nonviolent Jesus must represent an error by their Hebrew authors. Israelites "interpreted God's command to occupy the land in violent and even genocidal ways" that he never intended. To argue that God did so to eradicate Canaanite idols "casts him in the image of an insecure, tin-pot tyrant like Herod the Great, whose paranoia drove him to eradicate . . . competitors," Cowles claims. God does not intervene personally to judge sinners, he asserts; sin brings its own consequences.[3]

We will analyze Cowles's static, timeless Christology later, but now we notice that he projects back onto ancient Israel the new commands that Jesus taught as part of God's new covenant—which Old Testament Israel could not have known. He is guilty of anachronism. The word *genocide* is anachronistic when applied to events in 1400 B.C. The word *violent* (or *violence*) often "implies a violation of another's legal rights or property . . . a corruption or abuse of someone or something entitled to respect"; often the actor is a private person who has lost emotional control and used force that only governments can rightfully use.[4] When used of governments or of God, the word takes connotations of private illegality and, in a guilt by association, attaches these to public entities entitled to use force (but held accountable for its misuse) or to a holy God. Like the use of "Westophobia," this is an attempt to settle the issue by semantics.

How does God accomplish his goals in a history filled with human sin? Cowles does not say. He just sets out a present worldview he thinks is superior to past ones. Once past events create this nonviolent worldview, history is at an

---

[2]C. S. Cowles, "The Case for Radical Discontinuity," in C. S. Cowles, Eugene H. Merrill, Daniel L. Gard and Tremper Longman III, *Show Them No Mercy: Four Views on God and Canaanite Genocide* (Grand Rapids: Zondervan, 2003), pp. 14, 18.
[3]Cowles, "The Case for Radical Discontinuity," pp. 32, 35, 38, 40-41, and Cowles, "A Response to Eugene H. Merrill," in *Show Them No Mercy*, p. 98.
[4]*Webster's New Dictionary of Synonyms* (Springfield, Mass.: Merriam-Webster, 1984), p. 351.

end, its job done. God does not need to use future events to consummate his plan; Cowles's worldview *is* the consummation; judgment becomes obsolete. That places the twenty-first-century individual outside the uncontrollable stream of events and assumes his or her worldview to be largely immune to future changes. That is an unwarranted assumption.

The other three theologians who contributed to this book dissented from Cowles's views: Eugene H. Merrill ("he opens the door to . . . a decanonizing of three-fourths of the Bible"); Daniel L. Gard ("We cannot pick and choose which biblical texts we can accept as coming from God"); and Tremper Longman III ("Cowles in effect rejects the Old Testament as authoritative").[5] Although this debate is useful, we do not examine the judgment called "Yahweh war" or Old Testament Israel's attacks on the nations but God's judgments on the nations generally.

To the Old Testament we turn for a historical view. God's right to judge derives from his act of creation, to which it testifies. Its Hebrew writers set out a historical view of God and humanity. Its being anathema to philosophy helps to free us from a worldview apologetic. To talk of Yahweh bringing Alexander the Great's siege in 332 B.C. to judge Tyre for rejoicing in his chosen city Jerusalem's fall in 586 B.C.—as prophesied several months before Jerusalem's fall, recorded in Ezekiel 26 and prophesied in Zechariah 9:4 some 150 years before Alexander's siege—is to cut the ropes that tie us to philosophy and to set out on a voyage of historical thinking.[6]

We need this Old Testament testimony for our discussion of God's possible judgment of the United States. Some evangelicals believe the United States is God's new Israel, in covenant to obey him. They will easily believe we can be judged for violating this covenant, as Israel was. Other evangelicals deny this and the idea of God's judgment on the United States: no covenant, no judgment for breaking it. Ezekiel 26 and other passages reveal that Gentile, noncovenant nations are judged, too. I will not repeat the argument in *This Rebellious House* for why I believe the United States was not founded as an explicitly and exclusively Christian nation pledged to follow Christ.[7] Massachusetts and other seventeenth-century colonies saw themselves in a covenant; from 1775 to 1787,

---

[5]*Show Them No Mercy*, pp. 47, 55, 58.

[6]See Robert W. Manweiler, "The Destruction of Tyre," in *The Evidence of Prophecy: Fulfilled Prediction as a Testimony to the Truth of Christianity*, ed. Robert C. Newman (Hatfield, Penn.: Interdisciplinary Biblical Research Institute, 1990), pp. 21-30. See also the notes in the *NIV Study Bible*, pp. 1189 (for Jeremiah 39:2), 1227 ("Dates in Ezekiel" chart) and 1262 (for Ezekiel 26:14).

[7]Steven J. Keillor, *This Rebellious House: American History and the Truth of Christianity* (Downers Grove, Ill.: InterVarsity Press, 1996), pp. 81-102.

the states and the United States wrote new constitutions that did not contain such language. After surveying Scripture, we return to U.S. history to apply other scriptural reasons why God judges a noncovenanted nation. To meet the argument against judgment at its strongest point, we assume no national covenant and focus on what Old Testament scholars call the "oracles against the nations" (OAN).[8]

The Enlightenment sparked criticism of the Old Testament canon, based partly on philosophical reasoning that assumed accurate prophecy was impossible, so texts predicting events must be written after the events. German higher criticism looked skeptically on the OAN. The prophets' "major contribution" was "universal monotheism and moral values" . . . "the narrow nationalism of the foreign-nation oracles appeared to have little relevance for anyone." The OAN were "the dregs of the prophetic movement" in critics' eyes. Later form criticism and archaeological discoveries have undercut this a priori view.[9] In his commentary on Ezekiel, Daniel I. Block rejects a "scissors-and-paste approach." He identifies "at least seven discrete stages" from divine vision to a prophet's oral message to a final text but denies these had to be done by seven different persons or over seven centuries. He takes Exekiel's text as handed down in the canon, and we will follow suit with the other Old Testament prophets.[10]

Judgment and Salvation as Two Sides of God's Plan in the Old Testament

First, we look at the Old Testament concept of judgment in general. God's right to judge individuals and nations derives from his creation of the earth and its inhabitants. The Bible testifies to creation; it does not give a scientific or a deductive proof. A New Testament chapter on Old Testament faith begins, "By faith we understand that the universe was formed at God's command, so that what is seen was not made out of what was visible" (Hebrews 11:3). A deductive approach might argue that the self first must accept the axiom of creation. Yet the twenty-first-century self may believe in Christ first and, because he proves faithful, accept later Genesis 1–3, which may raise more doubts than does John 3:16. God's act of sending his Son into the world becomes a powerful reason to believe he must have made it. Believing one piece of testimony, seeing it and the Testifier prove true, we grow confident of his trustworthiness and believe the next piece.

---

[8] I take the term "oracles against the nation" (OAN) from Duane L. Christensen, *Transformations of the War Oracle in Old Testament Prophecy: Studies in the Oracles Against the Nations* (Missoula, Mont.: Scholars Press, 1975), p. 1.

[9] Christensen, *Transformations*, p. 1; see also pp. 2-7.

[10] Daniel I. Block, *The Book of Ezekiel: Chapters 1-24* (Grand Rapids: Eerdmans, 1997), pp. 18-23.

Several Old Testament passages present God's assertion that his act of creation gives him the right of judgment after the Fall. He sees the wickedness of "mankind, whom I have created," and threatens their destruction (Genesis 6:5-8). Much later, God addresses Cyrus, king of Persia, "Woe to him who quarrels with his Maker, / . . . Does the clay say to the potter, / 'What are you making?' / . . . do you question me about my children / or give me orders about the work of my hands? / It is I who made the earth / and created mankind upon it" (Isaiah 45:9, 11, 12). The Creator has strong rights of ownership, rule and judgment—and a strong desire to save what he created.

We should not read back into the Old Testament our American idea of judgment. We picture a passive, impartial, professional jurist independent of executive and legislative branches, who decides cases that others bring into court according to laws the legislature has passed (the verdict vindicates the law and maintains order more than it redresses wrongs against victims), relies on the executive to enforce the verdict, and corrects the other two branches' errors. We picture the state prosecuting a defendant, except in civil cases. We may regard the state as overbearing and sympathize with the underdog on trial or the John Dillinger who avoids capture and trial. In general, we tend to be reductionistic: we exclude entire realms such as foreign policy from the realm of justice; "justice" may mean only procedural fairness; verdicts may be based on narrow individual rights, with the broader social outcome and others' interests ignored.

These notions carry over into our idea of divine judgment. We picture a distant, passive God who suddenly acts where he had never acted before when we did such and such. Our surprise means he is unfair. His overwhelming power means he is unfair. The tragic event we see as unfair: the law and its penalty were unclear; there were no victims hurt by our sin; God never heard our rationalizing explanation, is not impartial, judges in his own case as the aggrieved lawmaker and complainant and acts as prosecutor, jury and sentencing magistrate.

In *The Biblical Doctrine of Judgment,* Leon Morris employed a detailed word study to recapture the Old Testament Hebrew idea. The verb *shaphat* and noun *mishpat* have other, related meanings, but when translated as "to judge" and "the judgment(s)" they connote an idea different from ours. *Shaphat* means to rule or to judge, but the Hebrews did not have our separation of powers, so lawmaking, law-applying and law-enforcing powers are all included. It denotes "power directed towards right ends," and social outcomes or realms like foreign policy are not excluded. *Mishpat* has more meanings, and the context is key. It is not a passive impartiality that delegates action to someone else but "a dynamic right-doing" that sees injustice, steps in to rescue the righteous victim and carries out a just verdict. "Judgment has a salvation aspect." Saving victims and judging wrongdoers are linked. Our laws uphold the status quo and custom; *mishpat* may mean a revolutionary reversal of current injustice. The Lord's judgments vindicate his holiness and can combine mercy and wrath, "to us . . . something of a contradiction." So his judgment is not "merely negative and destructive" but has "a creative element" in separating a righteous remnant from evildoers. It sifts out. Future-oriented, it is not merely a return to the status quo ante.[11]

In his political theology, Anglican theologian Oliver O'Donovan stresses this active sifting out of good from evil in the Old Testament concept: "Yhwh exercises his judgment by making the just and unjust causes manifestly distinct, ending the irresolution of public ambiguity which the cunning of the evil-doer has cast around his deeds."[12] This sifting-out process is part of judgment, a word we use mainly for the end of the process, when the evildoer is punished. For the rest of this book, we focus on sifting out—but the reality of curtain-dropping punishments, too, is not denied. As a historian, I find the long sifting-out process more usable for historical interpretation. It also bridges the divide between the curtain-dropping judgment preached from the pulpit and the ordinary course of events in the past or present that lack any such finality and so might be regarded as not judgments at all. That divide encourages a nonchalant dismissal of preacher's warnings that is quite unjustified. The truth that there is a God actively sifting my thoughts, acts and motives now is about as sobering as the truth that he will one day render a verdict. It avoids self-righteous finger pointing: he sifts all now, even if the curtain now drops only on a few.

In the Old Testament, very few Gentiles landed in the righteous camp: Rahab, Ruth, and a few others. The sifting out of a holy Hebrew remnant makes possible the proclamation of a saving gospel to Gentiles in New Testament times, however. Actively linked are salvation and judgment: the Lord judges the nations to save Israel from their hostility and judges Israel to preserve its purity so it can proclaim his saving power to the nations. God pilots his righteous program through a stream of events amidst human sinfulness that seems to imperil it at times—seems to, for he is sovereign. In the Old Testament he pulls on the

---

[11]Leon Morris, *The Biblical Doctrine of Judgment* (Grand Rapids: Eerdmans, 1960), pp. 7-25 (quotes from pp. 10, 18, 22, 23); R. Laird Harris, Gleason L. Archer and Bruce K. Waltke, eds., *Theological Wordbook of the Old Testament* (Chicago: Moody Press, 1980), 2:947-49. Hebrew uses other words: *dyn* (to vindicate and deliver through judging); *ribb* (to strive and rebuke, often in a lawsuit). "A word [*ribb*] which orginally means 'strife' does not picture God as mildly displeased with sinners." The Old Testament can describe judgment just with metaphors like a burning flame or a cup of wine. Morris, *Doctrine of Judgment*, p. 40; see pp. 26-41.

[12]Oliver O'Donovan, *The Desire of the Nations: Rediscovering the Roots of Political Theology* (Cambridge: Cambridge University Press, 1996), pp. 38-39.

right oar of salvation at this point, so to speak, and on the left oar of judgment at that point, as if to make it through a perilous rapids. He is in control, but salvation and judgment are the means of control that he chooses to use.[13]

We will look later at the Open Theist claim that God can be surprised by events. For now, we note that he retains a flexibility to deal with future events, not because he does not know what they will be but because his holiness will not allow sinners to trap him in a timeless box—a divine program that they think is committed to blessing them even if they turn wicked. Even a people who were chosen could not deduce from that fact security for the individual Hebrew, the temple or any one tribe or generation. Right after commissioning Moses as his chosen leader, God is about to judge Moses—with death—for disobedience in not circumcising his son (Exodus 4:21-26). Ten tribes were exiled in 722 B.C. for idolatry. When wicked Judah thought itself secure because the Lord's temple was in its midst and chanted, "the temple of the LORD," Jeremiah warned them the Lord could destroy his temple (Jeremiah 7:1-15). He did not have to fulfill his purposes through any one Judahite generation, and he exiled that one.

The progression of events seems counterintuitive. Like Gideon whittling his army down from thirty-two thousand men to three hundred men, the Lord used a narrowing-down rule: first all twelve tribes of Israel, then only two, and then a remnant of these two, and always a promise that in the future he would act through one man, the Son of Man, as we shall see. An active Judge sifts out a holy remnant from the general wickedness. No security for individual members of the chosen people; none for other peoples, collectively or individually.

It was arrogant to assume that God could not possibly be judging you because you were an Israelite, a Judahite, a priest or a prophet. Everyone was judged in a sifting-out process. And the process might have uncovered something in you that God must punish. King David showed this godly, humble attitude of not dismissing the possibility of God's judgment. When Absalom's rebellion drove him from Jerusalem and Shimei cursed him and threw stones at him as he fled, David's aide asked for permission to kill Shimei. David replied, "If he is cursing because the LORD said to him, 'Curse David,' who can ask, 'Why do you do this?'" (2 Samuel 16:5-10). He took curses and stones as God's judgment and humbled himself under the volleys.

Our presuppositions may cause us to object that Old Testament history was

---

[13]"Judgment and salvation are closely linked in the theology of these prophets," O. Palmer Robertson summarizes. "Salvation for God's people comes directly in association with the judgment of God's enemies." "The salvation of God ultimately shall include Gentiles as well as Jews." *The Books of Nahum, Habbakuk and Zephaniah* (Grand Rapids: Eerdmans, 1990), p. 24.

unfair. Wait. We haven't come to the Son of Man yet. And rebels have no right to complain of the strategy a government uses to reinstate its authority over them. The Old Testament portrays humanity in rebellion against our Creator, whose rights of ownership and rule we defy, as Southerners in 1861 rebelled against the Federal government, defied its laws, seized its forts and fired on its soldiers. Confederates could not complain that President Lincoln was unfair in focusing resources on capturing Richmond instead of attacking all Southern cities equally, or on controlling the Mississippi River instead of sending equal forces to all Southern rivers. Philadelphians could complain if he sent a gunboat up the Delaware River to shell that loyal city, but rebels relinquish many rights. Can we complain of unfairness if God chose to begin to reinstate his righteous reign with Israel as a beachhead?

Judgment is not the only category of divine action. The Creator showers natural bounty on the good and the evil alike. Yet our mortality, the resulting transitory nature of our works and accomplishments and the hard toil required for our survival are all God's general, all-encompassing judgments on fallen humanity (Genesis 3:17-19). At the opposite end of history, a general judgment again falls, Isaiah warned: "The earth dries up and withers. . . . The earth is defiled by its people; / they have disobeyed the laws, / violated the statutes / and broken the everlasting covenant. / Therefore a curse consumes the earth; / its people must bear their guilt" (Isaiah 24:4-6).

Principles of Divine Judgment in the Oracles Against the Nations (OAN)

Between history's start and finish, God judges in specific events that advance his plan and deal with specific evils. The OAN outline some examples. We will not try to link each of these prophecies to a specific fulfillment event, since we are not examining the issue of prophetic fulfillment but of divine judgment of noncovenanted nations. The OAN consist primarily of the following passages: (1) Isaiah 13–23; (2) Jeremiah 46–51; (3) Ezekiel 25–32; 35; (4) Joel 3:1-16; (5) Amos 1–2:3; (6) Obadiah; (7) Nahum 1–3; (8) Habakkuk 2:4-20; (9) Zephaniah 2:4-15; and (10) Zechariah 9:1-8. Many OAN warn that the Lord will judge a nation for how it treats his chosen nation, Israel. Since Israel's present and future status is a matter of interpretive controversy, we exclude these judgments from our consideration. We want to consider only those reasons for judgment that might still indisputably apply in our own time.

National pride or a ruler's arrogance is most often cited. (In an age of autocratic rule, the two are hard to separate.) Egypt boasts, "I will rise and cover the earth / I will destroy cities and their people," so the Lord will enact "a day of vengeance, for vengeance on his foes" (Jeremiah 46:8, 10). In Ezekiel 27:3, the Lord complains,

"You say, O Tyre, / 'I am perfect in beauty.' " Later he accuses the king of Tyre: "In the pride of your heart / you say, 'I am a god; / I sit on the throne of a god / in the heart of the seas.' / But you are a man and not a god, / though you think you are as wise as a god" (Ezekiel 28:2). "The pride of your heart has deceived you," warns Yahweh in Obadiah 3, and so he will bring Edom low. Israel's God is the universal sovereign who will not respect the ancient custom of a god for each nation but will judge nations for idolatry: Moab, for worshiping Chemosh; Egypt, for "the images in Memphis" and "the idols" (Jeremiah 48:13, 35; Ezekiel 30:13).

Sometimes specific deeds are the crime. Ninevah's cruelty to other nations beside Israel, its sexual immorality, its seduction of others and its occult practices would be judged (Nahum 3:1, 4, 19). Yahweh warned Babylon: "Because you have plundered many nations, / the peoples who are left will plunder you" (Habakkuk 2:8). Amos predicted that Moab's fortresses would be burned "Because he burned, as if to lime / the bones of Edom's king" (Amos 2:1-2). Ninevah would suffer because of one (possibly Ashurbanipal) "who plots evil against the LORD / and counsels wickedness" (Nahum 1:11).

The prophets used devices to indicate the essential justice of the Lord's judgments, as Patrick Miller points out. The sin may be compared with a seed that bears fruit, a given punishment. The "eye for an eye" formula may be cited. The Hebrew verb for the offense may be repeated in the judgment (Habakkuk 2:6-8). The means of sin (e.g., fire to burn the bones of Edom's king [Amos 2:1]) may be the means of judgment (fire to burn Moab's fortresses [Amos 2:2]). "The victim of the sin brings about the judgment on the sinner." The punishment may exemplify a general principle: Edom's fate, Obadiah concludes, illustrates the general rule that "your deeds will return upon your own head" (Obadiah 15). This wording may seem to leave God out as a personal actor. The sin may seem to be a "fate-effecting deed," a key term we will revisit, that means a deed that brings its own fate apart from any action by God. Yet the Old Testament's God-centered theology will not let us stop with the impersonal causes of "blowback." Links between the crime and the punishment stress the justice, not the impersonal nature, of the judgment. Miller gives six persuasive reasons for rejecting the idea of an impersonal mechanism. O. Palmer Robertson reminds us that this justness means "God's judgment is retributive and not always restorative. . . . his judgment has a character of rightness that has no further end," often, except to demonstrate "the reality that a person or a nation shall receive from God's hand exactly what he deserves." That reality is "repulsive to the modern mind" but true.[14]

---

[14]Patrick D. Miller Jr., *Sin and Judgment in the Prophets: A Stylistic and Theological Analysis* (Chico, Calif.: Scholars Press, 1982), pp. 115, 134; see pp. 1-5, 111-19, 121, 130, 132-34; Rob-

It is not always innocent victims who mete out punishment. How can God use fanatical killers without being himself contaminated by their evil? We looked at this issue in chapter 3. God counseled Habakkuk to have patience and faith; the Babylonians' turn was coming. Their overthrow would vindicate divine justice. "I will wait patiently for the day of calamity / to come on the nation invading us," the prophet concluded (Habakkuk 3:16). Using the idea of *deus abscon-ditus* ("hidden God"), Sundberg argues, "God accomplishes his will in the kingdom of this world through the things of the world, even things as terrible and evil as the sword."[15]

Daniel portrays a Last Judgment; the Old Testament teaches ongoing judgment in individuals' lives as well as on nations in history, as in the OAN (Daniel 7:9-10; Jeremiah 17:10-11). The two former cases are more fundamental, but we consider the latter case because of its applicability to September 11, because many people admit in theory a final judgment but treat it as so distant that it seems unreal and because an exclusive focus on individuals risks privatizing the faith.

Miller argues "that a notion of retributive justice is not incompatible with an understanding of divine judgment wrought out in the processes of history. The correlation of [human] sin and [Yahweh's] punishment" is not "capricious and irrational" or "unconnected to the nexus of events, as if it were an 'act of God'" in an insurance policy. "There is no such trivialization of the notion of judgment" but "a kind of synergism in which divine and human action are forged into a single whole." Judgment "does not run counter to the historical processes but happens within them." They remain human and truly historical; it remains supernatural. "The theological task is not to eliminate this word of judgment in history but to probe more deeply into understanding that reality past and present," he concludes.[16]

Daniel's Visions: a Series of Judgments of Empires Lead to a Goal, God's Kingdom

Daniel's prophetic visions occurred during and after the Babylonians' destruction of Judah and the first temple. Exiled to Babylon around 605 B.C., in a first and partial exile, he lived there during and after the fall of Jerusalem in 586 B.C. He was subjected to a pagan despot, Nebuchadnezzar, yet the Lord protected

---

ertson, *Nahum, Habakkuk and Zephaniah*, pp. 21, 22. Miller deals also with the judgments on Israel and on sins against Israel.

[15]Walter Sundberg, "'Evil' After 9/11: The Alien Work of God," *Word & World* (spring 2004): 204.

[16]Miller, *Sin and Judgment*, pp. 138-39.

him—proving Yahweh's sovereignty over pagan nations. God advanced his program in history without the help of a now-prostrate Judah.

Thus, Daniel's OAN are different. The Lord acts apart from Israel: a stone not made "by human hands" destroys the statue that represents human empires (Daniel 2:34, 45); the Lord brings temporary madness on the proud despot; a disembodied hand writes Belshazzar's doom on the wall; an angel protects Daniel from the lions; the Ancient of Days and "one like a son of man" destroy beasts and judge nations. Mistreatment of Israel is not a prominent reason for judgment on the nations. Their proud presumption and awful power are stressed more than their specific misdeeds. Judgment does not reinstate a prior status quo absent proud powers but pushes history along toward a *telos,* a final goal. Here is not an endless tit-for-tat of Egypt used to judge Babylon for its sins, and then the reverse. The succession of kingdoms—gold, silver, bronze and iron or lion, bear, leopard and beast—propels history in a linear direction toward God's final kingdom. Israel, Jerusalem, the temple and the Anointed One are part of this, but Daniel ends with an eschatological vision far beyond a return to Zion and a new temple.

Progress toward this final goal of an eternal, righteous kingdom reinforces the righteousness of God's judgments. They are just given the nations' sins but also wise in having an ultimate righteous purpose and end. They are not a perpetual, pointless repetition such as the author of Ecclesiastes wearily recites: "what has been will be again, / what has been done will be done again; / there is nothing new under the sun" (Ecclesiastes 1:9). There is something new: a divine ("coming with the clouds of heaven") and yet human-appearing figure ("one like a son of man"), the Omega point of history whom all peoples worship. The goal of human history, with all its back-and-forth judgments, is a person. This is not unique to Daniel. The Servant of Isaiah 52:13–53:12, the Branch of Isaiah 11 and Jeremiah 33:14-17, the messianic King of Zechariah 9:9-10—all of these titles and others point to a coming individual who will bring history to an end, with a meaning to it. That fits the Hebrew idea of judgment: not "merely negative and destructive" but "a creative element" of sifting out the righteous to create a new *shalom,* not the status quo ante.

Did God Intend That All His Judgments in History Be Hidden Secrets?

The prophets' OAN show that God is not afraid of revealing himself as a God who uses historical events to punish collective, national evil. Prophets' correlation of crime with punishment shows God revealing and justifying his judgments. Many passages show that the reasons for judgment will not be "secret things."[17] In Deuteronomy 29:24-28, the nations ask, "Why has the LORD done this to this land?" and they either find the answer themselves or it is told to them: "It is because this people abandoned the covenant of the LORD, the God of their fathers." It is no secret. The Lord warns Solomon that future destruction of the temple will be seen by other peoples as punishment for Israel's idolatry (1 Kings 9:7-9). When the king's palace in Jerusalem is destroyed, Jeremiah warns, "People from many nations will pass by this city and will ask one another, 'Why has the LORD done such a thing to this great city?' And the answer will be: 'Because they have forsaken the covenant of the LORD their God' " (Jeremiah 22:8-9).

That does not mean that all calamities in history are God's judgments on particular sins, much less that God always reveals to us the reasons for them. The OAN come from an inspired Scripture that alone is authorized to give God's interpretation of events. We must beware of false prophets who make false claims that God has revealed an interpretation to them. (Falwell was accused of doing that.) Jeremiah mainly condemned false prophets who deny that any judgment is coming on sin. Yet the false oracle—falsely claiming a calamity was a judgment—is also implicitly condemned. " 'Therefore,' declares the LORD, 'I am against the prophets who steal from one another words supposedly from me. . . . But you must not mention 'the oracle of the LORD' again, because every man's own word becomes his oracle and so you distort the words of the living God'" (Jeremiah 23:30, 36; see Jeremiah 23:9-24, 33-40). That personal bias, of "everyone's own word," is what we tried to avoid when we identified three tentative, nonpartisan causes for judgment on the United States.

A gift of prophecy may exist presently (1 Corinthians 12:10; Ephesians 4:11). Yet I do not claim to be a prophet or that the tentative interpretation of September 11 offered in chapter 3 is a divine revelation. I am a historian. As such, I tried to correlate known causes of the event with known categories of divine holiness and judgment. It was tentative, offered to avoid the equally presumptuous error of taking divine judgment off the table for this generation. To do that, as Cowles does, has a similar albeit unintended effect as the words of the false prophets who "keep saying to those who despise me, / 'The LORD says: You will have peace'" (Jeremiah 23:17).

---

[17]An outspoken statement of this is in Ezekiel 39:21-23, toward the end of the prophet's oracle against Gog, when the Lord states, "I will display my glory among the nations, and all the nations will see the punishment I inflict and the hand I lay upon them. From that day forward the house of Israel will know that I am the LORD their God. And the nations will know that the people of Israel went into exile for their sin, because they were unfaithful to me." No agnostic questioning here.

To answer this objection that judgment is now off the table, we must examine the New Testament. A seismic shift is there signaled in God's dealing with humanity: Gentiles are saved on an equal footing with Israelites! How does this shift impact divine judgment? Is it taken off the table? What, if anything, has changed? Before we proceed to the New Testament, we must recall that *mishpat* can mean sifting out the righteous from the wicked, so that God may do justice by saving the righteous. We Americans mainly use "judgment" to refer to the negative consequences the guilty receive at the end. We will partly conform to this English-language usage. It wrenches English too much to use "judgment" to refer also to saving the righteous. But we will start to use the Hebrew *mishpat* or sifting out to describe the longer, more painstaking process that characterizes human history.

Before turning to the New Testament, it may be helpful to consider how one historian has applied this idea of a sifting-out *mishpat* to nonscriptural history. In one talk, the mid-twentieth-century British historian and Christian thinker Herbert Butterfield applied a mainly Old Testament idea of judgment to the long career of Prussian militarism that ended in May 1945—and then to all nations and systems. "The moral judgments that lie in the very nature of history are often long-term affairs." Prussian militarism seemed triumphant in 1870-1871, but it became clear "whether in 1918 or in 1933 or in 1945, or in all these together, [that] a judgment has been passed on the militarism of Prussia." Germany would have avoided future woes "if even in 1918 she could at least have taken the verdict as the judgment of God and set out to discover what it was she had done to offend heaven." Yet he avoided British self-righteousness: "it is a dangerous illusion to imagine that if Germany can be proved to have sinned those who were fighting against her may be assumed to have been righteous. Perhaps the Allies were less-than-righteous tools that God used to judge Germany." Tools are not made holy through use, for communism was "the most terrible instrument of Divine judgment in our generation." In fact, "you cannot introduce the idea of judgment into history without quickly meeting with situations of a paradoxical kind."[18]

"The processes of time have a curious way of bringing out the faultiness that is concealed in a system which at first view seems to be satisfactory." There is "a relentless sifting and testing of anything we achieve." Greek city-states, a Roman empire, the medieval papacy, nineteenth-century liberal nationalist democracy—all were seen in their day as timeless ideals. "Yet the river of time is lit-

---

[18]Herbert Butterfield, "Christianity and History," in *Herbert Butterfield on History,* ed. Robin Winks (New York: Garland, 1985), pp. 49-50, 52.

tered with the ruins of these various systems." Butterfield stressed human sin producing the "fate-effecting deed" but concluded that the process is "a judgment of God."[19] Old Testament prophets would agree: God is an active judge who put nineteenth-century democratic, liberal nationalism through its paces to find out what it was made of, morally. When it displayed the sins of greed, envy, pride and hatred—thus leading to imperialism, a global contest for markets, an arms race and rival alliances—it was judged in the cataclysm of World War I. This *mishpat,* the sifting out of the long nineteenth century, was God's active work, just as in Old Testament times.

[19]Ibid., pp. 53-55, 56, 57.

5

Does the New Testament Render God's Judgment Obsolete?

Some Christian critics of the idea of God judging the nations now, and the United States on September 11, point to the New Testament to prove the idea obsolete. Many would agree that God judged nations in Old Testament times. They might concede Herbert Butterfield's application of Old Testament ideas to German militarism and Nazism but be reluctant to extend them further, perhaps by citing the agnostic response. Claiming the New Testament does not endorse such an idea, they point to Jesus' Sermon on the Mount commanding love of enemies, his refusal to allow the disciples to battle the temple guards, the gospel of salvation on offer in the New Testament and the scattering of Israel, thus leaving no chosen nation to defend and none to inflict God's judgment on enemy nations.

C. S. Cowles vigorously asserts that argument. We start with his case. In looking at the New Testament, we take the text as it stands, avoid texts that are apocalyptic and, therefore, of disputed interpretation (Revelation) and focus on the Gospels and Acts, the New Testament historical books. Critics' strongest points are based on Jesus' teaching in the Gospels, so we will consider their case in this, its strongest and clearest texts. We consider first whether the New Testament renders obsolete God's active judgments in history. Then we look at judgments on nations as opposed to those on individuals or the church.

An Argument That Jesus Ended God's Active Judgment in History

Cowles uses a "Christological hermeneutic" to reinterpret Old Testament texts on Yahweh war as Israel misunderstanding Yahweh. Jesus came "to pull back the curtain and let us see the beautiful face of God, 'full of grace and truth,' " bringing "a radical shift in the understanding of God's character." Preaching at

Nazareth, Jesus omitted Isaiah's word about "the day of vengeance of our God," and the people tried to kill him for it (Isaiah 61:2; Luke 4:19-20, 28-30). When James and John wanted fire from heaven to slay the inhospitable Samaritans, he gave "the most incisive critique of God as destroyer" (Luke 9:52-55). He "directly countermanded Moses in forbidding the use of violence of any sort" when he rebuked Peter for wielding the sword to prevent his arrest (Matthew 26:52-54; John 18:10). In voluntarily becoming a servant, Jesus revealed a God who does not judge to maintain sovereignty, for "his sovereignty is the sovereignty of self-emptying, cruciform love" (Philippians 2:6-7).[1]

Cowles correctly dismisses an ahistorical hyper-Calvinism that sees no discontinuity whatever between Old Testament and New Testament and claims their "differing historical locations, perspectives, and personalities . . . mean nothing." Instead, Cowles argues, "human history moves along lines of relative continuities until a singular point emerges," perhaps "in a person such as Abraham, Plato, or Copernicus," after which "a sea change in thinking and behavior occurs." Jesus' life was a "uniquely singular . . . axial point of human history" after which "we can categorically affirm that God is not a destroyer . . . does not engage in punitive, redemptive or sacred violence . . . [and] does not proactively use death as an instrument of judgment." Instead, sin is the fate-effecting deed that is "inherently self-destructive" and brings death. He quotes Mennonite theologian C. Norman Kraus on "the objective, intrinsic consequences of sin in the created order as God's judgment"; creation's rationality means "consequences are inherent in the actions themselves." Cowles accepts Jesus' role in a "final judgment" but places this outside history, at the end of time, and implies that sins, not a judge's verdict, will be the fate-effecting deeds there too.[2]

First, a few general comments are in order. Cowles's case makes Jesus' message into a timeless principle that cannot be altered (even by Christ presumably) until time ends and the Last Judgment commences; therefore, deductions can be made from it with unalterable certainty. Jesus becomes a Hebrew Socrates announcing a new First Principle in philosophy, from which followers then deduce inferences. Cowles approvingly quotes one: Alice Mc-

---

[1]For Cowles's comments on the above passages, see C. S. Cowles, "The Case for Radical Discontinuity," in C. S. Cowles, Eugene H. Merrill, Daniel L. Gard and Tremper Longman III, *Show Them No Mercy: Four Views on God and Canaanite Genocide* (Grand Rapids: Zondervan, 2003), pp. 23-26, 28, 39, 41, and Cowles, "Response to Merrill," ibid., p. 99.
[2]Cowles, "The Case for Radical Discontinuity," pp. 20, 26, 27, 31-32. The phrase "fate-effecting deed" is from Patrick D. Miller Jr., *Sin and Judgment in the Prophets: A Stylistic and Theological Analysis* (Chico, Calif.: Scholars Press, 1982).

Dermott's reasoning that " 'the incredible notion of God made flesh . . . cannot logically be sustained, if any single life [is] expendable. . . . If any one life can be dismissed as meaningless, so too can the life of Christ.' "[3] To use a unique historical event, even one so "axial" as Jesus' life, as a philosophical axiom is unwarranted. Scripture gives valid incarnational inferences: for example, that God loves the world (John 3:16-17). We are not authorized to deduce our own. McDermott's is disproven by Jesus' view of the meaningless, expendable life of his betrayer: "It would be better for him if he had not been born" (Mark 14:21). An event's centrality does not remove it from the realm of history to that of philosophy. We may wish Jesus' life set a fixed principle that God will not judge, as Israelites hoped their fixed chosen-nation status exempted them from God's judgment. Jesus warned of such presumption (see, e.g., John 8:31-59). We cannot put God in a box, an axiom, exempting us from judgment.

Second, Cowles's specific cases do not prove Jesus ruled judgment off the table. After he omitted Isaiah 61:2 in his synagogue reading, the crowd "spoke well of him"; it was after he mentioned two Old Testament examples of God blessing Gentiles to warn Nazareth about its unbelief that they "were furious" (Luke 4:19, 22, 24-28). After his rebuke of the Sons of Thunder, he instructed the disciples to shake dust off their feet when leaving a town that rejected the message, warned that "it will be more bearable on that day for Sodom than for that town" and singled out two Galilean towns for a worse fate than Tyre and Sidon's "at the judgment" (Luke 10:10-14). Ordering Peter to put down the sword did not signal God's renunciation of judgment's sword. His rationale to Peter fell well short of that: a curt "No more of this!" (Luke 22:51); a refusal to use swords to avoid "the cup the Father has given me" (John 18:11); a proverbial saying ("all who draw the sword will die by the sword") and an assertion of a power ("twelve legions of angels") that he will forego lest Scripture not be fulfilled (Matthew 26:52-54). His remarks addressed the specific historical situation and did not announce a new philosophy that God will no longer personally, actively judge evil.

Jesus' Coming: A Decisive Historical Moment for Salvation or Judgment

Jesus' life and ministry represented a brief historical moment fraught with decisive and fateful choices for individuals and Israel. The fulfillment of Old Testament prophecies came on that generation, which faced a crucial decision that would reverberate for millennia (e.g., Isaiah 9:1-2; Malachi 3:1). The divine iden-

---

[3]Cowles, "Case for Radical Discontinuity," p. 43.

tity of the Promised One meant salvation and judgment as two sides of one coin. The Son of God could save, but rejecting the Son's saving acts and words was far more serious than rejecting prophets' words. "God did not send his Son into the world to condemn the world, but to save the world throught him," John wrote. "Whoever does not believe stands condemned already because he has not believed in the name of God's one and only Son" (John 3:17-18). A Savior with enough power to save was one with enough majesty to render any rejection of him an act subject to judgment.

Leon Morris expresses it best, as *mishpat:* "It was as little the purpose of Jesus to judge men at His first coming as it is the purpose of the sun to cast shadows. But if the sun shines on a landscape shadows are inevitable." Blocking its intense light creates an area of relative darkness. "And when the Son of God comes into the world bringing salvation it is inevitable that He will judge men by that very fact. . . . There is a sifting process. The offer of salvation . . . separates between those who respond to the gracious offer and those who do not."[4]

We look at seven aspects of Jesus' life in the Gospels: prophecies around the time of his birth; his basic message; the parables; disputes with rulers and Pharisees; his relationship to Jerusalem and the temple; the Son of God's mission; and his death and resurrection.

Luke recorded three songs recited before and shortly after Jesus' birth: Mary's, Zechariah's and Simeon's. All three resonate with Hebrew concepts of salvation and judgment. Mary celebrated *mishpat* as an upside-down reversal of the current state of affairs. "He has brought down rulers from their thrones / but has lifted up the humble" (Luke 1:52). The Holy Spirit's act of conception in her womb was God's *mishpat,* a lifting up of "the humble state of his servant" (Luke 1:48). Zechariah stressed salvation from enemies, but that means judgment on enemies. Simeon revealed that Israel will not be exempt: "This child" will cause the "rising of many in Israel" to salvation and the "falling" of many to judgment. God's sign "will be spoken against," even in Israel, "so that the thoughts of many hearts will be revealed" (Luke 2:34-35). A *mishpat* occurred as individuals' inner thoughts for or against this child were exposed.

The New Testament does not use Hebrew words for judgment; however, in classical Greek literature, the verb *krino* ("to judge") and the nouns *krima* and *krisis* ("judgment") have the "basic meaning to separate, sift" and then acquired other meanings, including "to judge, pronounce judgment." In the New Testa-

---

[4]Leon Morris, *The Biblical Doctrine of Judgment* (Grand Rapids: Eerdmans, 1960), p. 50. There may be some hyperbole in Morris's first sentence, but it is a clarifying comparison.

ment, these words "are used with the same complex meanings" as in Greek literature and in the Septuagint (the Greek Old Testament translation). The Greek words can mean a judicial condemnation if the context so indicates. There is no linguistic reason to think the New Testament's different language brings a different view of judgment.[5]

John the Baptist "prepared the way" by warning that the coming One would bring a sifting-out *mishpat*: "His winnowing fork is in his hand, and he will clear his threshing floor, gathering his wheat . . . and burning up the chaff" (Matthew 3:12). Matthew recorded the first words of Jesus' public ministry—"Repent, for the kingdom of heaven is near"—as an exact repetition of the Baptist's first words (Matthew 3:2; 4:17). Mark 1:15 quoted Jesus stressing the historical moment of decision: "The time has come. . . . The kingdom of God is near. Repent and believe the good news." The kingdom was near in the person of the King, whose holiness demanded sinners repent but whose authority could grant forgiveness to those who did. Luke presented the reading in Nazareth as the historical moment: "Today this scripture is fulfilled in your hearing" (Luke 4:21). In John, private dialogues with prospective disciples came first; then two acts opened the public ministry: one symbolizing salvation (turning water into wine at the marriage feast); one symbolizing judgment (driving moneychangers from the temple).

As deliberately vague or ambiguous or difficult sayings, the parables were a form of judgment on an unrepentant generation whose "heart has become calloused" (Matthew 13:11-15; Luke 8:10). Many contained prophecies of judgment, sometimes on the listeners. "The teachers of the law and the chief priests looked for a way to arrest him immediately, because they knew he had spoken this parable [of the tenants] against them" (Luke 20:19). The vineyard owner (God) was about to use death as a punishment for the rebellious tenants.

Jesus' dialogues with Pharisees and Jewish leaders stressed judgment. That many poor people, Galileans and despised Samaritans accepted him while the leaders and self-righteous guardians of religion rejected him was *mishpat,* a great reversal. Jesus warned that the nation's decision about him carried grave consequences. First-century Jews did not have an independent nation, but they had leaders able to make a religious decision on his claims. Dialogues in John reveal the momentous "rising" or "falling" choice for Israel as God's "son" was now brought face to face with the unique Son of God.[6] An Israel truly in a son-

[5]W. Schneider, "Judgment" *(Krima),* in *Dictionary of New Testament Theology,* ed. Colin Brown (Grand Rapids: Zondervan, 1976), 2:362-67.
[6]John 5:16-47, 6:25-59, 8:31-59, 10:22-39. For Israel as God's son, see Exodus 4:22-23.

like relationship to Yahweh would surely not reject God's Son.

The dispute narrowed to the temple and Jerusalem, as Peter Walker reminds us. Jesus claimed to be a new temple superseding the temple soon to be destroyed (not by him); the rulers threatened death to him but asserted a continuance of the temple. "The fate of the two temples is about to be decided. The custodians of each have pronounced the doom of the other."[7] Jerusalem's fate was linked to the temple's fate. Foreseeing that rejecting him meant the city's doom, Jesus wept over Jerusalem (Luke 13:34-35; 19:41-44; 23:27-31). Contrary to Cowles, Jesus' ministry was not God's surrender of judgment as an instrument. It resulted in judgment on those who rejected it.

Jesus' sense of his mission included his role as judge. "I have come to bring fire on the earth, and how I wish it were already kindled!" (Luke 12:49). Disputing Pharisees who objected to his healing on the sabbath, he said, "the Father judges no one, but has entrusted all judgment to the Son," and elaborated, "he has given him authority to judge because he is the Son of Man" (John 5:22, 27). The context was the final resurrection but also the first-century situation. "In this Gospel . . . there is a sense in which judgment takes place even now" (Morris); Jesus "traces his authority as the Son to call the dead to life *now* to the power given the Son of man to execute judgment."[8] That is clearer in John 9:39: "For judgment I have come into this world, so that the blind will see and those who see will become blind."

God's judgment surrounded Jesus' death and resurrection. As John Stott reminds us, Jesus' ransom saying ("the Son of Man did not come to be served, but to serve, and to give his life as a ransom for many" [Mark 10:45]) and institution of the Lord's Supper ("This is my blood of the covenant, which is poured out for many" Mark 14:24) showed that "Jesus applied Isaiah 53 to himself" and saw his death "as a sin-bearing death," a death from enduring God's judgment on sin.[9] If God did not shrink from judging sins placed upon Jesus, by subjecting his Son to such a painful, humiliating judgment as crucifixion, then he will not shrink from judging the guilty themselves. For believers, this logic from the greater to the lesser is a comfort: if God gave us his Son, will he withhold lesser things from us (Romans 8:32)? But the logic also disproves Cowles's claim that God "does not proactively use death as an in-

---

[7]Peter W. L. Walker, *Jesus and the Holy City: New Testament Perspectives on Jerusalem* (Grand Rapids: Eerdmans, 1996), p. 11 (quoting Geddert).

[8]Leon Morris, *The Gospel According to John*, rev. ed. (Grand Rapids: Eerdmans), p. 279; Herman Ridderbos, *The Gospel of John: A Theological Commentary* (Grand Rapids: Eerdmans, 1997), p. 201.

[9]John R. W. Stott, *The Cross of Christ* (Downers Grove, Ill.: InterVarsity Press, 1986), pp. 146-47.

strument of judgment."[10] Jesus calls his imminent crucifixion the time for "judgment on this world; now the prince of this world will be driven out" (John 12:31). Herman Ridderbos interprets this time as "the hour of the world's judgment because by rejecting Jesus it rejects God's only begotten Son (3:18) and crucifies the Son of Man. . . . It is the hour for the expulsion of the ruler of this world because . . . in Jesus' exaltation he loses his claim on the world and is thus driven from the center of his power."[11]

From beginning to end, Jesus' life and teachings involved a sifting-out based on responses to him; a forgiveness for penitent, believing tax collectors and sinners but a catastrophic "falling" for the people who proudly claimed a son-like special relationship with God but rejected the Son; a judgment on the temple and Jerusalem "because you did not recognize the time of God's coming to you" (Luke 19:44); a judgment on Jesus for the sins of others; yet this sacrificial death qualifying Jesus to be humanity's judge later.

John Stott defines God's judging wrath to exclude egotistical, biased, self-centered aspects of human anger. "It does not mean that God loses his temper, flies into a rage, or is ever malicious, spiteful or vindictive" as we are. "The alternative to 'wrath' is not 'love' but 'neutrality' in the moral conflict." (Often, judgment means rendering a decision between contending parties, and sin usually produces a victim.) "And God is not neutral. On the contrary, his wrath is his holy hostility to evil, his refusal to condone it or come to terms with it, his just judgment upon it."[12]

An Intermediate View of the New Testament and God's (Retributive) Judgment

There are other views situated between Cowles's rejection of judgment and Stott's acceptance of the traditional concept of it. In *Christ and the Judgment of God*, Stephen H. Travis presents a middle way. Looking at his view can clarify some issues. His main concern is with retribution, the idea that God judges to pay back sinners for their sins, not to correct them or to accomplish some positive end. He acknowledges that a stress (like Cowles's) on judgment as the sinner's fate-effecting deed might "degenerate into a belief that 'an inevitable process of cause and effect' virtually takes the place of God." No, God personally opposes evil just as he offers salvation as a personal relationship with himself.

---

[10]Cowles, "Case for Radical Discontinuity," p. 30.

[11]Ridderbos, *Gospel of John,* p. 439.

[12]John R. W. Stott, *Romans: God's Good News for the World* (Downers Grove, Ill.: InterVarsity Press, 1994), p. 72. Stott also sees the wrath as being revealed in the present (p. 75).

Travis admits that there is "New Testament *language* which 'looks retributive' " and that the church has long interpreted it as such. Yet, he claims such language "is best understood in relation to a non-retributive *theology* of judgment." This theology centers on a "relationship to God and to Christ." Once that "is seen as central, retributive concepts become inappropriate." Judgment is "exclusion from relationship to God," not retribution, and final salvation is "an intensification of the relationship with God." So, he backs partly away from the traditional view.[13]

Travis's view is not persuasive, for retribution and relationship are not two mutually exclusive categories here. There are other problems: language describes and constitutes a theology; his argument seems shaped by what Palmer Robertson saw as the "repulsive" aspect of retribution "to the modern mind"; he sets very high standards ("no specific *doctrine* of degrees of reward and punishment") or unclear ones (how frequently must an idea be mentioned to be significant?) in order to minimize retribution; he tries to examine retribution apart from the atonement, and they are hard to separate in the New Testament.[14] Yet the main problem is that a "relationship to God and to Christ" can involve exact retribution ("But whoever disowns me before men, I will disown him before my Father in heaven" [Matthew 10:33]). Atonement is the New Testament concept linking retribution and relationship to God, and it centers on Christ: Christ bore the sinner's retributive judgment, and the sinner who comes into relationship with him by accepting him is saved. The logic works in reverse also. The sinner who refuses the atoning sacrifice whom God has sent, and that relationship, faces a retribution that goes beyond punishment for misdeeds—a judgment that "is exclusion from relationship to God" and that is not just self-imposed. God and Christ disown him as he did them. That is why Jesus' coming provoked a *krisis,* a sifting out, in Israel and beyond.

Key Statements by Jesus on Judgment in Luke 12 and Luke 13

Luke 12 is a key chapter giving Jesus' views on judgment. He warns of God's "power to throw you into hell" (Luke 12:5). He tells a would-be plaintiff, "Man, who appointed me a judge or an arbiter between you?" (Luke 12:14). He warns that God can suddenly demand the life of the sinner (Luke 12:20). He urges watchfulness and faithful stewardship, "because the Son of Man will come at an

---

[13]Stephen H. Travis, *Christ and the Judgment of God: Divine Retribution in the New Testament* (Basingstoke, U.K.: Marshall Pickering, 1986), pp. 2, 124, 168-69; see also pp. 9-11.
[14]Travis, *Christ and the Judgment of God,* p. 152; see also pp. 2, 162-64, 167, 168.

hour when you do not expect him" and will punish faithless servants (Luke 12:35-48). He gives a principle for judgment: "From everyone who has been given much, much will be demanded" (Luke 12:48). He states his eagerness to bring judgment ("fire on the earth") and the reality that his presence means division between people, a sifting out even within families (Luke 12:49-53). He accuses his listeners of hypocrisy for being so quick to perceive approaching weather but so slow to perceive the imminent judgment of "this present time" (Luke 12:54-56). He advises a quick settlement and repentance while people are on their way to the judge, before the irreversible courtroom proceedings begin (Luke 12:57-59). "Three horizons of God's judgment are identified" in Luke, argues John Nolland, "human history, after death, final judgment."[15] All three are present in Luke 12, and none is denied by Jesus.

They form the context for the text most often cited after September 11, Luke 13:1-5. Apparently on the same occasion as the above remarks, "some present . . . told Jesus about the Galileans whose blood Pilate had mixed with their sacrifices"—at the temple and probably due to acts of political rebellion. His questioners may have been asking Jesus to interpret this sign of the "present time" in terms of first-century politics, especially Jewish hatred of Roman rule. If so, he did not take the bait but brought up God's judgment on sin: "these Galileans" were not "worse sinners than all the other Galileans." To further distance the discussion from politics, Jesus added the nonpolitical case of Siloam's falling tower. That also added Judeans as sinners to avoid favoritism to groups. He did not deny their deaths were a judgment on their sins. He denied they had more sins than others. "In the situation created by Jesus' presence and his preaching of the kingdom of God, *all* need to repent," Nolland summarizes. "He moves the focus away from [our] judgment of others with his call to put one's own house in order."[16] But impending judgment is why our house needs to be in order.

Relative New Testament Silence About God's Judgments on the Nations

And yet, although a prophet, Jesus issued no oracles against the nations and neither did his apostles. Does the New Testament concept of judgment thus apply only to individuals, religious leaders, the church or Israel—not to nations? The burden of proof would seem to lie with those who argue that the New Testament reverses or makes obsolete the Old Testament teaching about God judging the nations. And an argument from silence is not an adequate proof of such a sweeping reversal.

---

[15]John Nolland, *Luke 9:21-18:34*, Word Biblical Commentary 35B (Dallas: Word), p. 718.
[16]Ibid., pp. 717-19.

Good reasons exist for this silence. Jesus' public ministry was to Israel not to Gentile nations. He could have issued oracles against the Roman Empire and its officials, who had the Galileans killed as they offered sacrifices, but that would raise nationalistic hopes that he avoided. It would raise the wrong issues at his trial: rebelling against Rome, not claiming to be the Son of God. Denouncing Rome conflicted with his coming as a humble servant.[17] When people told him of Pilate's action, they may have wanted him to condemn Pilate. They certainly did not mention divine judgment on sinners. Yet that was Jesus' only application. When Herod Antipas executed John the Baptist, John's disciples told Jesus and may have expected a retaliatory act or a judgment-invoking word. Jesus "withdrew by boat privately to a solitary place" (Matthew 14:13). At his trial, Jesus implied that Pilate was guilty of a lesser sin for unjustly condemning him to death but to charge Pilate openly with guilt would be implicitly to plead for his own release, contrary to the Father's will, and that he refused to do (John 19:11).

The apostles issued no OAN either. Their gospel message was to individuals and small groups, not entire nations. They did not specify how rulers should conduct affairs and did not threaten punishments for disobeying commands they did not give. Oliver O'Donovan notes, "There was no revealed political doctrine in the New Testament prescribing how the state was to be guided."[18] The apostles shepherded small, persecuted churches without political influence in the empire. To include political advice or warnings in the Epistles would have been fruitless. The New Testament world enjoyed the Pax Romana that greatly facilitated gospel preaching. Few international military conflicts raged for New Testament prophets to view with alarm or to point to as God's judgment, in their known world, and they had no divine call to stir up any. Paul urged Timothy and the churches to pray "for kings, . . . that we may live peaceful and quiet lives in all godliness and holiness" (1 Timothy 2:2). Not Israel's peace in the land, but churches' peaceful ministry, was the goal. Interestingly, Paul indicates "the saints will judge the world," but like their Lord they must suffer first and not prematurely take upon them this future role (1 Corinthians 6:2).

---

[17]"The fashion for aligning Jesus with zealot revolutionaries . . . has now deservedly passed" (Oliver O'Donovan, *The Desire of the Nations: Rediscovering the Roots of Political Theology* [Cambridge: Cambridge University Press, 1996], p. 95). For more on Jesus and the Zealots, see Ernst Bammel and C. F. D. Moule, eds., *Jesus and the Politics of His Day* (Cambridge: Cambridge University Press, 1984). For a recent, perceptive account of Jesus' attitude toward Rome that also denies that he opposed Roman rule, see Christopher Bryan, *Render to Caesar: Jesus, the Early Church and the Roman Superpower* (New York: Oxford University Press, 2005).

[18]O'Donovan, *Desire of the Nations*, p. 219.

These reasons for New Testament silence do not amount to a denial that God judges peoples and nations in the course of history. An active, righteous God enacting *mishpat* for the suffering of the earth was a central Old Testament concept that is never renounced in the New Testament.

G. W. Trumpf insightfully refuses to take silence as a repudiation of judgment. He grants Luke more authorial independence than an evangelical belief in inspiration can accept, but he also draws out more examples of God's retributive judgments in Luke-Acts. Luke did not mention "the defeat of Herod Antipas' army" in A.D. 37 as God's judgment on him for executing John the Baptist (as the Jewish historian Josephus did), but Luke reported Herod Agrippa's death in 44 as God's judgment on him for not rebuking the crowd that hailed him as a god. Trumpf argues that because Luke did not identify which Herod, "his ugly end stands as an implied retribution on 'Herodianism' in general." Luke identified Herod as a persecutor of the church, so his death can be seen as a judgment for that evil too (Acts 12:1-4, 22-23). Paul's correct prophecy of the high priest Ananias's assassination during the Jewish revolt (66-70) "implicitly pays back the Jewish high priesthood" for its role in the deaths of Jesus and Stephen, according to Trumpf.[19]

Trumpf claims that Luke allowed "no retributive measure of any kind . . . in his Gospel" (future judgment is predicted), for he wanted "the *positive* divine offer of salvation [to] precede and outweigh notes of negativity." He hints that Luke wrote his second work, Acts, to show how Simeon's "falling" and "rising" prophecy came true. Evangelicals will see Jesus, not Luke, as responsible for a lack of retribution in Luke's Gospel, and the church's missionary success, not retribution, as the main story in Acts. Given his focus on apostles and churches, not major imperial events, "Luke is left only with the intermittent 'manifestations' of God in his protagonists' experiences," and that limits talk of judgment on nations. "Luke proceeds slowly towards a clear exposition of Christ as cosmic judge," and "it is not until" Cornelius's conversion "and especially in the great Areopagus sermon—that it is revealed with clarity . . . that Jesus is God's appointee as arbiter over 'every nation on the face of the earth' and 'their allotted times.' "[20] Paul's closing remarks at Athens are highly significant in stressing Christ's role as judge.

Does the Last Judgment "render all human efforts to fathom divine judgments" in history before the end "either futile or utterly provisional"? Theologians' overwhelming stress on the Last Judgment and their neglect of any inter-

---

[19]G. W. Trompf, *Early Christian Historiography* (London: Continuum, 2000), pp. 62, 76-77.
[20]Ibid., pp. 70, 75, 77. The Scripture references are Acts 10:42; 17:26, 31.

vening ones has given a de facto answer: Yes. Trompf says no, in Luke's case. "God's final Judgement . . . evidently does not leave the historian with nothing to say about divine judgements *during* this order," for Luke narrated events not just as "'God's actions in history' but for their fuller eschatological implications." Judgments on a Herod Agrippa or an Ananias were consistent with, even foreshadowings of, the Last Judgment. The evangelical historian, who believes Luke's words were inspired by the Holy Spirit in a way that his cannot be, will not be so reassured that Acts shows historians have something "to say about divine judgements *during*" this age.[21] Yet, he or she can say something tentative and "provisional" about them, just as about other interpretive issues.

Trompf demonstrates that New Testament writers did not take judgment off the table for their generation. Early church fathers who wrote on history, such as Eusebius, did not regard the New Testament as rendering God's judgments in history obsolete. The New Testament added a new human error to be judged: rejection of a gospel far superior to the limited light Israel had offered to the Gentiles. In his *Ecclesiastical History,* Eusebius contended (in Trompf's words) "that the unprecedented disruption and dissection of the Roman world" from 303 to 313 "was the direct result of the persecution of the Christians." Augustine's *City of God* attempted to explain historical events in terms of God's retributive judgments, or, rather, to disprove the pagan charge that the sack of Rome in 410 was the pagan gods' judgment on Rome for its official conversion to Christianity. In book 20, now past his immediate apologetic problem, Augustine asserted that "even now God judges"; but he sidestepped the national or imperial level to concentrate on "voluntary and personal acts of individuals"; he concluded that "we do not know by what judgment of God this good man is poor and that bad man rich": he turned to the Last Judgment, whose date is uncertain but whose outcome is certain.[22]

The New Testament does not state that God's judgments against the nations have ended, but it does not specifically identify them either. Obvious reasons for that silence argue against construing it as a signal such judgments have ended. This category of divine action is not ended by the New Testament. Yet writers like Cowles are correct in perceiving that something about judgment changes with the New Testament. In the next chapter, we will consider just what that something might be.

---

[21]Ibid., pp. 70, 75.
[22]Ibid., p. 123; Saint Augustine, *The City of God,* trans. Marcus Dods (New York: Random House, 1993), pp. 710-12.

6

History's Meaning: The Son of Man in His Descent, Ascent and Return

We have come to the midpoint in our journey from the September 11 attacks, back to Scripture to find principles of judgment and forward to apply those principles to U.S. history. We have seen the need for a more historical view of Christianity, but if history is seen as a meaningless jumble of events, then we will be shoehorned back into a worldview philosophical approach that does have coherence and meaning. Before interpreting U.S. history, we need to find a central meaning that can anchor our interpretation. We also need to apply Old Testament principles about God's judgments to this nation. New Testament silence on this issue raises some problems that must be resolved. Yet, we are not helpless. Old Testment principles still generally apply where they are not specifically superseded by the New Testament, but critics of Old Testament judgment have a valid point in seeing some New Testament changes.

Jesus' self-designation as Son of Man gives us the most complete New Testament context for judgment. When dealing with C. S. Cowles's views, we called him Jesus, partly to meet the critics at their strongest point. They stress his humility, meekness and nonviolence by using his human name alone, without titles indicating status, power or authority. (Jesus or *Yeshua* is a title of sorts, for it means "Yahweh saves.") Still, we found a Jesus of judgment and salvation. What additional insight will we derive by using his favorite title, and why zero in on one title? "Son of Man" most aptly describes Jesus of Nazareth as a historical figure who undergoes change over time in his role and status, in universal human history, not merely Israel's. "Son of God" connotes changelessness and eternal existence outside of time. "Messiah" or "Christ" connotes a Davidic king of Israel, not a universal ruler. These distinctions, however, must not be carried too far. Christ rules the nations; the Son of God became incarnate and entered our time-bound world. Jesus united all these titles in one person, so they cannot be fully separated for analysis. Yet "Son of Man" gives the historical context of salvation and judgment, as long as we do not misconstrue it to minimize his divine nature or to contrast a human Son of Man with a divine Son of God.[1]

Jesus called himself the Son of Man about fifty times in the Gospels. No one else called him that except the crowd in John 12:34, and they quizzically quoted his self-designation back at him. The term is not used outside the Gospels except by Stephen (Acts 7:56). The early church did not use this title of its Lord.[2] That cautions us against using it for theological topics such as justification or redemption, but we are inquiring about God's judgments in history, not a usual New Testament topic, so it seems valid to use this title here.

Scholarly Microscopic Analysis: *ho huios tou anthropou* and *bar (e)nasha*

An interminable, inconclusive scholarly debate rages over the exact denotations and connotations of the Greek *ho huios tou anthropou* ("the son of the man") and the Aramaic *bar (e)nasha* that lies behind the Greek. N. T. Wright calls it "that bane of scholars' lives." Delbert Burkett quotes cries of scholarly frustration: "a can of worms"; "a veritable mine field"; "scholarly discord reigns supreme." One scholar complains that in "modern methods of critical analysis . . . material tends to be divided into smaller and smaller units" that "obscure rather than clarify," for often "patterns" can be seen only when "the material" is "considered as a whole." The minute analysis of trees, leaves and the chlorophyll in leaves has obscured the forest.[3]

Burkett summarizes the most common interpretations of "Son of Man": (1) a "genealogical interpretation" stresses "his descent from a human parent," mainly Adam or Mary; (2) a view that the Aramaic idiom denoted "human" and connoted "an element of lowliness and humility" or the opposite, "the pre-eminent man, the ideal man, and the man who is the goal of human history"; (3) a view based on Daniel 7:13 that regarded the Son of Man as a messianic and apocalyptic figure who was "a superhuman being."[4] This debate is reminiscent of the story of the blind men examining the elephant, which they described differently depending on whether they touched ear, trunk, leg or tail. The Son of Man can

---

[1]"The two titles are used together repeatedly with no clear distinction or transition," argues Ridderbos; *Gospel of John: A Theological Commentary* (Grand Rapids: Eerdmans, 1997), p. 93.
[2]Delbert Burkett, *The Son of Man Debate: A History and Evaluation* (Cambridge: Cambridge University Press, 1999), p. 1.
[3]N. T. Wright, *Jesus and the Victory of God* (Minneapolis: Fortress, 1996), p. 394; John Bowker, "The Son of Man," *Journal of Theological Studies* 28 (April 1977): 20-21; Burkett, *Son of Man Debate*, p. 2; Francis J. Moloney, *The Johannine Son of Man* (Rome: Libreria Ateneo Salesiano, 1976), p. 33.
[4]Burkett, *Son of Man Debate*, pp. 7, 14, 17, 29; see also pp. 6-10, 13, 17-19, 22-23, 25, 28-29.

have *all* these characteristics: a descent from Adam (via Mary) qualifying him as the second Adam representing humanity before God (Romans 5:12-19); in the initial stages of his life, he is seemingly a lowly, humble man who later is exalted to pre-eminence as "the goal of human history"; and, as such, he is Messiah, the apocalyptic "one like a son of man" of Daniel 7:13-14 and a superhuman being "coming with the clouds of heaven." There is no need to take an ahistorical view of the Son of Man as unchanging in his status. Allowing for change over time, we see so-called discrepancies as successive stages in his career.[5]

We need not take an overly historical view, as Wright does in limiting the title to what first-century Jews understood by it. Jesus used it to escape the preconceptions of his contemporaries, who were puzzled by it: "Who is this 'Son of Man'?" (John 12:34).[6] Our approach will not satisfy scholars who have analyzed the title or who want to forget an interminable debate. Yet the title is so important to Jesus' self-revelation that, absent a scholarly consensus, we must forge ahead without one.

The Dramatic Heights-to-Depths-to-Heights Trajectory of the Son of Man

We see, then, the Son of Man like a comet hurtling across the dark night of human history, in a dramatic trajectory from startling Old Testament prophecies of his transcendent majesty down to a lowly birth and a humiliating death on a cross to God the Father's right hand to await a spectacular return and reign. This historical figure who plumbs the depths and scales the heights cannot be abstracted into a timeless principle that God's "way of being in the world is [that of] . . . a creative, life-giving, life-enhancing servant" and "his sovereignty is the sovereignty of self-emptying, cruciform love."[7] Cowles is temporarily correct: the cross is a stage in his career; the preaching of the cross forms a long period in history. It is not the only stage in his career or the final period in history. We cannot freeze the motion picture to produce only the frame we wish to see.

---

[5]Burkett (p. 25) points to writers who have combined various aspects of these interpretations. This is largely the view taken in Chrys C. Caragounis, *The Son of Man: Vision and Interpretation* (Tübingen: J. C. B. Mohr, 1986), pp. 200-201, 242-43, 249-50. While calling it "a many-sided concept" (p. 215), whose sides are combined in Jesus, Caragounis dismisses the role of any Aramaic idiom and stresses Daniel 7.

[6]In discussing the Mount Olivet Discourse, Wright ridicules the idea of "a transcendent figure [who] is about to come floating, cloudborne, towards earth" (p. 516). Yet, if we accept the historicity of his cloud-borne ascension (Acts 1:9), it is hard to see what problems a similar descent poses. For Wright on the Discourse, see *Victory of God,* pp. 360-65, 512-19.

[7]C. S. Cowles, "Response to Eugene H. Merrill," in C. S. Cowles, Eugene H. Merrill, Daniel L. Gard and Tremper Longman III, *Show Them No Mercy: Four Views on God and Canaanite Genocide* (Grand Rapids: Zondervan, 2003), p. 99.

Scholars classify Jesus' Son-of-Man sayings into three types: earthly life, sufferings and exaltation. These vividly portray his heights-to-depths-to-heights trajectory.[8] "The Son of Man has no place to lay his head," Jesus told a would-be disciple (Matthew 8:20; Luke 9:58). He "came eating and drinking" with common people and sinners (Matthew 11:19). He and his disciples depended on donations. Yet he forgave sins and was Lord of the sabbath.[9] Despite his intrinsic authority, he had to suffer death to fulfill Scripture and to attain his full exaltation. "For even the Son of Man did not come to be served, but to serve, and to give his life as a ransom for many" (Mark 10:45) in the most humiliating manner: "They will condemn him to death and will turn him over to the Gentiles to be mocked and flogged and crucified" (Matthew 20:18-19). When Pilate brought out Jesus, with crown of thorns and purple robe, to mock his royal claims and announced, "Here is the man!" John may allude to the Son of Man, now near the bottom of his descent.[10] His resurrection and ascent are dramatic (Luke 24; Acts 1:1-11). Before the high priest, he applied Daniel 7:13-14 to his return: "And you will see the Son of Man sitting at the right hand of the Mighty One and coming on the clouds of heaven" (Mark 14:62).

Herman Ridderbos notes that this "self-designation is an expression of the utterly transcendent character of Jesus' messiahship" that "far surpasses those features" of the Old Testament "messianic king." Francis Moloney observes that in John, people make "a series of confessions" that Jesus is "Rabbi, Son of God, King of Israel" or Messiah. Then Jesus employs "Son of Man" as the last, fullest or clearest explanation of his identity and mission that corrects mistaken notions they attached to other titles: "the Son of Man is a title used by Jesus himself to correct an insufficient acclamation of him by onlookers." This title "speak[s] of the place, among men," where God's revelation through his Son "will occur. . . . The Son of Man is where revelation and judgment take place. . . . Jesus, the Son of Man, is the revealer and . . . [thus] he is the judge."[11] We might add that the Son of Man is also a place in time, in history, where God's saving revelation and judgment occur.

His mission is salvation and judgment, two sides of one divine program. In John 5:22-27, Jesus is the giver of life (Savior) and the Judge.[12] In John 3:13-21,

---

[8]Burkett, *Son of Man Debate*, p. 43; Caragounis, *Son of Man*, p. 146; Seyoon Kim, *"The 'Son of Man' " as the Son of God* (Tübingen: J. C. B. Mohr, 1983), p. 7.
[9]Matthew 9:6; Mark 2:10; Matthew 12:8; Mark 2:28.
[10]Moloney, *Johannine Son of Man*, p. 207. But see Ridderbos, *Gospel of John*, pp. 600-601.
[11]Ridderbos, *Gospel of John*, p. 93; Moloney, *Johannine Son of Man*, pp. 37-38, 85-86, 109, 158; see also pp. 52-53, 139-40, 181.
[12]Moloney, *Johannine Son of Man*, pp. 77-78, 83.

the Son of Man must be lifted up as Savior, but because he is sent of God, a failure to believe in him brings judgment. The Son of Man's descent to the cross is needed for a substitutionary atonement that saves: he must be a man born of a human parent, a son of man, to bear the punishment for human sins; he must live a sinless life so that he has no personal sins to bear and can bear others' sins; and he must be God (the one "coming with the clouds of heaven" in Daniel 7 is divine), whose life is infinitely worthy and whose death is a sufficient payment for innumerable horrible sins.[13] This divine, transcendent, proffered salvation is so grand that rejection of it is a fate-effecting deed that brings judgment, by itself as it were, despite the Son of Man's descent to save, not judge.[14] This salvation's brilliant light makes more culpable the love of darkness shown in rejecting it (John 3:18-20).

Why Must the Coming World Ruler Suffer Before Reigning?

History is more than individual choices, and it contains nations, too. In Daniel 7:14 the "one like a son of man" is given "dominion" over nations; in Daniel 2:34 and 45 it is arguably he who is the stone "cut out, but not by human hands" that smashes the statue, the final human empire to be superseded by his divine one. In Old Testament prophecies, a future world ruler suffers a prior humiliation and rejection: "his appearance was so disfigured beyond that of any man / and his form marred beyond human likeness— / so will he sprinkle many nations, / and kings will shut their mouths because of him"; "to him who was despised and abhorred by the nation, / . . . 'Kings will see you and rise up / princes will see and bow down'" (Isaiah 52:14-15; 49:7). In Psalm 22:25-28, the righteous one's sufferings lead to a "great assembly" when "all the families of the nations / will bow down before" the Lord. In Philippians, in Paul's hymn to Christ's humiliation and exaltation, his obedience unto death is followed by God's vindication of him by "exalt[ing] him to the highest place" (Philippians 2:9). The suffering and the glory are closely juxtaposed.

We are not told exactly and explicitly why the Son of Man as coming world ruler and judge must suffer and be rejected first. The Son of God is worthy to rule by reason of his divine attributes. Yet God the Father has chosen that the Son of Man suffer first.[15] Jesus simply stated the "must" or related it to a need to fulfill Scripture; before the cross, he said that the Son of Man must suffer and die; after

---

[13]John R. W. Stott, *The Cross of Christ* (Downers Grove, Ill.: InterVarsity Press, 1986), pp. 149-61.
[14]See, e.g., Ridderbos, *Gospel of John*, p. 139; Moloney, *Johannine Son of Man*, pp. 83-85; Leon Morris, *The Gospel According to John*, rev. ed. (Grand Rapids: Eerdmans, 1995), pp. 279-80.
[15]Luke 24:26 (Jesus uses the term "Christ" perhaps because this is after the resurrection).

the resurrection, he teaches that he had to suffer these things to enter his glory.[16]
Substitutionary atonement cannot be divorced from glory and rule. The redeemed share his reign and are part of his glory. God the Father's exaltation of
the Son of Man includes the glory of being "the firstborn among many brothers"
(Romans 8:29). His path of obedient, humble suffering before glory becomes
his disciples' path, too. F. F. Bruce translates *archegos* (Hebrews 2:10) as "the
Pathfinder, the Pioneer of our salvation . . . who blazed the trail of salvation,"
for the trail "which His people must tread must first be trodden by the Pathfinder."[17] One writer suggests that Jesus took on himself the suffering of the
saints (Daniel 7:21, 25): as "substitute for his people," Jesus "combined in his
new conception of the Son of Man, the exalted traits of the Danielic 'S[on of]
M[an]' with the humiliation and suffering of the saints, and thus gave a new
meaning to the idea of exaltation and royal rule—one that goes via suffering."[18]

To link this to Old Testament *mishpat,* we can add that, in entering history
as its meaning, the Son of Man submits to the sifting-out process that is human
history. He submits to being tempted and tried, according to the Father's will,
so as to be sifted out as the perfectly righteous one, not so he can then immediately receive the reward due the righteous but to bear the judgment due those
who had failed God's test, "the righteous for the unrighteous," and thus offer
them salvation from judgment (1 Peter 3:18). Yet, at the bottom of his descent,
his last week highlights aspects of royalty and its corollary, judgeship, that go
beyond what seems necessary for a substitutionary atonement: the triumphal
entry; his judicial expulsion of moneychangers from the temple; his application
of Daniel 7:13-14 to himself, which triggers the guilty verdict; the Romans' use
of a crown of thorns and purple robe to mock him; the inscription on the *titulus*
("The King of the Jews"); the priests and scribes' mocking demand that he prove
his kingship by coming down from the cross (Mark 15:32; for the guilty verdict,
see Mark 14:62-63). Here is not only a substitute who suffers but also a ruler
who is humiliated and a judge who is condemned.

The coming ruler earns the right to reign and to judge. The Son of God is seen
by those in heaven's courts to be entitled to reign and judge, but the Father con-
descends to demonstrate this to us who live in history by requiring the Son of Man
to be sifted out through the most excruciating descent, from which furnace he

---

[16]Mark 8:31; Luke 24:26. See also Matthew 17:12; 26:54; Mark 8:31; 9:12; Luke 9:22; 18:31-32;
John 3:14. I am indebted to Caragounis, *Son of Man,* p. 146 and footnotes, for a list of the
Son of Man sayings.
[17]F. F. Bruce, *Epistle to the Hebrews,* New International Commentary on the New Testament
(Grand Rapids: Eerdmans, 1964), p. 43.
[18]Caragounis, *Son of Man,* pp. 200-201; see also p. 213.

emerges as pure gold, a startling figure whose right to reign is transparent.[19] This great reversal from a cross to God's right hand is God's *mishpat*: the lowly righteous one is now exalted. Peter confronts the Sanhedrin with this reversal: "whom you crucified but whom God raised from the dead" (Acts 4:10). Gaining glory and rule through righteous suffering is undoubtedly meant as a condemning contrast to the way most rulers gain power. In the parable of the tenants, Jesus critiqued Jewish rulers' conduct (Mark 12:1-12). To his disciples, he critiqued "the rulers of the Gentiles" who "lord it over them. . . . Not so with you" (Matthew 20:25-26).

Israel's official (Sanhedrin) rejection of him, the Romans' crucifixion of him that represented an official Gentile rejection and the utterly demeaning nature of his death meant that he was "cut out, but not by human hands" but by God's act alone (Daniel 2:34, 45). Israel did not create his status as ruler, much less did the Gentiles. The Son of Man's rejection by his own nation and his own creation made his trajectory to glory all the more astonishing, clearly God's work. In the incarnation, humanity did not find its lost idealism and its true self and then regain its rule over creation through its chosen representative, the Son of Man. "The starting point of faith," Ridderbos notes, "does not lie in the fact that the world returned to God in the ascent of the Son of man and so found its lost self, any more than" his incarnational descent meant that "God again put the world on the track of true humanity."[20] No, God the Father cut out this Son of Man, sent him down to us, sifted him out and showed him to be the worthy substitute and ruler, judged our sins in his person, raised him, exalted him and will return him to us—all on his own initiative without our aid.

For a judge to be sentenced, for a ruler to be mocked as powerless, is especially humiliating. For a rightful judge and ruler to submit to it out of obedience to his Father and love to us is glorious.

In Revelation 5:9, his dying to redeem people from all nations makes him "worthy" to open seals releasing judgment on all nations. His suffering renders his verdicts transparently, convincingly just. When the judge is the savior who took the penalty and offered a pardon the defendants rejected, they cannot complain the verdict is unfair. His trajectory is highly visible. That may help produce repentance but makes unbelief more culpable. Paul stated it at Athens, a highly visible cultural center: repent; the judge is appointed, as proved by a dramatic resurrection (Acts 17:30-31).

Finally, extreme depths and extreme height in this trajectory combine to make for finality. The Son of Man is the final, Omega figure of human history. No one

---

[19]For a postresurrection description of the Son of Man, see Revelation 1:13-16.
[20]Ridderbos, *Gospel of John*, p. 138.

else can descend from such an exalted role in heaven to such depths, endure such punishment for sins and ascend to such heights at God's right hand. Do not wait for some new figure to trump that! This Son of Man has an irresistibly attractive power for his love to the death draws people of all nations to him.

We, Not God, Need to Come Out of Philosophy, Back into History

Stressing history and the Son of Man's career does not diminish God's attributes of omniscience, immutability, omnipresence, sovereignty, omnipotence and so on. The Son of Man is the place—a person in space and time—where God reveals himself, for salvation and for judgment, but not as himself limited by space and time or a body. Jesus, the incarnate Son of God, per the Nicene Creed, is "very God of very God . . . being of one substance with the Father" *and* "was made man." Two natures are not mixed together in him, divinity somehow becoming partly human. Our approach is not Open Theism, although it may appear similar. Open Theism also emphasizes a rejection of Greek philosophy and a return to a Hebrew historical view. In Open Theism "God is in the dock," in C. S. Lewis's words. God is taken out of Greek philosophy and placed firmly into history. We are taking humanity out of a static Greek philosophy and placing it back in history, a stream of events bringing divine judgment and a decision for or against God's salvation. Ironically, the Son of Man represents the relational, vulnerable God that Open Theists seek.

In *Most Moved Mover,* Clark Pinnock's chapter on "Overcoming a Pagan Inheritance" of Greek philosophy argues: "we need to be more affirming of God as a living person involved in history and less as a remote absolute principle"; in the "'biblical-classical synthesis . . . the ontological categories of Greco-Roman philosophy have been united with the personal-dramatic categories of biblical faith'"; Augustine's use of "neo-Platonic ideas" has "put God in a kind of box" that "spelled God's immunity to time, change, and real relations with creatures"; yet "the gospel does not view God in terms of changeless thought and timeless being but in reference to historical events"; "conventional attributes [of God] rise and fall together," for "if God is personal and enters into relationships, God cannot be immutable in every respect, timelessly eternal, impassible, or meticulously sovereign"; believing God was impassible (incapable of suffering) meant the early fathers "had great difficulty handling Jesus' suffering"; "the gospel brought something new to light: God is a radically self-giving God and descends to the lowest condition"; "Besides redefining what humanity means, the revelation redefines what divinity means."[21]

---

[21]Clark H. Pinnock, *Most Moved Mover: A Theology of God's Openness* (Grand Rapids: Baker Ac-

As in Cowles, Jesus' suffering becomes a timeless principle defining God the Father. The Son of Man as the place of the Father's mediating revelation to humanity is collapsed, and the man Jesus defines all that God the Father can possibly be. (Despite Pinnock's concern for "God's own self-disclosure," Jesus' self-designation "Son of Man" is never mentioned in the book.[22]) To refute Pinnock's view is beyond the scope of this book. Yet we must stress that the Son of Man is a mediator through events between two parties, God and humanity, not someone who mediates through semantics by "redefin[ing]" the two parties, God and humanity. God's ongoing and impending judgment on sinful humanity makes his trajectory necessary. Humanity's problem is its sinfulness and God's holiness, not its ignorance or God's "immunity to time, change, and real relations with creatures." True, the Hebrew idea of God did not stress abstract philosophical perfection, but it did stress absolute moral perfection: "For the LORD your God is a consuming fire" (Deuteronomy 4:24). The Son of Man comes into history to redeem us from history's imminent judgments and render us suited to come into God's presence, not to make God suited for our historical world.

Jesus has not established a timeless principle that God is always, only "self-emptying, cruciform love." Hans Urs von Balthasar argued that this gospel is not a "universal philosophical sun" that "neither rises nor sets and is without time and without history." It is "always shining *just for this present time*"; its light "always carries with it (even for us!) the threat of denial and withdrawal."[23] What about Hebrews 13:8 ("Jesus Christ is the same yesterday and today and forever")? Bruce interprets this in the context of the preceding verse on imitating Christian leaders, some of whom had died, but Christ the high priest had yesterday been perfected through his sufferings, was today representing believers in heaven and forever lived "to intercede for them" (Hebrews 7:25).[24] This is not a timeless state, for he had not been high priest in eternity past, had been made "perfect" through sufferings on earth in time and had ascended to heaven about A.D. 29, and they would be there too some day.

---

ademic, 2001), pp. 65-79 (quotes from pp. 65, 69, 70, 72, 73, 74). The quote about "ontological categories" is from Donald G. Bloesch, but he may not endorse Pinnock's views.

[22]Ibid., p. 27. Pinnock uses the term "Son" evidently to mean Son of God. I cannot find "Son of Man" anywhere.

[23]Cowles, "Response to Eugene H. Merrill," p. 99; Hans Urs von Balthasar, *A Theology of History* (New York: Sheed and Ward, 1963), p. 69. For this quote, I am indebted to Morris, *Gospel According to John*, p. 533 n. 97. Balthasar fails to use the "Son of Man" title, which forces him to view the Son of God's existence in time as a philosophical category of "uninterrupted reception . . . of his very self, from the Father" (p. 26).

[24]Bruce, *Hebrews*, pp. 394-99.

The Son of Man's Disciples Follow His Path of Preaching Judgment and Salvation

The Son of Man cannot have redefined God to remove his Old Testament character as an active, righteous judge. Oliver O'Donovan notes that, for Israel, an end to *mishpat* was a tragedy, "the lapsing of a juridical function that always needs to be exercised." Israel's leaders might let it lapse, but not Israel's God. Paul assures us that God's judgment is a present reality: "The wrath of God is being revealed from heaven against all the godlessness and wickedness of men who suppress the truth by their wickedness" (Romans 1:18). Douglas Moo interprets this verse to mean "there is an anticipatory working of God's wrath in the events of history," and wrath "falls more deservedly than ever before on people now that God's righteousness in Christ is being publicly proclaimed."[25]

We face another question: is there continuity or discontinuity between the Gospels on the Son of Man's life and the later New Testament on the church and its mission? Liberals see discontinuity and privilege the Gospels' kingdom message of aiding the poor; conservatives stress individual morality based on the cross and resurrection and downplay the kingdom.[26] We focus on the Son of Man in his descent, ascent and return. What unites the period of his earthly mission and that of his disciples' mission is a shared path from obedient suffering to glory, his substitutionary atonement that launches disciples on this path they could never otherwise take and their path-following sonship that forms a major part of his glory as "firstborn among many brothers" (Romans 8:29). Personal morality and helping the poor are both commanded in his and their preaching.

"Through the Spirit the church recapitulates the whole saving event" of the Son of Man's trajectory, writes Oliver O'Donovan.[27] After being empowered by the Spirit at Pentecost (like Jesus at his baptism), the disciples take up his cause in defiance of the rulers who crucified him. Like him, they pray to God for help and cite the Old Testament on "the nations conspir[ing]" and "the kings of the earth tak[ing] their stand / . . . against the LORD / and against his Anointed One" (Psalm 2:1-2). They name Herod and Pontius Pilate as hostile rulers who joined with the Sanhedrin (it had just warned Peter and John to cease proclaiming Christ) "to conspire against" Christ. They pray for boldness and for miracles that

---

[25]Oliver O'Donovan, *The Desire of the Nations: Rediscovering the Roots of Political Theology* (Cambridge: Cambridge University Press, 1996), p. 39; Douglas J. Moo, *The Epistle to the Romans* (Grand Rapids: Eerdmans, 1996), pp. 101-2; see also pp. 99-100.
[26]O'Donovan, *Desire of the Nations*, pp. 120-22.
[27]Ibid., p. 161.

attest to the truth of their witness. And their prayers are answered (Acts 4:24-31). A new trajectory begins, from suffering to glory, for the two-sided goal of salvation and judgment. Disciples are not given timeless philosophical principles to try (in vain?) to achieve. A Pathfinder empowers them to follow his path. When Paul tells the "mystery of our religion," he does not present a philosophy but the Son of Man's life: "he appeared in a body / was vindicated . . . / was seen . . . / was preached . . . / was believed . . . / was taken up in glory" (1 Timothy 3:16). Taking his path by his power, disciples are sifted out as righteous and escape condemnation in the final judgment but not chastening along the path.[28]

This new church bowing to another King, a newly enthroned Son of Man, is not a private club meeting for spiritual contemplation and posing no threat to rulers of the material realm. Here, O'Donovan's political theology helpfully reroutes us around the millennia-old privatization of the faith.[29] Like the Son's life, the believers' presence is handwriting on the wall telling nations and kings that God has weighed them, found them wanting and numbered their days. "A community lives under the authority of him to whom the Ancient of Days has entrusted the Kingdom." They have their own new holy day (Lord's Day), justice system, family laws and mandate to disobey rulers who forbid them to preach Christ.[30] They preach judgment on a Gentile empire and a Jewish court. Like their Lord, they do not seize power but exude power from a rival authority, and rulers find this threatening. Paul's and Barnabas's foes in Thessalonica cry to the magistrates, "They are all defying Caesar's decrees, saying that there is another king, one called Jesus" (Acts 17:7). Martyrdom resulted when disciples refused to join in the imperial cult involving worship of the emperor.

Judgment did not come yet. The city that rejected the Son experienced an astonishing display of God's mercy and an outpouring of God's salvation in the three thousand converted on Pentecost and two thousand more after the healing at the temple gate, and in the startling conversion of the persecutor, Saul (Acts 2:41; 4:4; 9:1-19, 26-30).

Preaching the gospel harvested the fruits of the Son's sufferings and added to his glory by adding new followers and conforming the old ones more closely to him. The Father and the Son were in no untoward hurry to glorify him the other way, by immediately "put[ting] all his enemies under his feet" (1 Corinthians 15:25; Psalm 110:1). The disciples' trajectory, too, had stages, and it was

---

[28]This, I take it, is what Balthasar means by the Son being "raised to become the norm of our being and the norm of our concrete history" (*Theology of History*, p. 12).
[29]O'Donovan, *Desire of the Nations*, p. 162. My approval of his applying theology to the public realm should not be taken as approval of his interpretations of Scripture or theology.
[30]Ibid., pp. 158-59, 183-84, 186.

not yet time for that one, their reign with him. In postascension appearances to Paul, Ananias and John, the Lord focused on the gospel, its progress among Gentiles and the state of his churches. He said nothing about being eager to judge the nations. He did offer to Thyatira's overcoming disciples the future reward of ruling the nations, but they were not to seize that rule straightaway (Revelation 2:26-27).

Their gospel warned of judgment as had his kingdom message. They must follow his path. "No servant is greater than his master," Jesus told them. "If they persecuted me, they will persecute you also" (John 15:20). His warnings to Pharisees and rulers brought hatred down on him, and his disciples' warnings would too: "a time is coming when anyone who kills you will think he is offering a service to God" (John 16:2). They must imitate him by warning of judgment. Paul did at Athens; derision, not death, was the result (Acts 17:31-32). Paul warned the high priest, "God will strike you, you whitewashed wall," using the Greek adjective Jesus had used (Acts 23:3; Matthew 23:27). They were not traveling orators sent to argue a new self-evident, risk-free syllogism, but testifiers willing to take the risks he took.

Proclaiming the gospel effected a sifting out based on people's response to it. Judgment began with his followers: Barnabas gave the entire sales proceeds to the church; Ananias and Sapphira dishonestly withheld part and died (Acts 4:36-5:11; 1 Peter 4:17). By stoning Stephen and persecuting the church, Jerusalem drove away the gospel, and Christ ordered Paul, "Leave Jerusalem immediately, because they will not accept your testimony about me" (Acts 22:18). The persecutor Herod Agrippa was struck dead for accepting the crowd's worship of him as a deity, whereas Paul and Barnabas saved themselves by strongly protesting a similar misidentification by Lystra's crowd. A clear continuity linked Jesus' command to disciples proclaiming the kingdom to "shake the dust off your feet" when departing any town that refused to listen, and Paul and Barnabus' shaking "the dust from their feet [in protest against]" Antioch's refusers and persecutors (Matthew 10:14; Acts 13:51). The Son of Man's followers did not end judgment but added new causes of it, including a refusal to heed God's new message.

The new causes were the sin of rejecting it (2 Thessalonians 1:8); preventing others from hearing it (1 Thessalonians 2:15-16); falsely claiming to believe it (Jude); teaching a false gospel (2 Peter 2:1-3). It did not leave people where they were before. This fork in the road forced a decision: go toward faith that brings righteousness or toward unbelief that increases sin. Widespread acceptance of the gospel can contribute to peace and order in a society and thus slow the pace of history (major, tragic events), but it does not slow history's stream of events into a motionless pool of timeless principles. A sifting out continues, and the wickedness of some ripens over time, and judgment sometimes comes in the form of major and tragic events.

His Followers Must Warn That the Son of Man Does Judge the Nations at His Return

This present stage in the Son of Man's trajectory is not the final one. At God's right hand, he awaits a final triumph, while his gospel is preached worldwide. "Yet at present we do not see everything subject to him. But we see Jesus, who was made a little lower than the angels, now crowned with glory and honor because he suffered death" (Hebrews 2:8-9). Here is the already/not yet tension: Christ is already crowned but not yet visibly reigning as Lord. In the New Testament, the Son of Man is not clearly portrayed as actively judging the nations currently. He is seated "at God's right hand—with angels, authorities and powers in submission to him" and is "far above all rule and authority" (1 Peter 3:22; Ephesians 1:21). We are not told exactly how his exalted power is exercised in history. The martyr Stephen saw "the Son of Man standing at the right hand of God" while the Sanhedrin or its supporters stoned him (Acts 7:56). John saw a decidedly regal one "like a son of man" while he was exiled by the emperor on Patmos (Revelation 1:12-16). Yet Christ did not judge the rulers who stoned or exiled. He waited, not impatiently, to descend to earth to reign. His followers must wait, too, and not seize power to avoid treading his path of suffering before glory. Alluding to Psalm 110:1, Paul stated, "For he must reign until *he* has put all his enemies under his feet" (1 Corinthians 15:25, 27, emphasis added). Here, God the Father seems to put the enemies under Christ's feet. Of course, given the unity of Father and Son, this may be a distinction without much difference. Certainly the Son of Man's gospel is not presented as a threat: believe, or a Ruler will judge you instantly. That does not deny present risks of judgment that history poses for everyone or the future judgment that Jesus linked to the Son of Man's coming (Luke 17:22-27; Matthew 24:27, 44-51).

Without getting bogged down in millennia-old disputes over how to interpret last things, we can conclude that the Son of Man's return will bring judgment on the nations. In Psalm 2:8-10, God (the Father, presumably) promises to "make the nations your inheritance," predicts that the Son "will rule them with an iron scepter" and "dash them to pieces like pottery" and warns kings to submit. Several New Testament writers apply this passage to Christ. And Daniel predicted a stone that "will crush all those kingdoms" and "one like a son of man" whom "all peoples, nations and men of every language" worshiped (Daniel 2:44; 7:13, 14). Nations provisionally judged now will be finally judged then. Some argue that this occurs at the end of history, at the Last Judgment; others, in history before the end. Since the Son of Man is a historical figure, I tend to agree with the latter view, but we need not resolve that issue, since judgment of nations, not its exact timing, is our theme.

Cowles ridicules the traditional view of Christ riding the white horse in Revelation 19: "like Clark Kent, emerging from the telephone booth as Superman, Jesus at his return will cast aside his servant garments" to become "a fierce, merciless, and physically violent eschatological terminator. . . . Having failed to reconcile the world to the Father through the power of Calvary's love, he will come again . . . and will smash his enemies into oblivion."[31] Having defined away the judgment side of God's two-sided historical program, having defined Jesus as a timeless principle of love, having wished away a history full of evil actors deserving judgment, these critics are shocked at judgment. There are several problems with this dismissal. The Son of Man never was merely a Clark-Kent-like Everyman but always was a future world ruler. Arguably, his "servant garments" were cast aside at his ascension—or, perhaps, at his crucifixion as a criminal, not a servant. His descent was far too deep to be merely an act of service or emotional reconciliation. Cowles's view has God in the dock, charged with failure to reconcile the world, rather than sinners guilty of refusing "the ministry of reconciliation" (2 Corinthians 5:18-20). And he ignores the sifting-out process yet to come in history. Refusing the message takes on an ever more sinister aspect over time. Refusal also is not a timeless philosophical principle but one that displays historical development, until the final rebellion against God is so evil, the final opponent so blasphemous (2 Thessalonians 2:3-12) and the Son of Man so contrasted with antichrist by the former's loving, obedient suffering and sacrifice that the Son of Man's coming in judgment will be clearly seen as just. Today's blurred picture will come into sharp focus.

That will be the final word giving meaning to history. We have it now so we can escape the meaninglessness of living for a soon-to-be-superseded meaning. God's judgment on sin is our main risk in history, so the Son of Man's trajectory is the meaning of history, the one we need, the final one. By faith to be caught up in his saving death on the cross, and to follow his path, is the only way to escape judgment. The all-encompassing dimensions of this Son of Man—very God descending to a criminal's cross and ascending to God's right hand as Lord of the universe—and the stated necessity of all this for salvation—and the uniqueness of this trajectory as an historical event, not some philosophical category in-

---

[31]Cowles, "Response to Tremper Longman III," p. 193.

cluding similar cases—all these factors make it an exclusive way to salvation. "How shall we escape if we ignore such a great salvation?" (Hebrews 2:3).

New Complications of God's Judgment on the Nations in This Present Period

The fact of a future judgment on the nations sets a context for events in the present and near future. The gospel is preached to individuals, not to nations per se: "In the New Testament, while social and communal responsibility is not overlooked, the emphasis in judgment is on what the individual does or does not do," unlike the Old Testament, where "judgment falls on" nations. Yet, "the New Testament makes it clear that God is engaged upon a present activity of judging."[32] Widespread revivals or widespread rejection impact a nation in a sociological way. Ideas in the gospel and in rival beliefs have ideological, saving or condemning, effects upon a nation.

God's judgments become more complicated. Disciples are scattered among many nations, so his rescue of disciples in one may imperil disciples in others. God uses judgments to chasten disciples for their good. One event may save some and judge others. Judgment may speed or slow the gospel's progress in different areas. O'Donovan notes that "to trace the outline of Christ's dawning reign on earth requires that one trace the false pretension" of antichrist also.[33] Judgment keeps "the false pretension" of a Napoleon from rising to the level of an antichrist so the gospel has longer to work or it may allow a rise at the end (2 Thessalonians 2). Separation of powers, election of leaders and levels of government divide responsibility. Herod Agrippa was alone responsible for persecuting the church and claiming deity. The Nazi regime was a many-headed monster that secured some democratic approval from the German people.

One complication is fifteen hundred years of "Christendom . . . an era in which the truth of Christianity was taken to be a truth of secular politics" and "confessionally Christian government[s]" were secular like other nations and also professedly "obedient to Christ." O'Donovan ends this era at 1791, when the First Amendment to the U.S. Constitution prohibited religious establishment.[34] Did God judge Christian nations differently? How were conflicts between two such nations judged? Did he regard the ending of this national confession as apostasy or as honesty? Were leaders who de-coupled government from Christianity guilty of rejecting the gospel, thus exposing themselves and

---

[32]Leon Morris, *The Biblical Doctrine of Judgment* (Grand Rapids: Eerdmans, 1960), pp. 45, 49.
[33]O'Donovan, *Desire of the Nations*, p. 214.
[34]Ibid., pp. 195, 244-45.

the nation to judgment? Christianity has preferred peace and order for the preaching of the gospel and for its ministries. The governments of Christendom were to maintain that. Paul urges prayers "for kings and all those in authority," not that they be judged but "that we may live peaceful and quiet lives in all godliness and holiness" (1 Timothy 2:2). War and civil disorder limit the gospel, so God may limit them instead of allowing war and disorder as judgments. Complications make it harder for us to comprehend or identify God's judgments, not for him to decide or execute them. Dividing policy making between twenty officials or three branches or two layers cannot confuse him. We have to sort through complications as we turn to the history of the United States, the first nation to adopt the idea "that religious questions were not open to public arbitration" and to create "a state freed from all responsibility to recognise God's self-disclosure in history," that is, his disclosure in the Son of Man.[35]

Rulers and governments face a radically altered situation. The Son of Man has set a new standard of suffering before glory that implicitly judges their arrogance of power. His ascension numbered their days of power. That is the gospel to rulers that relativizes their power and pretensions. A sifting-out choice is thrust on them: submit or resist in ways now more culpable due to *who* is being resisted. O'Donovan argues, "The most truly Christian state . . . makes the confession of Christ's victory and accepts the relegation of its own authority. It echoes the words of John the Baptist: 'He must increase, I must decrease' (John 3:30)."[36] Or, the disobedient state can set the state against Christ's victory and relegate his authority to private affairs, while the state sets up a public cult that demands citizens' ultimate allegiance as did the Roman emperors' cult. That is idolatry. God will ultimately judge such idolatry. For now, we turn to the post-1791 history of the United States, to see what the response of its governing elite was to this choice.

---

[35]Ibid., pp. 244, 245.
[36]Ibid., p. 219.

7

Was the Burning of Washington (1814) God's Judgment?

The heights-to-depths-to-heights trajectory of the Son of Man gives us the context in which to examine God's judgments in U.S. history. Apart from that context, claims that God judged the nation will be dismissed as whining by Christians peeved at being denied their alleged Constantinian right to rule the nation. That is not the issue. As we saw, the Son of Man's followers must share his rejection, not calling down judgment on those who reject them, any more than he did. The Son of Man who patiently endured the agony and humiliation of crucifixion, the Roman soldiers' mocking him with a royal robe, is not peevishly losing his temper because a nation neglects to highlight his name in its constitution. That does not mean God the Father has ceased his sifting out and judging in history. For God not to judge would be an unthinkable act of abdication, a denial of his righteousness and sovereignty.

Psalm 2 proclaims that God is not threatened by human rejection of his plans: "The kings of the earth take their stand, . . . / against the LORD / and against his Anointed One. . . . / The One enthroned in heaven laughs; / the LORD scoffs at them" (Psalm 2:2, 4). The first purported example of God's judgment in U.S. history that we examine falls more into this category of farce than tragedy. We have a feeling that a cosmic joke is being played. The humor comes largely in a stark contrast between human self-exalting grandiosity and simple, bungling incompetence.

After September 11, commentators pointed to the burning of the public buildings in Washington, D.C., including the Capitol and White House, in August 1814, as the last time enemies invaded our soil and destroyed or damaged key national symbols. We look first at events leading up to this disaster, from 1801 to 1813, when Thomas Jefferson's party was in power, in order to ascertain its causes and what human failings might have been judged then. We start from our scriptural presupposition, now, that this crisis likely was a divine judgment, and see if that idea makes sense or helps to explain events. If so, it was more a judgment on the nation's ruling class, as symbolized by the capital where the elite enacted laws, rather than on the American people. Fires that temporarily disabled the national government had some effect on ordinary citizens, but the decentralized country carried on without its national leaders, as state and local governments functioned. The burning capital seems more the result of a "fate-effecting deed," but the Old Testament indicates we should not preclude an acting God.

Embarrassment as a Judgment Perhaps Suited to Gentlemen-Founders

To examine the ruling class of gentry, we must re-enter a lost world of knee breeches, powdered wigs, three-cornered hats and equally unfamiliar notions. The ideas of the American Revolution (1775-1783) percolated through society and gradually democratized it, but the nation in 1801 resembled 1770s America. Gentlemen were still in power. "Gentleman" was not a synonym for a disciple of the Son of Man, although he might be one. Human pride defined that status: not having to work for a living, especially not with one's hands; inheriting the status or obtaining it by one's achievements in business, a profession or land-holding; conspicuously spending wealth and displaying superior manners; condescending to speak to one's inferiors; stressing reputation and honor above all. "Honor was the value genteel society placed on a gentleman and the value that a gentleman placed on himself," concludes historian Gordon Wood. "Honor suggested a public drama in which men played roles for which they were praised or blamed." This was quite opposite to the Son of Man's willingness to suffer the humiliations of spitting, thorns, a mock robe and a cross. We see role playing as hypocrisy, in light of Jesus' critique of Pharisees; they saw it in classical Greco-Roman terms as that love of praise from worthy men that motivated a man to act worthily. Given this stress on an honorable façade, the obvious way to spark humor was to expose pretense, as the era's playwrights knew, which was an effective judgment, too, striking them at their most vulnerable point and at the pride that was their sin.[1]

The Founding Fathers were gentlemen who accepted these values and, often, some related philosophical ones: a Deism that softened Christianity's clash with classicism by dropping the divinity of Jesus and stressing religion as ethics; the Enlightenment that softened Christians' mutual clashes by adopting

---

[1]Gordon S. Wood, *The Radicalism of the American Revolution* (New York: Knopf, 1992), p. 39; see pp. 24-42; Forrest McDonald, *Novus Ordo Seclorum: The Intellectual Origins of the Constitution* (Lawrence: University Press of Kansas, 1985), pp. 89-98.

this less contentious Deism, privileging reason above faith and separating church from state; a republicanism that made a cult out of the republic, with a new definition of virtue (self-sacrifice for the public good), a new stress on independence and a utopian hope of bringing gentry virtues of "politeness, grace, taste, learning, and character" to an entire people.[2] Those who founded a new utopian social order would win enduring fame and honor beyond all others. Gentlemen self-consciously sought this lasting fame as founders and self-approved their own search as a worthy goal.

Most state constitutions mentioned God in their preamble and "required officeholders to profess some kind of religious faith"; the 1787 Federal Constitution did neither, apart from the dating "in the year of our Lord." This "perfectly secular text" was devoid of "manifest religious content" because the state governments were regarded as the main ones, closest to the people and best suited to handle religion, a matter closest to the people's hearts; because the Founders tried to reassure minority denominations that feared established churches; and because the Enlightenment's political science was secular and rational. Protests against this absence of the name of God or Christ were of no avail. Much later, during the Civil War, Christians campaigned in vain to add these words to the preamble: "Recognizing Almighty God as the source of all authority and power in civil government, and acknowledging the Lord Jesus Christ as the Governor among nations, His revealed will as the supreme law of the land, in order to constitute a Christian government."[3]

Founders were not limited to ideas, as if they cared not whether their new order ruled a drawing room or a universe. It ruled the eastern edge of a continent. One predicted, "a mighty empire . . . will arise on this continent where she [Britain] cannot hinder its progress." On the nation's Great Seal (on our dollar bill), they placed the Latin phrase *Novus Ordo Seclorum,* which can have a spatial meaning—"A New Order in the Universe"—or a temporal one— "A New Order Among the Ages." They did not believe in building small.[4] Nor did Thomas Jefferson. "His slaves carted away the top of" his mountain near Charlottesville, "creat[ing] for him a presentation-platform" on which his

---

[2]Here I rely mainly on Wood, *Radicalism,* p. 195; see pp. 95-225.

[3]Stephen Botein, "Religious Dimensions of the Early American State," in Richard Beeman, Stephen Botein and Edward C. Carter II, *Beyond Confederation: Origins of the Constitution and American National Identity* (Chapel Hill: University of North Carolina Press, 1987), pp. 317, 329; see pp. 315-30. Botein minimizes the role of Enlightenment thought in this secularity.

[4]Marc Egnal, *A Mighty Empire: The Origins of the American Revolution* (Ithaca, N.Y.: Cornell University Press, 1988), p. 14 (quoting Laurens); Roger G. Kennedy, *Mr. Jefferson's Lost Cause: Land, Farmers, Slavery and the Louisiana Purchase* (New York: Oxford University Press, 2003), p. 28.

model home, Monticello, faced west to teach that region the Enlightenment values its architecture embodied.[5]

Thomas Jefferson Reduces the History-Making Son of Man to a Philosopher of Ethics

In examining the Enlightenment, its preference for philosophy over history and its disdain for Old Testament prophecy, we also examined Jefferson. Let us hear his views in his words. He saw "the Christian philosophy,—[as] the most sublime & benevolent, but most perverted system that ever shone on man." Hebrews' ideas of God "were degrading & injurious" and "their Ethics" were "imperfect . . . & repulsive & anti-social, as respecting other nations," for God would not choose one nation to advance a history of salvation. Jesus had "every *human* excellence" and "never claimed any other" but was a moral philosopher who "corrected the Deism of the Jews" to be more cosmopolitan, "inculcating universal philanthropy . . . to all mankind, gathering all into one family." Unfortunately, unlike other philosophers, "he wrote nothing himself" and died "at about 33 years of age, his reason having not yet attained the *maximum* of its energy"; thus, the task of "writing his life & doctrines fell on the most unlettered & ignorant men; who wrote, too, from memory" and distorted his teachings.[6]

Angered at attacks on his religious views and hopeful that an ethical, Unitarian religion would promote social harmony in the republic, Jefferson sought to "cut out the morsels of morality" in the New Testament and construct "a digest of his [Jesus'] moral doctrines . . . leaving out everything relative to his personal history and character." In 1803, he wrote a "Syllabus" on Jesus' "Doctrines" (quoted above). Evenings, at the White House in February-March 1804, he took two New Testaments, clipped out verses he felt were Jesus' words and compiled "The Philosophy of Jesus." Some sayings on judgment did not make the cut, including Luke 12:49-53, where Jesus brings the sifting out that divides families. The passage about the tower of Siloam (Luke 13:1-5) is here, but Jefferson misinterpreted it as teaching "misfortune no proof of sin." Jesus' trial he pieced together from several Gospels, omitting Jesus' use of Daniel's prophecy of the Son of Man coming on the clouds. Using the scissors-and-paste method, Jefferson edited the Son of Man's trajectory down to a series of lectures on morality.[7]

[5]Kennedy, *Mr. Jefferson's Lost Cause,* p. 6.

[6]Thomas Jefferson to Dr. Joseph Priestley, March 21, 1801, and Jefferson to Dr. Benjamin Rush, April 21, 1803, both in *Thomas Jefferson: Writings* (New York: Library of America, 1984), pp. 1085, 1122, 1124, 1125; see also pp. 1086, 1123, 1126.

[7]Eugene R. Sheriden, "Introduction," pp. 14, 22, 27-28, 30; Thomas Jefferson, "The Philosophy of Jesus," pp. 59, 91, 98-99, 102-3, 119; and Dickinson W. Adams, ed., *Jefferson's Extracts from*

Jefferson hoped for an agrarian, Unitarian republic. "Those who labour in the earth are the chosen people of God, if ever he had a chosen people," he claimed. Western small farmers were his ideal citizens, and Unitarians were to become the religious rule in the westwardly expanding nation.[8] Jefferson regarded history as philosophy teaching political truths by examples. He wanted his ideal citizens' education to be "chiefly historical" in its beginning grades. "History . . . will enable them to judge of the future; it will avail them of the experience of other times . . . ; it will qualify them as judges of the actions and designs of men" so as to preserve the republic, which would be tested by its rulers' scheming ambitions. His ideal farmer-citizens were "its only safe depositories."[9] Incomprehensible to him would be our ideas: (1) the Son of Man's personal history was itself the meaning of history; (2) God did the testing and sifting, for his purpose, to glorify the Son; (3) the republic's citizens were not the judges but the judged; and (4) history was essentially theological, not political. To him, this would be like saying that an exalted Plato would return one day to judge those who had not accepted his *Republic*.

The Son of Man Steals Away Jefferson's Western Sheep at Cane Ridge, Kentucky

Jefferson stood in the Senate chamber on March 4, 1801, to take the oath of office. In his inaugural address, with sunny optimism, he proclaimed "this Government, the world's best hope." Despite fears "that a republican government can not be strong enough," he believed it "the strongest Government on earth," for it was "the only one where every man, at the call of the law, would fly to

---

the Gospels, in *The Papers of Thomas Jefferson: Second Series* (Princeton, N.J.: Princeton University Press, 1983). In 1819 or 1820, Jefferson completed his "Life and Morals of Jesus," sometimes called The Jefferson Bible. Excised, reports Edwin Gaustad, were miracles, angels, claims of divinity, the resurrection and the ascension. The boy Jesus goes to the temple, stays an extra three days and is questioned by his parents. "Didn't you know I had to be in my Father's house?" Jesus responds. "But they did not understand what he was saying to them" (Luke 2:49-50). Gaustad wittily adds, "Neither did Jefferson, so he dropped the exchange." Edwin S. Gaustad, *Sworn on the Altar of God: A Religious Biography of Thomas Jefferson* (Grand Rapids: Eerdmans, 1996), p. 125 (see pp. 114-31). See also *Jefferson: Writings*, pp. 1080-81, 1121, 1122-23, 1526-27, 1530.

[8]*Jefferson: Writings*, p. 290 (from *Notes on the State of Virginia*, query 19); Drew R. McCoy, *The Elusive Republic: Political Economy in Jeffersonian America* (Chapel Hill: University of North Carolina Press, 1980); Gaustad, *Sworn on the Altar*, p. 146. By the Louisiana Purchase (1803), he so expanded the nation's land area that it would take centuries, he thought, before the West would be settled and the United States forced to become a manufacturing nation (McCoy's point).

[9]*Jefferson: Writings*, p. 274 (query 14 in *Notes on the State of Virginia*). See also Jefferson to John Norvell, June 14, 1807, on pp. 1176-77.

the standard of the law, and would meet invasions of the public order as his own personal concern." To unify the nation, he masked divisions with "the irresolution of public ambiguity" (O'Donovan's words): "We are all Republicans, we are all Federalists." This vast republic was "enlightened by a benign religion" that incorporated Calvinist, Catholic and Deist into Jefferson's religion of reason and ethics, his universal philosophical sun. An "overruling Providence" shone on all, regardless of belief or unbelief, for "it delights in the happiness of man here and his greater happiness hereafter."[10]

As he spoke, Kentucky was experiencing "religious stirrings" after revivals at Gasper and Red Rivers during the summer of 1800 and scattered ones over the winter. These revivals occurred during days of preaching before communion services that attracted hundreds of people and spilled out of meetinghouses. The emotional responses, evangelical doctrine, non-genteel participants, outdoor primitive settings in frontier Kentucky and the names Cabin Creek and Stony Creek and Indian Creek all shouted a contrast to Jefferson's Enlightened speech to an audience of gentry inside the Capitol. Despite his claim that "corruption of morals in the mass of cultivators" was unknown, about half of Kentucky's cultivators were unchurched, and vice was well-known. At Cane Ridge, five months after his speech, the most famous revival of the Second Great Awakening blazed for a week.[11] Cane Ridge was not a driving force causing the Awakening but a symbol of it and a well-documented instance of it.

On Friday, August 6, 1801, people came by wagon, on horseback and on foot to Cane Ridge meetinghouse, where the first preaching occurred that night. "By Saturday the roads were jammed with people." Ten thousand were likely on the grounds for Saturday and Sunday, but only nine hundred took part in the main event, the Sunday communion service, for the great drama came in the intense questioning of whether one was saved and fit to take communion. One minister reported thousands "assembled in the woods, ministers preaching day and night, the camp illuminated with candles, on trees, at waggons, and at the tent; persons falling down, and carried out of the crowd, by those next to them, and taken to some convenient place, where prayer is made for them; some Psalm or Hymn suitable to the occasion, sung . . . some

---

[10]*Jefferson: Writings*, pp. 493, 494; Oliver O'Donovan, *The Desire of the Nations: Rediscovering the Roots of Political Theology* (Cambridge: Cambridge University Press, 1996), pp. 38-39.
[11]Paul K. Conkin, *Cane Ridge: America's Pentecost* (Madison: University of Wisconsin Press, 1990), p. 67; see pp. 57-62, 64, 71; *Jefferson: Writings*, 290; Steven J. Keillor, *This Rebellious House: American History and the Truth of Christianity* (Downers Grove, Ill.: InterVarsity Press, 1996), pp. 121-23.

mourning, some rejoicing, and great solemnity on every countenance."[12]

It was as if the full weight of eternity settled down on a small section of Kentucky. Gone was Jefferson's "benign religion," his public ambiguity, where Providence shone on saint and sinner alike. God's sifting out intensified, as a deep conviction of sin or an ecstasy of forgiving grace threw people down by the hundreds. "Some parts of the ground were literally strewn like a battlefield." Individual dramas of feared judgment then realized salvation through faith in Christ reverberated, as one person's saving release convicted another, whose faith led him to exhort loudly that sinners repent. Will I be saved or lost for eternity? In a democratic drama, women, children, black slaves and white laymen exhorted—three hundred at once—as well as twenty clergy, one of whom reported: "the darkness of the night, the solemnity of the place, and of the occasion, and conscious guilt, all conspire to make terror thrill through every power of the soul, and rouse it to awful attention."[13] Physical jerks, erroneous doctrines and foolish exhortations marred such revivals, but terror at God's holy judgment befitted the human crisis of an eternal soul in a mortal sinful body in an unpredictable stream of events in a holy God's control—more than did Jefferson's unworried philosophical optimism.

The Son of Man stole Western sheep (and Eastern ones) away from Deistic, Enlightened, genteel Founders. The republic's history would be marked by paradox: an elite's hopes of a new order to end the age of Constantinian, monarchical Christendom amid the most Christianized people on earth, in a land where the winds of the gospel blew more freely than anywhere or any time. The republic's future, its West, would not be Unitarian; the republic would be tested to see if it was "the strongest Government on earth"; Jefferson's government, like all systems, would undergo "a relentless sifting and testing," in Herbert Butterfield's words.

This paradox of an often secular elite ruling a religious people was the key cause of the judgment enacted from 1801 to 1815, for this elite tended to lead where the people would not follow and to choose a means to peace, a cause of war and a strategy for war that the people did not understand or support. Jefferson's Republicans were closer to and more understanding of the common people than were their opponents, the Federalists. Urban workers, minority ethnic groups like the Scotch-Irish and less elite denominations like the Baptists and Methodists tended to vote Republican. What follows is not an argument that Federalists could have better handled the crises of the Napoleonic Wars but that

---

[12]Conkin, *Cane Ridge*, p. 93; see pp. 83, 87-88, 89, 90-91.
[13]Ibid., pp. 94, 95; see also pp. 91, 93.

these wars occasioned God's "sifting and testing" of the nation's leaders, who were Jefferson's Republicans at the time. God does not grade on the curve, so the hypothetical Federalist score is irrelevant.

The Napoleonic Wars Grind the Republic Between Two Powerful Belligerents

In 1800, the nation's capital was a work in progress. A "half-finished White House stood in a naked field overlooking the Potomac, with two awkward Department buildings near it," wrote historian Henry Adams. "Across a swamp, a mile and a half away, the shapeless, unfinished Capitol was seen, two wings without a body." The nation's leaders "clustered together in eight or ten boarding-houses . . . and there lived, like a convent of monks" who could only go from house to office and back again, for the city had nothing else. The republic's president lodged there "like a pelican in the wilderness," wrote one editor.[14] Costly improvements to the government or capital were not contemplated by Jefferson's political philosophy, which called for reliance on state governments, a strict view of the constitution and the federal government's limited powers, low taxes and low expenditures leading to paying off the national debt. That meant a weak army and navy (strong ones cost money), a foreign policy of neutrality without alliances requiring a strong military and a focus on westward expansion. Jefferson believed cutting off trade with foreign nations could be an alternative to war. This philosophical ideal history would put to the test.[15]

The Napoleonic Wars were the "relentless sifting and testing" of Jefferson, his friend and successor James Madison and their Republican system. Britain's navy blockaded France, and France's navy seized neutral vessels that had stopped in Britain. Neutrals like the United States were caught in a Catch-22: "To sail toward France without first calling at England meant seizure by the Royal Navy; to touch at England and then sail to France meant confiscation by Napoleon." More insulting to U.S. honor was the Royal Navy's stopping and boarding U.S. merchant ships to remove sailors who had deserted (and some who had not) from the Royal Navy. The British seemed to mock independence, especially when H.M.S. *Leopard* fired on the U.S. Navy's *Chesapeake*

---

[14]Henry Adams, *History of the United States of America During the Administrations of Thomas Jefferson* (New York: Library of America, 1986), pp. 23-24; Botein, "Religious Dimensions," p. 325.

[15]*Jefferson: Writings*, pp. 494-95 (his first inaugural address), pp. 1006-7 (Jefferson to Madison, March 24, 1793), p. 1014 (to Tench Coxe, May 1, 1794), p. 1045 (to Thomas Pinckney, May 29, 1797); Adams, *History of Administrations of Thomas Jefferson*, pp. 99-102.

in June 1807 and killed several American sailors.[16]

Jefferson's Republicans did not believe in spending money on a seagoing navy, or in accepting Britain's high-handed acts on the seas or in resolving this seeming contradiction. The United States had gained independence by being too large for the British army to conquer, and that fact did not establish the new nation's freedom at sea. After 1783, Britain re-established economic dominance over the United States, which exported cotton to British mills and imported British manufactured goods, both of which went by sea. Jefferson's anti-slavery hopes failed to keep cotton-raising slavery out of the Southwest; that aided British millers' and brokers' mastery.[17] Jefferson's and Madison's foreign policy writhed in agony on a historical rack: tied between two warring nations, almost powerless from military weakness, wrenched first this way, then that, by the changing policies and fortunes of war, while the national unity was torn asunder.

The wrenching began in the fall of 1801, when France and Britain signed a peace agreement, but in May 1803, they were at war again; in April 1803, the Louisiana Purchase removed Napoleon as a neighbor, lessening dependence on Britain and making the Royal Navy's acts seem more intolerable to American honor; the *Leopard's* outrage rankled for four years while the two nations argued over terms; Jefferson rejected a treaty negotiated in 1806, and the British did likewise in 1809; they differed over maritime definitions (when was a sailor an American citizen and when was a blockade a blockade). France's seizure of U.S. ships annoyed, but Britain's control of the seas let it annoy America more often, more deeply.[18]

In December 1807, Jefferson applied his philosophical concept of embargo as a "peaceable coercion" to force Britain to give way. The embargo made it illegal for a U.S. vessel to leave for a foreign port and blocked foreign vessels from coming to U.S. ports. To Jefferson, "peaceable coercion" was part of the new order of the ages, "another useful lesson" from the new Republic, "another example to the world," a point of honor. Embargoes prevent wars.[19]

The embargo hurt the economy. Wheat fell from $2 to 75¢ per bushel; cotton

---

[16]Patrick C. T. White, *A Nation on Trial: America and the War of 1812* (New York: Wiley, 1965), p. 12.

[17]For British "textile colonial-imperialism" and the failure of Jeffersonian anti-slavery, see Kennedy, *Jefferson's Lost Cause,* pp. 87-117.

[18]For details on the events leading up to the War of 1812, I am indebted to Robert A. Rutland, ed., *James Madison and the American Nation 1751-1836: An Encyclopedia* (New York: Simon & Schuster, 1994).

[19]*Jefferson: Writings,* p. 1006 (Jefferson to Madison, March 24, 1793), p. 1014 (to Tench Coxe, May 1, 1794).

exports in 1808 fell to one-fifth their 1807 level; shipping activity was cut in half. A British traveler in 1808 described New York: "Not a box, bale, cask, barrel, or package was to be seen. . . . Many of the counting houses were shut up . . . , the streets, near the water-side, were almost deserted; the grass had begun to grow upon the wharves." Jefferson had inflicted a self-judgment of biblical proportions on his own country. Citizens did not meekly submit to it. In some regions, the cry of unity became, "We are all smugglers." Republicans violated their principles by enforcing the federal (unconstitutional) edict against states, expanding federal powers, ending individuals' economic freedom, using the military against U.S. citizens and erasing custom revenues that enabled the government to repay its debts. Jefferson's embargo divided the country more than had any disputed Christian doctrine.[20]

A Leader's Nightmare: Looking Back to See Few Followers

The failed embargo was dry-docked for good on March 1, 1809, three days before Jefferson's second term ended, with his popularity radically diminished. Unfair but not inaccurate as a sign of public opinion was Josiah Quincy's memorable quip about Jefferson being "a dish of skim milk curdling at the head of our nation." The cards of forbearance and of embargo had been played to no avail by the time Madison became president, and his supporters felt the war card must come next.[21] To them, British insults were not just against America's honor but also were a monarchy's disrespect for the honor of republicanism. A war was needed to vindicate a philosophy, but a people might not fight eagerly for that end.[22]

Out of touch with many Americans' Christian faith, Republican leaders in the White House and in Congress (War Hawks such as Henry Clay and John Calhoun shared Madison's deistic views) were out of touch with many Americans' opinion on war. They had not seized on the *Chesapeake* tragedy, which created the necessary but temporary popular support for war against Britain. Instead, Madison seized on Napoleon's deceitful claim in November 1810 to

---

[20]Adams, *History of Administrations of Thomas Jefferson*, pp. 1099-1110, 1116-17, 1118 (quoting Lambert), p. 1120; Douglass C. North, *The Economic Growth of the United States 1790-1860* (New York: Norton, 1966), pp. 37-38, 40, 231; White, *Nation on Trial*, pp. 47-53.
[21]Adams, *History of the Administrations of Thomas Jefferson*, p. 1172 (quoting Quincy), 1239; J. C. A. Stagg, *Mr. Madison's War: Politics, Diplomacy and Warfare in the Early American Republic, 1783-1830* (Princeton, N.J.: Princeton University Press, 1983), pp. 4, 7, 30-31, 71, 78, 92.
[22]This point is made in Roger H. Brown, *The Republic in Peril: 1812* (New York: Columbia University Press, 1964), pp. 76-80; and Steven Watts, *The Republic Reborn: War and the Making of Liberal America, 1790-1820* (Baltimore: Johns Hopkins University Press, 1987), p. 283.

have ended France's attacks on U.S. shipping, in order to pressure Britain to do likewise or face a war. Americans knew France captured U.S. ships after November 1810, but Madison refused to admit the obvious: he was wrong. He planned to invade Canada to force Britain to respect America's maritime rights, but invading others proved less motivating for Americans than anger at being attacked *(Chesapeake)*. Congress wanted war but not the taxes to pay for it, so taxes were to begin only after war was declared. New England, the Federalist Party, the Congregationalist clergy and other groups opposed the war. These Americans and many others abhorred fighting, in effect, on the same side as Napoleon's infidel France against Britain, the home of the evangelical missionary movement.[23]

Republican leaders' insensitivity to their highly Christian citizenry was evident. Britain, too, was experiencing evangelical revival; Napoleon was seen by prophecy-minded believers as the antichrist or a close model. Wouldn't God judge a people who fought against evangelical Britain while benefiting, indirectly, from Napoleon's successes? Jedidiah Morse pointed to the folly of fighting "a nation which embosoms a great multitude of devout men and women, precious pledges of her safety, and formidable for her defence against all assailants; whose prayers, like a cloud of incense, daily ascend up before the throne of God for protection."[24] Those prayers were answered, partly, in the assistance given to Britain by America's internal divisions.

Days after the Senate narrowly approved the declaration of war, news came that the anti-American prime minister of Britain had been assassinated and that efforts were underway to repeal a major grievance against Britain, the Orders in Council. The orders had been repealed already, but the news had not yet crossed the Atlantic.[25] (During the war, the weeks-long duration of the Atlantic crossing would serve to enhance suspense, like a plot device.) Leaders put the cart (war) before the horse (public support for war) in hopes the sight of a cart would cause the horse to push. Madison's ally Richard Rush argued that he had to "put the machine of power in motion," hoping "thousands will run

---

[23]Adams, *History of the Administrations of Thomas Jefferson,* pp. 946-54; Stagg, *Mr. Madison's War,* pp. 71, 86-87, 91, 92, 99, 109, 110-11, 138; Henry Adams, *History of the United States of America During the Administrations of James Madison* (New York: Library of America, 1986), pp. 179-84, 264-73, 321, 439, 441, 448-49; White, *Nation on Trial,* pp. 40-42, 75-80. For evangelical opposition to a war against Britain, see William Gribbin, *The Churches Militant: The War of 1812 and American Religion* (New Haven, Conn.: Yale University Press, 1973), chaps. 1 and 2. There were Baptists, Methodists and other evangelicals who supported the war, and Gribbin tells their story too.
[24]Gribbin, *Churches Militant,* pp. 49-50.
[25]Stagg, *Mr. Madison's War,* pp. 111-14, 118.

after its wheels," but "everybody is pulling it to pieces."[26]

The cart got stuck in 1812, and few Americans were willing to push. General William Hull surrendered Detroit to the British, who also took Fort Dearborn (Chicago); an American invasion force was repulsed near Niagara when New York's state militia refused to cross the border into Canada; a similar refusal in November (plus "an extremely serious throat infection" among many troops) halted a larger force that had set out to seize Montreal. Volunteering declined due to defeat, and partisan bickering increased. Apart from a naval victory on Lake Erie and a raid on York (present-day Toronto) that saw the burning of public buildings in that provincial capital, the year 1813 saw little improvement in military fortunes. A weak national government was ill-suited to mobilize a decentralized people to attack Canada to defend sailors at sea. Where local threats existed—from Indians in the Northwest or the British at New Orleans—the people responded with courage. In 1814, the British could send troops to America after the collapse of Napoleon's forces in March. The republic began to look like a new order for the decades.[27]

Washington Burns: "The Capital of the Union Lost by Cowardice" (and Incompetence)

As the summer season for warring opened, Madison's cabinet was disunited and without a realistic hope of invading Canada. A British fleet with forty-five hundred British soldiers and marines on board landed on August 18 at Benedict, Maryland, only thirty miles from the capital. The British fleet's conspicuous control of Chesapeake Bay encouraged hundreds of slaves to run away. Americans' practice of slavery looked to be part of an impending judgment. About three hundred ex-slaves joined the new Colonial Marines and aided in the attack on Washington.[28]

The result was pure farce. Secretary of War John Armstrong doubted the British would attack the capital and did nothing to fortify it. Residents knew better, protested at the White House on July 28 and angrily threatened "to prevent Mad-

---

[26]Ibid., pp. 109-110 (quoting Rush); Henry Adams ridiculed this "experiment of thrusting the country into war to inflame it" . . . "the United States were first to force themselves into a war they dreaded, in the hope that the war itself might create the spirit they lacked" (Adams, *History of the Administrations of James Madison*, p. 439).

[27]Stagg, *Mr. Madison's War*, pp. 204-7, 246-51, 268 (quoted), 270-71, 346, 382-83, 389.

[28]C. J. Bartlett and Gene A. Smith, "A 'Species of Milito-Nautico-Guerilla-Plundering Warfare': Admiral Alexander Cochrane's Naval Campaign against the United States, 1814-1815," pp. 188-89, in *Britain and America Go to War: The Impact of War and Warfare in Anglo-America, 1754-1815,* ed. Julie Flavell and Stephen Conway (Gainesville: University Press of Florida, 2004).

ison and his family from leaving the area should they try to do so." Fearing a British attack, Madison gave orders to prepare a defense but did not insure they were carried out. To command Washington's defenders, he appointed Brigadier General William Winder, a lawyer who had blundered into the British lines during his one prior battle. Madison thought Armstrong was still in charge of Washington's defense; Armstrong felt Madison had relieved him and given the job to Winder, who rode around like a jockey scouting the countryside so rapidly and incessantly that his superiors lost touch with him; Secretary of State James Monroe rode out to do scout duty and watch the British (one day he forgot to bring his telescope). Meanwhile, forty-five hundred British troops marched on Maryland roads and encountered so little resistance that they decided to attack Washington, which they had thought impossible.[29]

A comedy of errors ensued. Winder retreated to the Navy-Yard bridge to make a stand, although firing this quarter-mile-long bridge would have prevented a British crossing. On Wednesday morning, August 24, Winder wrote Armstrong, "I shall remain stationary as much as possible, that I may be the more readily found." But he did not. Hearing that the British were marching to Bladensburg, the key approach by land to the capital, he finally did move his three thousand troops there by noon, to join three thousand militia. Madison, Monroe, Armstrong and the attorney general also rode up to the battlefield-to-be. The cabinet officers and the diminutive president, "absurdly wearing a pair of duelling pistols buckled at his waist, [were] headed straight for the bridge—and the British." A Republican president showed up to fight a duel for the republic's honor, with the cabinet as his seconds. A scout warned them to return to avoid capture. Their unorganized, undisciplined army also turned around and fled. They should not be blamed, what with the last-minute "who's in charge here" talk among the cabinet, Winder's open planning for a retreat route and the best U.S. troops being stationed too far in the rear to render much assistance.[30]

Starting Wednesday night, the British burned the Capitol, White House and State, Treasury and War Department buildings. They spared private residences

---

[29]Stagg, *Mr. Madison's War,* pp. 407-16; Anthony S. Pitch, *The Burning of Washington: The British Invasion of 1814* (Annapolis, Md.: Naval Institute Press, 1998), pp. 30-34, 36, 39-40, 55-56; Adams, *History of the Administrations of James Madison,* pp. 993-1005. For Madison's version of this controversy, see *James Madison: Writings* (New York: Library of America, 1999), pp. 697-706.

[30]Stagg, *Mr. Madison's War,* pp. 416-17; Pitch, *Burning of Washington,* pp. 64-69; Adams, *History of the Administrations of James Madison,* pp. 1005, 1006 (quoting Winder), 1007-10; Christopher T. George, *Terror on the Chesapeake: The War of 1812 on the Bay* (Shippensburg, Penn.: White Mane Books, 2000), p. 95; see also pp. 93-94, 96.

and businesses. Still, enough flames lit up the night sky to create "an almost meridian brightness," recalled one resident. "You never saw a drawing room so brilliantly lighted as the whole city was that night." The president, one cabinet member and two dragoons fled on horseback to the Virginia shore toward Leesburg. They repeatedly looked back at the burning city. "If at intervals the dismal sight was lost to our view," the attorney general recalled, "we got it again from some hill-top or eminence where we paused to look at it." Madison rejoined his wife at a tavern, but they could not stay the night due to reports of British pursuit. Ironically, the God of nature seemed the only one defending the capital: a fierce rainstorm before dawn on Thursday and "a violent late summer storm of hurricane force" early on Thursday afternoon both extinguished some of the flames.[31]

Citizens did not absolve leaders for failing to defend the capital. When Madison returned on Saturday afternoon, graffiti was scrawled on the Capitol's walls: "James Madison is a rascal, a coward and a fool" and "The capital of the Union lost by cowardice." Fears were expressed for Armstrong's safety if he remained in the city.[32] The outer walls of the Capitol and White House were standing, albeit blackened. They "lay open to the skies, their roofs burned off, their singular works of art reduced to rubble or cracked and blistered beyond repair. Scorched walls enclosed piles of ash." Madison had to go live with his brother-in-law on F Street, where a strong guard was posted to protect him (not only against the British).[33]

Disillusionment spread along the East Coast. The cabinet decided the citizenry needed to be reassured that the nation's government was back in its capital, but the elite misunderstood the people again. The September 1 proclamation they persuaded Madison to issue, against the "extended devastation and barbarism" of the British, mainly alarmed the citizenry. Having seen the government's inability to defend the capital, Americans in coastal cities assumed it could not defend them either. The idea of one national defense fell apart; each locality looked out for its own defense. A financial crisis hit. "The nation's rudimentary banking structure collapsed, and the federal government was left without the means to remit or withdraw money." Banks would lend to state and local

---

[31]George, *Terror on the Chesapeake*, p. 111, see pp. 105-11; Pitch, *Burning of Washington*, pp. 104-28 (quote from Mary Hunter on p. 124, and quote from Attorney General Richard Rush on p. 125); Adams, *History of the Administrations of James Madison*, pp. 1013-15.

[32]Pitch, *Burning of Washington*, pp. 162-63, 164, 167-69; Adams, *History of the Administrations of James Madison*, pp. 1021-22. Madison confirms rumors of threats against Armstrong and himself; *Writings*, p. 703.

[33]Pitch, *Burning of Washington*, pp. 163-64; Stagg, *Mr. Madison's War*, pp. 428-30, 436; Rutland, *James Madison and the American Nation*, p. 90.

governments for local defense, but the federal government tried to keep up "the fiction of federal supremacy." Preoccupied with the capital, the administration "lost sight of the larger course of the war." It temporarily ceased to be a national government. Several cabinet members resigned. A Federalist governor of Massachusetts sounded out the British on peace terms. New Englanders held their antiwar Hartford Convention in mid-December. Americans worried that secession from the Union was New England's ultimate goal.[34] The plot device of a six-week Atlantic crossing reappeared. Unbeknownst to Federalists in Hartford or Republicans in Washington, the verdict was already in, and it would deliver the latter and condemn the former.

Madison was saved by the bell. On Christmas Eve 1814, British and American negotiators signed a peace agreement in Ghent, Belgium. A wounded government avoided another year of war. The treaty restored the prewar situation. Neither nation lost territory or surrendered disputed claims. "The present war appears destined by the God of heaven, to answer the purposes of a judgment—a trial—and, a benefit," wrote a pro-war pastor in January 1815.[35]

Partly, this trial was "blowback," a payback for Americans burning York. Partly, it resulted from Jeffersonian Republicans' fate-effecting deeds due to their disdain for their citizens' evangelical faith and their overconfidence in citizens' faith in *their* philosophy. As a result, they were insensitive to Americans' horror at aiding the infidel Napoleon against missionary Britain; they tried, in vain, to have Americans avoid war and trade to prove their philosophy of "peaceable coercion"; they tried to persuade Americans to fight a war for republicanism's honor; they refused to violate their philosophy by building a navy to defend sailors and instead violated many Americans' sense of morality by invading Canada to defend American sailors at sea. Thus, their war was unpopular, and Americans did not rush to enlist in it.

Does that mean that the burning of Washington was God's judgment on this elite? This case is harder to assess than September 11 in many ways. We have a long-term cause—elite disdain for Christian faith—that could provoke God's judgment. We have a prior sifting out, as revivals lead more citizens to that faith while the elite remained more loyal than ordinary citizens to the Deism popular during the Revolutionary years. Yet, we focused on this long-term cause, and there were others. We focused on this aspect of Jefferson's Republicanism, and there were others. Not all disasters like Bladensburg are judgments from God.

---

[34]Stagg, *Mr. Madison's War,* pp. 424, 427, 432; see also pp. 423, 425-26, 431, 472-73, 478-96.
[35]Watts, *Republic Reborn,* p. 289 (quoting Alexander McLeod); Adams, *History of the Administrations of James Madison,* pp. 1200-1223.

And yet, the disaster's focus on the elites, its embarrassing nature and its relative exemption of ordinary Americans (except in Washington) does point toward divine judgment on them.

The God of heaven may have judged gentry republicans' pretensions by subjecting them to a severe trial and their capital to an army of arsonists, but the nation where a gospel wind blew freely survived. It courted destruction by warring against the world's superpower but survived. God had his own plans for it. Its citizens had not rushed to enlist to "meet invasions of the public order" but might prove more self-sacrificing for Christ than for the republic. We turn to the Civil War, a less murky example of divine judgment, at least according to Abraham Lincoln.

8

Was the Civil War God's Judgment for Slavery? (Part 1)

We turn to slavery and the Civil War, quite the opposite of the short-term, embarrassing tragicomedy of August 1814. Just as commentators compared September 11 with the British burning Washington, so they observed that its thousands of victims made it the bloodiest day in U.S. history, surpassing the battle of Antietam on September 17, 1862 (the number of victims was revised downward so that turned out not to be true). Another reason for examining this war is that Abraham Lincoln's second inaugural address (1865) contains the most explicit statement ever made by a U.S. president about God's judgment on the nation.[1] The history of American slavery offers us an excellent case study of God's *mishpat,* his sifting-out process encompassing far more than the final, negative consequence of civil war. The duration and complexity of this *mishpat* and the deep-seated ambiguities that it clarified will take us two chapters to unravel. Finally, this historical event featured conflict between philosophical and historical approaches to slavery, so we may further contrast worldview and historical approaches to our Christian faith.

Introduction: Defects in a Secular Analysis of Slavery and Civil War

Two historians introduce a 1998 book on religion, the debate over slavery and the two contending sides by quoting from Lincoln's address: "Both read the same Bible, and pray to the same God. . . . The prayers of both could not be answered. . . . The Almighty has His own purposes." Lincoln, they conclude, here "recognized a crucial fact that historians" also have noted and "have sought

---

[1] See, e.g., Walter Sundberg, "'Evil' After 9/11: The Alien Work of God," *Word & World* (spring 2004): 204, 206.

to explain—that the antebellum sectional controversy over slavery developed within a society profoundly pervaded by evangelical Protestantism."[2] The quote undercuts their point. For Lincoln, the presence of evangelicalism was not a "crucial fact" but merely a given, a humdrum, matter-of-fact condition that everyone saw. The "crucial fact" that Lincoln, more than most contemporaries, perceived was that "the Almighty has His own purposes" and that judging the nation for the sin of slavery was his purpose in the war.

Historians' failure to go beyond believers' text (the Bible) and behavior (prayer, preaching, voting, etc.) to inquire into their God's actions and purposes has other consequences. Historians overemphasize unrealistic aspects of the moral perfectionism preached by some evangelicals during and after the Second Great Awakening that we saw dramatized at Cane Ridge.[3] The sermons' section on human responsibility for the sins of slavery falls within historians' realm of observable human behavior, so they emphasize that part. The section on divine sovereignty in judging sins falls outside historians' list of researchable topics, so they minimize or omit that part. Yet that distorts the entire, two-part message and interprets these evangelical calls—"you do something about slavery or God will"—as failures, when they were not if God did do something. From the democratic perspective, talk of judgment can be seen (especially now) as just talk that only signifies "I'm *really* opposed to this evil." If it fails to persuade others (as it logically should fail, if that is all it is), then it fails utterly. Since judgment is not a real category in this view, clergy who issued such warnings used unfair, theocratic tactics to dictate to a democracy, as Stephen A. Douglas charged. Denying God as an actor in history distorts the clergy's position; they did not say that *they* would act but that *God* would act. They did not say the United States *ought* to be a theocracy but that the universe, including the United States, *is* under God's governance.

Not treating divine judgment as a real category encourages determinism, the belief that Americans never had an option of ending slavery voluntarily because it was an entrenched foundation on which their politics and economics partly rested. If the cost-benefit analysis counts only political and economic costs, then it can seem an impossibly costly choice. If we regard the threatened divine judgment as a possible outcome, with severe costs of its own,

---

[2] John R. McKivigan and Mitchell Snay, eds., *Religion and the Antebellum Debate over Slavery* (Athens: University of Georgia Press, 1998), p. 1.

[3] One example is Douglas M. Strong, *Perfectionist Politics: Abolitionism and the Religious Tensions of American Democracy* (Syracuse, N.Y.: Syracuse University Press, 1999), although this study may be accurate in its emphasis, due to the different theology of the "come-outer" groups it examines.

then we can conceive of decision points when those who took the warnings seriously might have estimated the costs of retaining slavery to be greater than the costs of removing it—even if they could not have guessed the actual war costs: some 620,000 lives and $20 billion ("about 10 times the value of all slaves in the country in 1860").[4]

Not treating divine judgment as a real category reduces Christians to persons who hold to a certain worldview based on a text and who experience cognitive dissonance and mental, emotional or social discomfort when their actions do not measure up to their high ideals, but those are the only costs and are no different from what others pay. In this view, evangelicals faced the same dilemma as the most famous philosophically discomfited anti-slavery idealist, Thomas Jefferson: how to act consistently with their ideals. Yet they claimed that a different dynamic was at work, involving a higher judge more than higher ideals. That dynamic produced more real anti-slavery action than resulted from Jefferson's philosophy.

To treat judgment as a real category is not naively to treat every warning of it as a nonpartisan calculation. Some talk of judgment did mean "I'm *really* opposed, and since you won't listen to other arguments, I'll try this one." In *God Against Slavery*, a collection of sermons, Congregationalist minister George Cheever hurled warnings like thunderbolts for polemical effect but did not closely follow Scripture. He distorted Jeremiah's warning of judgment (Jeremiah 34:8-22) into an attack on slavery per se, when the Lord was angered by Judah's refusal to free Hebrew slaves after seven years, which Judah had promised to do.[5] We must critically assess all warnings of judgment.

Some argue that while ignoring judgment may have its costs, treating it as a real category has higher costs that outweigh the benefits, for we cannot know if the Civil War was God's judgment. We cannot know for sure that other interpretations of the past are correct, but we make them anyway. We have testimony of contemporaries who predicted judgment in the form of civil war, who experienced the war as a judgment and who looked back on it as one. Lincoln is the most prominent, well-qualified witness. We base interpretations of the past on testimony, and this category is not so different as to outlaw it. Aided by scriptural ideas, we will examine events in chronological order to see if the cat-

---

[4]Cost estimates taken from James West Davidson, et al., *Nation of Nations: A Narrative History of the American Republic* (New York: McGraw-Hill, 1990), pp. 598-99.
[5]George B. Cheever, *God Against Slavery: And the Freedom and Duty of the Pulpit to Rebuke It, as a Sin Against God* (reprint, New York: Negro Universities Press, 1969), pp. iii, 72-76, 107-8, 162-64. For Cheever and other anti-slavery debaters, see Mark A. Noll, *The Civil War as a Theological Crisis* (Chapel Hill: University of North Carolina Press, 2006), pp. 40-50.

egory of divine judgment makes sense of the Civil War. The story begins with the ambiguity of no clear-cut slave and free regions or pro-slavery and anti-slavery factions, continues through a sifting out to the creation of clear regions and factions and ends with crisis. Throughout, Christians warned of God's judgment in our narrow sense of final, negative consequences, but the entire process was God's *mishpat.* One caveat is that the sifting out was not to save one good group and judge the bad one—the entire nation was judged, Lincoln noted—but to cause a crisis that would free slaves and judge the nation. (During the war, the good anti-slavery side may have shown the most brutality.[6])

Before Nationhood: Beginning Cracks in Public Ambiguity and Acceptance of Slavery

Slavery existed in all thirteen colonies, in a continuum that stretched from South Carolina (slaves were about 70% of the population) to Virginia (about 40%) to the middle colonies of New Jersey, New York and Pennsylvania (about 8%) to New England (2%), and without significant anti-slavery agitation anywhere except Quaker Pennsylvania. Northern merchants and shipowners engaged in the slave trade. The great preacher and writer, Jonathan Edwards, always owned a household slave or two; in this hierarchical society, a Christian like Edwards regarded the slave as part of a continuum of relationships between superiors and inferiors, with the slave arguably not too different from the white servant. The New Testament neither condemned nor explicitly endorsed slavery as a social institution; it commanded proper behavior for individual masters and slaves. Disciples lacked power to alter Rome's institutions; similarly, colonists' subjection to England discouraged serious anti-slavery efforts. Edwards's slave, Leah, was converted in the 1734-1735 revival and joined his church, but few other ministers sought to convert slaves, and many masters opposed preaching the gospel to them.[7] Before 1740, ambiguity on slavery meant an unexamined, taken-for-granted consensus that did not differentiate between specific aspects of slavery. Most whites knew a slaveholder or could become one, and they knew slavery was not condemned in the New Testament, resembled other forms

---

[6]That is the argument in Harry S. Stout, *Upon the Altar of the Nation: A Moral History of the Civil War* (New York: Viking, 2006).

[7]Alan Taylor, *American Colonies* (New York: Viking, 2001), pp. 238, 333, 336, 357; George M. Marsden, *Jonathan Edwards: A Life* (New Haven, Conn.: Yale University Press, 2003), pp. 255-58; James D. Essig, *The Bonds of Wickedness: American Evangelicals Against Slavery, 1770-1808* (Philadelphia: Temple University Press, 1982), pp. 10-11; Gordon S. Wood, *The Radicalism of the American Revolution* (New York: Knopf, 1992), pp. 86-87. Edwards did oppose the African slave trade.

of servanthood and was London's responsibility.

The religious earthquake of the First Great Awakening of the 1740s produced cracks in this ambiguity. Revivalists such as George Whitefield and Samuel Davies preached to slaves, resulting in the first large-scale conversion of African Americans.[8] The Son of Man had now redeemed many blacks who were, however, still held in bondage by professed Christians who were supposedly following him in his path of self-denial but were not denying themselves the luxury of forcing others to do their manual labor. The situation Paul addressed in Philemon—a Christian master and Christian slave—was becoming more common; Paul hinted that emancipation was the preferred outcome. Thousands of black disciples now prayed to the Son of Man for their freedom—prayers certain to carry weight with their Redeemer. Slavery now existed in a more Christianized society, and perpetuating it in that social context was morally different from acquiescing to Roman slavery in Nero's empire.

Large-scale conversions create new situations. In Oliver O'Donovan's words, "A community lives under the authority of him to whom the Ancient of Days has entrusted the Kingdom." Their obedient presence is handwriting on the wall warning society that God is testing and judging. That active Judge does not let his Scriptures be used against him, as a shield for evildoers, who chant, "The New Testament sanctions slavery, the New Testament sanctions slavery," as a cover for sexual exploitation of female slaves, splitting families and outlawing slave marriages and literacy. The New Testament did not launch a social movement against Roman slavery, but neither did it exonerate the institution so as to prevent God from judging it in the future. The Son of Man's work relativized that institution and all others and put it under his reign—to be radically reformed or ended—not to have its evils continue as though he had never lived.

While the Awakening's white evangelicals did not oppose slavery per se, they rediscovered the radical dimensions of following the Son of Man's path through humiliation and lowliness to glory—and of his gospel that raised the lowly and humbled the proud. A new community obeyed his authority, baptized slaves, admitted them to membership and taught them in defiance of the gentry. In an almost sentimental way, some evangelicals now delighted to mingle with the lowly slaves—to rejoice in how God had given grace to these "poor out-casts of men," to show their humble following of the Son of Man by associating with his humblest followers and to reproach the gentry elite who often

---

[8]Essig, *Bonds of Wickedness*, pp. 10, 12; Taylor, *American Colonies*, pp. 357-58. The number of black converts is hard to estimate.

mocked them and their revivals.[9] Less sentimentally, evangelical preachers warned of judgment to come on masters who abused their slaves. "Go to now, ye rich Men, weep and howl for your Miseries that shall come upon you!" wrote Whitefield, quoting James 5:1. "The Blood of them spilt for these many Years in your respective Provinces," he warned colonists, "will ascend up to Heaven against you." Preachers condemned mainly failure to preach to slaves and cruel mistreatment of them. Yet this was embryonic anti-slavery preaching.[10] Critiques of masters' behaviors differentiated acts formerly included under the blanket term "slavery": failure to preach to slaves, to allow slave marriages, to prevent family breakups due to slave sales, to teach slaves to read and write, to sell slaves, and so on. A public ambiguity—many meanings under the one word *slavery*—was starting to show cracks.

After this focus on the individual, the collective crisis of the dispute with England (1765-1775) and the War for Independence (1775-1783) caused evangelicals to address slavery as a national sin that might be causing God to judge America. New England fast-day and election-day sermons gave ministers a chance to address sin's national dimensions. Many now listed slavery as one national sin incurring God's judgment. In one sermon, Jacob Green cited the oracles against the nations in Amos 1–2 as a warning to America. A New England deacon identified slavery "to be a God-provoking and a wrath-procuring sin."[11] Cautiously, we must doubt their view that the American Revolution was God's judgment on American slavery in the narrow sense of his punishment for it. No one at the time identified slavery as a cause of the war; nor did the war affect slavery greatly. Britain had not yet ended slave trading or slavery in its other colonies, so the two warring parties did not differ on this issue. Yet, the war was part of God's judgment on slavery in our broader sense of *mishpat:* he used the war to begin to sift out an anti-slavery faction and region.

Revolutionary Era: Philosophy and Religion Give Americans a Choice About Slavery

If Americans had no choice but to continue slavery, then they had no collective guilt (individuals might have guilt for mistreatment of slaves), and judgment could be seen as unjust. Arguably, that was the case while Britain ruled them,

---

[9]Rhys Isaac, "Evangelical Revolt: The Nature of the Baptists' Challenge to the Traditional Order in Virginia, 1765 to 1775," *William and Mary Quarterly* 31, no. 3 (July 1974), p. 361; Essig, *Bonds of Wickedness*, p. 34; see chap. 2.

[10]Essig, *Bonds of Wickedness*, p. 11; see pp. 12-14. This is the start of the "nuanced biblical attacks on American slavery" that Noll notes in *Theological Crisis*, p. 49; see pp. 45-50.

[11]Essig, *Bonds of Wickedness*, p. 22; see pp. 20-24.

but independence brought national responsibility. Some historians assert that the new nation was locked into slavery for economic, political and demographic reasons. James L. Huston claims "that the concentration of valuable property in one region thwarted any attempt at compromise"; however, he skirts around the Revolutionary era's gradual emancipation in the North and efforts to prohibit slavery in the territories.[12] These efforts indicate real choice. Taking the costs of judgment seriously opens up arenas of choice, which might seem closed if only political, economic and social costs are seen as real.

In the 1770s and 1780s, a temporary coalition of evangelicals and Enlightenment idealists like Jefferson led the drive to independence and created two different, but not incompatible, rationales for anti-slavery action.[13] The Enlightenment's philosophical stress on human equality, human rights, an end to nonmerit-based hierarchies and a rational reordering of society rather than a blind acceptance of traditions (plus the inconsistency of Americans fighting for freedom while holding blacks in slavery) sparked a new questioning of slavery.[14] An evangelical stress on a radical conversion freeing believers to follow humbly the rejected, self-denying Son of Man had a similar effect. We need not weigh these two rationales to see which more strongly motivated Revolutionary-era anti-slavery efforts. For a time, the two were mutually reinforcing. Rather, we compare one's philosophical stress with the other's religious-historical stress, in keeping with our discussion in previous chapters. The difference is not that religious believers were more consistent than philosophical idealists in practicing their beliefs. Nor is it that believers talked of God's judgment while philosophers did not.

In the 1780s, Jefferson mentioned divine judgment twice. In *Notes on the State of Virginia* (1781-1782), he regretted the effects of slavery on Virginians. "Indeed I tremble for my country when I reflect that God is just: that his justice cannot sleep for ever." A philosopher and scientific observer, he thought an overturning of slavery "possible" due to demography ("numbers") or to "nature and natural means only," but "it may become probable by supernatural interference!" "The Almighty has no attribute which can take side with us in such a contest" between slave and master. Yet his philosophical optimism reasserted itself.

---

[12]James L. Huston, *Calculating the Value of the Union: Slavery, Property Rights and the Economic Origins of the Civil War* (Chapel Hill: University of North Carolina Press, 2003), p. xiv; see pp. 3-23. For a stress on demographics, see William W. Freehling, *The Road to Disunion: Secessionists at Bay 1776-1854* (New York: Oxford University Press, 1990). Huston does not totally neglect the Revolutionary era but applies his property-rights, economic determinism to it.

[13]For this coalition, see Steven J. Keillor, *This Rebellious House: American History and the Truth of Christianity* (Downers Grove, Ill: InterVarsity Press, 1996).

[14]See, e.g., Wood, *Radicalism*, pp. 96, 186-87.

"We must be contented to hope" anti-slavery "considerations" would "force their way into every one's mind." Ideas would force themselves on the knowing (and slave-owning) self. He persuaded himself that "a change [was] already perceptible" that would produce "a total emancipation . . . with the consent of the masters." Despite his "trembl[ing]," he would not act then but only trust that ideas would act later. In another piece, he lamented the inconsistency of slaveholders fighting for freedom but counseled "patience" and trust in "an overruling providence" who might end slavery "by his exterminating thunder" or "by diffusing light & liberality among" slaveholders who would voluntarily liberate them.[15]

Here was a passive acceptance of fate, rather than the immediate repentance and reform that prophetic warnings of judgment demanded. Here was a Providence useful for casting one's duties upon. Here was some disquiet about time running out but more philosophical optimism that slow processes would free slaves and make risky actions unnecessary. A gentle amelioration seemed like a universal philosophical sun; philanthropists could tinker with it for the indefinite future, when, in fact, the best opportunity for action was ending.

Both passages were intended for French readers. In letters to Americans, Jefferson was more passive, equivocal, procrastinating and evasively optimistic that some "natural means" would solve the problem without a need for him to act. Recent historians have concluded that Jefferson did nothing about slavery despite his protestations of anti-slavery feelings (and earlier biographers' myth of an anti-slavery Jefferson). He may have felt cognitive dissonance due to the mismatch between ideals and practices, but his luxurious lifestyle and resultant debts caused him to make family-dividing sales of his slaves. He did what his mind abhorred. He did not tremble at divine justice enough to forego French wines.[16] Evangelicals were also inconsistent. Yet their theology of judgment was more apt to have God declaring, "You act—or I will" and less apt to allow evasions about "natural means" or self-vindicating ideas defeating slavery despite sinners' refusal to repent of it.

The Revolutionary Era: New Governments Make New Choices on Slavery Possible

The evangelical-Enlightenment critique of slavery did produce gradual emanci-

---

[15] *Thomas Jefferson: Writings* (New York: Library of America, 1984), pp. 289, 592.

[16] See, e.g., Paul Finkelman, *Slavery and the Founders: Race and Liberty in the Age of Jefferson* (Armonk, N.Y.: M. E. Sharpe, 1996), chaps. 5-6; Roger G. Kennedy, *Mr. Jefferson's Lost Cause: Land, Farmers, Slavery and the Louisiana Purchase* (New York: Oxford University Press, 2003), chaps. 2-3 and epilogue; and David Brion Davis, *The Problem of Slavery in the Age of Revolution* (Ithaca, N.Y.: Cornell University Press, 1975), pp. 173-84.

pation laws in the North, where slavery was less entrenched. A need to remake former colonies into new state governments facilitated a new choice about slavery. These new state laws typically freed slave children born after a certain date (e.g., the date the law passed) once they reached a certain age (twenty-one or twenty-eight years old). The state offered no compensation on grounds that slave offspring were a bonus to the owner, not property he had purchased or inherited. These laws were not idealism in action: older slaves stayed in bondage for decades; owners sold young slaves south before their emancipating birthday; slavery lingered in New Jersey into the 1840s. Yet, gradual emancipation in the North advanced the sifting out as "the sections began to tread diverging paths" and "the nation became a house divided against itself." It confirmed Americans had a choice.[17]

In establishing rules for new settlements and governments in the Western territories, the new national government had a choice and the power to act. On April 19, 1784, the Continental Congress narrowly voted to delete a proposed ban on slavery in all Western territories after 1800; if one New Jersey delegate, John Beatty, had not been sick and absent, the ban would have been in the 1784 Ordinance. Southern slaveowners would have had sixteen years to settle the area and to lobby for a reversal of this policy. Yet that means that Congress would have faced other moments of decision, not that it had no real choice in 1784.[18]

In the Northwest Ordinance of 1787 that set the rules for the area north and west of the Ohio River, Congress did choose to exclude slavery from that region. No flaming anti-slavery zeal motivated most delegates. Southern delegates feared potential competition from slaveowning tobacco plantations that might develop in the Northwest Territory; many delegates wanted to expedite land sales in that area to pay off the nation's debts. This fateful measure began to draw a line to separate a free region (the Northwest) from a slave region (the Southwest). It did not prevent Americans from having to make future decisions: residents of Ohio, Indiana and Illinois later had to campaign and vote to retain the ban on slavery. Yet the 1787 choice was a real, if not a final, one.[19] The pres-

---

[17]Freehling, *Road to Disunion,* pp. 131-34; Arthur Zilversmit, *The First Emancipation: The Abolition of Slavery in the North* (Chicago: University of Chicago Press, 1967), p. 200.

[18]Don E. Fehrenbacher, *The Slaveholding Republic: An Account of the United States Government's Relations to Slavery* (New York: Oxford University Press, 2001), pp. 253-54; Davis, *Slavery in the Age of Revolution,* pp. 153-54 n. 74 (arguing this ban had "no chance of success"); Kennedy, *Mr. Jefferson's Lost Cause,* pp. 75-77, 249-50; Finkelman, *Slavery and the Founders,* pp. 42, 123-24.

[19]Fehrenbacher, *Slaveholding Republic,* pp. 254-55, 256-58; Peter S. Onuf, *Statehood and Union: A History of the Northwest Ordinance* (Bloomington: Indiana University Press, 1987), chap. 6; Finkelman, *Slavery and the Founders,* chaps. 2-3.

ence of slaves south of the river did not preclude a choice there. At Kentucky's 1792 constitutional convention, nineteen anti-slavery delegates faced twenty-three pro-slavery ones—losing odds but not so hopeless that Kentucky never had a real choice.[20]

These choices existed before Eli Whitney's invention of the cotton gin (1793) sparked a vast expansion of cotton plantations and, thus, of slavery. The most opportune time for anti-slavery action was nearing an end. In vain were philosophical hopes that gradual "diffusion" of slaves across more territory or the end of the slave trade would end slavery by "natural means."

The Federal Constitution: A Choice to Build a Divided House on Ambiguity

Also prior to Whitney's gin was the Constitutional Convention (1787). Debate has raged over whether the Constitution was a pro-slavery, anti-slavery or neutral document. It was ambiguous on slavery because it was a series of compromises on many contentious issues, some of which related to slavery. Definitions are in order. A document or an expression is ambiguous if it has "two or more possible meanings" or is "of uncertain signification" or is "susceptible of different interpretations."[21] A lack of clarity may be intentional or unintentional. A compromise may contain ambiguous sections if mediators cannot persuade the two parties to surrender a point clearly; however, it may not last once the double meaning is discovered. The entire compromise may be ambiguous, if it is unclear which side stands to gain the most by it. That was the Constitution's major ambiguity: on the whole, was it more pro-slavery or anti-slavery?

As a document giving practical guidance for courts, voters and officeholders, the Constitution contained few words with unclear meanings. Compromises were clearly worded. Slaves counted as three-fifths of a person in allocating representation in the House of Representatives (Southerners wanted a full person, while Northerners did not want them counted). Congress could not outlaw the slave trade before 1808. Fugitive slaves must be returned to their owners even if they reached a free state. Some ambiguity arose because "slave" or "slavery" never appeared, only euphemisms: "other Persons," "such Persons as any of the States now existing shall think proper to admit," a "Person held to Service or Labour in one State, under the Laws thereof."

---

[20]Kennedy, *Mr. Jefferson's Lost Cause*, p. 77; Asa Earl Martin, *The Anti-Slavery Movement in Kentucky Prior to 1850* (reprint, Westport, Conn.: Negro Universities Press, 1970), pp. 14-17. Three antislavery delegates changed their votes according to Martin, making the final margin sixteen votes to twenty-six votes.

[21]*Webster's New Twentieth-Century Dictionary of the English Language Unabridged*, 2nd ed. (New York: Simon & Schuster, 1979), p. 56.

This last, fugitive-slave clause shows how politicians used the Constitution in ambiguous ways: "Northern delegates could return home asserting that the Constitution did not recognize the legality of slavery" in the "technical linguistic sense": delegates dropped the word *legally* from "held to Service or Labour" and substituted an acknowledgment that a state's laws held "Persons" to labor, whether or not other states called that legal. "Southerners, on the other hand, could tell their neighbors" the Constitution did recognize slavery by commanding the return of fugitive slaves, under whatever name.[22] Rhetorical tactics led to other ambiguities. Southern defender and Northern skeptic were the same person in Madison's *Federalist No. 54*, published under the pseudonym Publius. Addressing Northern complaints about the three-fifths ratio, he presented a defense of the ratio as hypothetical comments of "one of our southern brethren" and concluded, "I must confess, that it fully reconciles me to" the ratio. He was the Southerner commenting *and* the Northerner convinced by the argument![23] Political leaders casting a different meaning over the same provision in different regions created ambiguity during the long battle over slavery.

Some warned that slavery could not be so easily fudged. Virginia's George Mason warned that slavery "bring[s] the judgment of heaven on a Country. As nations can not be rewarded or punished in the next world they must be in this. By an inevitable chain of causes & effects providence punishes national sins by national calamities." A delegate to Massachusetts' ratifying convention cautioned that "this lust for slavery, [was] portentous of much evil in America, for the cry of innocent blood, . . . hath undoubtedly reached the Heavens, to which that cry is always directed, and will draw down upon them vengeance adequate to the enormity of the crime."[24]

Delegates used the Convention's secrecy to mask underlying deals struck at Philadelphia (slavery was only one contentious issue), including the deal whereby New England delegates accepted slavery-protecting provisions in exchange for Southerners agreeing to give the national government the right to regulate foreign and interstate commerce. Delegates' notes (including Madi-

---

[22]Paul Finkelman, "Slavery and the Constitutional Convention: Making a Covenant with Death," pp. 223-24, in *Beyond Confederation: Origins of the Constitution and American National Identity*, ed. Richard Beeman, Stephen Botein and Edward C. Carter II (Chapel Hill: University of North Carolina Press, 1987).
[23]*The Federalist Papers by Alexander Hamilton, James Madison and John Jay* (New York: Bantam, 1982), pp. 276, 279.
[24]Forrest McDonald, *Novus Ordo Seclorum: The Intellectual Origins of the Constitution* (Lawrence: University Press of Kansas, 1985), p. 50 (quoting Mason); Jack P. Greene, *Colonies to Nation: 1763-1789* (New York: McGraw-Hill, 1967), p. 541; Finkelman, "Making a Covenant with Death," p. 225 (quoting Samuel Field of Massachusetts).

son's) reveal this deal. A behind-the-scenes deal need not be publicly acknowl-
edged by the New Englanders who thereby strayed from their region's growing
anti-slavery consensus.[25]

The grand deal was not explicit: "the bargain involved more than commerce
and slavery; it concerned the Union itself."[26] A new, stronger, more permanent
national house was built without addressing the growing division between slavery and freedom caused by Northern anti-slavery movements. The deal was
ambiguous: Northerners could think that the house was not committed to
slavery—changing conditions might gradually end it or this stronger government might do something about it, and the document never used the word;
Southerners could think that the house was not necessarily strong or permanent—if the government unexpectedly gained the power to do something about
slavery, they could exit the house as they threatened several times to leave the
Convention. William Gienapp notes that "the most crucial ambiguity of the Constitution was whether a state had the right to leave the Union." The Articles of
Confederation specified a "perpetual Union" of sovereign states; the Constitution did not declare that it was permanent or that states surrendered their sovereign right to leave.[27] No one had to decide about slavery. In a broad sense, it
was not a true compromise: many Southerners did not give up their right to
leave, and many Northerners did not give up their right to do something about
slavery at some time.

A further, rich source of ambiguity was embedded in the Constitution's complicated division of power: between executive, legislative and judicial branches;
between state and national levels of government; between ambitious political
rivals who were to check each other's power. Who was in charge here? Who
was responsible for slavery? Final responsibility was so divided up that every
government or official could point to some other one as truly responsible, especially for a broad social institution like slavery. Moreover, the nation could
simultaneously be ending slavery in some states and strengthening it in others.
Could it then be judged for slavery, if one section was virtuously combating it?
The entire nation of voters never would vote as a body on any question or of-

---

[25]Finkelman, "Making a Covenant with Death," pp. 205, 213-14, 220. In *Slaveholding Republic*
(pp. 21-46), Fehrenbacher disputes Finkelman's conclusions, but Finkelman gives the key
day-by-day, vote-by-vote sequence while Fehrenbacher relies on broad statements and tech-
nicalities that are not persuasive. However, Finkelman's subtitle, "Making a Covenant with
Death," is an unfortunate exaggeration derived from William Lloyd Garrison.

[26]Finkelman, "Making a Covenant with Death," p. 189.

[27]William E. Gienapp, "The Crisis of American Democracy: The Political System and the Coming
of the Civil War," in *Why the Civil War Came*, ed. Gabor S. Boritt (New York: Oxford University Press, 1996), p. 85.

fice. The election of a president was many separate state elections (due to the Electoral College). This system was not deliberately designed to evade responsibility for slavery. Yet the Constitution became a fundamental, defining document that established a status quo that was presumed to be just. Some protection for slavery was written into it, and any national effort to end slavery could now be portrayed as the violation of a sacred pledge. All the sanctions of legal precedent, social conservatism and established custom were now enlisted on slavery's side.

Politics and Economics Build on the Constitution and Limit Choices on Slavery

The Constitution set ground rules for politics and economics, on which political and business leaders then built. The brief Revolutionary-era window of opportunity, when basic rules of the game could be reformed and remade, was closed. Choice and change were not impossible, nor had all rules ever been open to change, but the costs of choice and change increased. This era of possible choice was not a universal philosophical sun that neither rose nor set; it shone only for two decades. Whitney's cotton gin caused it to set. Even with "a hand-operated gin, one person could clean 50 pounds of cotton in a single day, instead of the one pound that was possible without it." The gin made upland, short-fiber cotton suitable for growing and marketing. The amount of cotton raised in the United States increased 2,233 percent from 1790 to 1800. That dramatic increase was from a small starting point (1.5 million pounds in 1790). The explosion continued, to 160 million pounds (1820), 1 billion pounds (1850) and 2.275 billion pounds (1860). Britain's cotton-textile mills bought the majority of it and sold the textiles worldwide, to India and Africa (partly in exchange for new slaves), as well as the U.S. By 1830, American cotton made up 76 percent of the British supply. That census year, the number of slaves topped 2 million (it was 697,000 in 1790), many in the new Southwest. This global industry was hugely profitable, apart from some depressed years. For the U.S. economy (1815 to 1860), "cotton was the major expansive force"; after 1835, cotton exports were often more than half of U.S. exports. New York City rose to preeminence by becoming "the financial center for the cotton trade." Thousands of investors, shippers, manufacturers and planters had sizeable investments in slavery by 1840.[28]

---

[28]Ronald Bailey, "The Other Side of Slavery: Black Labor, Cotton and Textile Industrialization in Great Britain and the United States," in *Eli Whitney's Cotton Gin, 1793-1993*, ed. David O. Whitten (Washington, D.C.: Agricultural History Society, 1994), pp. 35 (quoted), 37 (table 1); Douglass C. North, *The Economic Growth of the United States 1790-1860* (New York: Norton, 1966), pp. 63, 67, 233 (table A-8).

Cotton was only one crop raised predominantly on slave plantations. By 1860, slaves were worth $3 billion, more than the nation's investment in railroads and manufacturing plants and equipment.[29]

The larger this investment was, the greater the resistance to ending slavery. That was part of God's sifting-out judgment. Because the nation refused in the 1780s to take steps to end slavery across the nation, that option was ended in the South, which became locked into slavery and headed toward an eventual confrontation with the anti-slavery North. And, the more slavery expanded into the Southwest, the larger the pro-slavery region became and the more protracted and damaging the final confrontation was likely to be.

Politics also built on the Constitution's foundations, although political parties appeared to have the opposite effect, to prevent a sifting out into two rival regions. Jefferson's Democratic-Republicans became the Republicans and, confusingly, the Democrats. A new opposition party, the Whigs, formed in the 1830s. Whigs and Democrats were national parties with supporters South and North, pro-slavery and anti-slavery. Both had to cultivate a studied ambiguity on the slavery issue in order to compete for the presidency in all regions. Historian David Potter described both parties "as strong unifying agencies. . . . They promoted consensus rather than divisiveness . . . and avoided sharpening the cutting edge of disagreement to dangerous keenness." Each was a big-tent coalition, not a tightly defined ideology, and each "often practiced the arts of evasion and ambiguity in order to gain the broadest possible base of support." They stressed "ties of personal loyalty to a leader" or "the sentimental bonds" of team spirit during campaigns, "and party regulars valued party harmony above party policy." They blocked a sifting-out process. "When the slavery question began to take shape as a public issue, both parties, sensing its divisive potential, vigorously resisted its introduction into politics."[30]

Finally, Adam Smith explained why it would be nearly impossible to end slavery in a republic like the United States. He argued, "The persons who make all the laws in that country are persons who have slaves themselves. . . . These will never make any laws mitigating their usage." Another agent of liberation might be a strong church, "but it was absolutely necessary that the authority of the king and the clergy should be great."[31] Americans rebelled against a king and

---

[29]Huston, *Calculating the Value of the Union*, pp. 24-29.

[30]David M. Potter, *The Impending Crisis 1848-1861* (New York: Harper & Row, 1976), pp. 225-27.

[31]Smith, quoted in Robert P. Forbes, "Slavery and the Evangelical Enlightenment," p. 74, in *Religion and the Antebellum Debate over Slavery*, ed. John R. McKivigan and Mitchell Snay (Athens: University of Georgia Press, 1998).

fragmented the church's authority into many denominations, none with decisive influence on the nation. In competing for members in the South, denominations softened or abandoned anti-slavery ideas and seemed to surrender some of the Son of Man's authority (over his disciples' behavior in their local churches) to the secular powers in the process.

Perhaps Smith (had he lived until 1865) would have seen emancipation, despite no strong king or church, as proof of a third actor: God. As we saw in the Old Testament, God could righteously overturn precedent, the status quo and long-established property rights. God could sort out political and governmental ambiguity. He was not fooled by the Constitution's omission of the word *slavery* or politicians' claims that they could do nothing about it. Two competing political parties did not paralyze him into inaction for fear that if he acted in judgment some Americans would say "God is a Whig" while if he did not act others would say "God is a Democrat." He acted, as we shall see. Or, if you assume he does not act in history, then how did such a deeply entrenched, profitable institution end, when there was no other actor powerful enough to end it and willing to end it?

9

Was the Civil War God's Judgment for Slavery? (Part 2)

What caused the Civil War may seem obvious: slavery. To the historian, writes Michael Holt, "the greatest puzzle in American history [is] exactly what caused the Civil War?"[1] As we saw, another puzzle is what or who ended such an entrenched institution as slavery. On the surface, the war ended it, but that returns us to the first question. Slavery was a necessary, background cause of the war, but it had existed in the United States for seventy years without provoking a war. Nor was it the triggering cause—Lincoln's election was that. Few Northerners saw ending slavery as the "cause" they fought for at first. Few believed the U.S. government could end slavery in Southern states, nor did most want to fight a war to end it. An early Union victory ending the war (or a Confederate one) would have kept slavery from immediate extinction. In 1850, the issue of slavery seemed to be shelved. Constitutional compromises, cotton's profitability in a global textile industry and two parties committed to keeping slavery out of national politics stalled any national anti-slavery movement.[2]

---

[1]Michael F. Holt, *Political Parties and American Political Development from the Age of Jackson to the Age of Lincoln* (Baton Rouge: Louisiana State University Press, 1992), p. 319.

[2]Historians fine-tune the explanations: the North's faster, more extensive modernization led an urban-industrial North to battle a rural-agricultural South; a generation of blundering politicians stumbled into war; slaveholders' code of honor caused the South to fight a great duel against Northern attacks on its honor; the war was "an understandable product of America's democratic political system" that failed in the 1850s; and other secular explanations abound. Probably no interpretation fully satisfies most of those who did not author it: Southern cotton fueled Northern textile industrialization; blunderers and duelists restrained themselves before 1860; and the system had resolved the slavery issue in 1850. See James M. McPherson, *Ordeal by Fire: The Civil War and Reconstruction* (New York: Knopf, 1982), pp. 13-22; Bertram Wyatt-Brown, *Yankee Saints and Southern Sinners* (Baton Rouge: Louisiana State University Press, 1985); Kenneth S. Greenberg, *Masters and Statesmen: The Political Culture of American Slavery* (Baltimore: Johns

We will see if our model of God's sifting-out activity to clarify public ambiguity represents a satisfying interpretation; even though not one subject to proof
anymore than the others are, it may appear a more plausible explanation for
more events. We hypothesize God's separating *mishpat*, human attempts to rec-
reate unity built on ambiguity about slavery and God's breaking down that
unity. How did a system constructed to prevent a divisive sifting out get sifted
out into two warring sides anyway? Arguably, God used men's political ambitions, the peculiarities of the nation's political system and a small righteous remnant with its come-outer separatism. Crucial, too, was the nation's westward expansion, which kept splitting that ambiguous unity, as a solved problem kept
getting pushed into frontiers where it was unsolved. We cannot unravel the
moral complications of westward expansion, but it certainly kept breaking
things that were fixed.

Old Debates over New Western Territories Recreate Old Divisions: Part 1

We start with the Louisiana Purchase that acquired from France the territory
from the Mississippi to the Rocky Mountains. Thomas Jefferson sent to Congress proposed laws that included "a rigorous slave code." The French and
Spanish had allowed slavery in lower Louisiana (Orleans Territory). In acts
creating Orleans and Louisiana territories, Jefferson's party leaders "omitted all
reference to slavery," for the rule had been set "that slavery was legal in any
federal territory" unless "excluded by federal law." Silence meant slavery.[3]
Federalists broke this ambiguous silence. To bring Northern-style gradual
emancipation, James Hillhouse offered an amendment to free slaves after their
twenty-first (males) or eighteenth (females) birthday (post-nati), but only
those imported into the area. In another moment of choice, his amendment
lost, eleven to seventeen. He tried to restrict importation of slaves from existing states to the new area. Southerners argued not that slavery was a positive
good but that "diffusion" of a fixed slave population to new areas improved
slaves' condition and prevented slave revolts. Later, one admonished Northerners, "It is wrong to reproach us with the immorality of slavery—that is a

Hopkins University Press, 1985); Holt, *Political Parties*, pp. 314-15; William E. Gienapp, "The
Crisis of American Democracy: The Political System and the Coming of the Civil War," in *Why
the Civil War Came*, ed. Gabor S. Boritt (New York: Oxford University Press, 1996), p. 81.
[3]Don E. Fehrenbacher, *The Slaveholding Republic: An Account of the United States Government's Relations to Slavery* (New York: Oxford University Press, 2001), p. 260; Adam Rothman,
Slave Country: American Expansion and the Origins of the Deep South (Cambridge, Mass.:
Harvard University Press, 2005), pp. 26-27.

crime we must answer at the bar of God—we ought not therefore to answer it here—for it would be unjust that we should be punished twice for the same offence." That interesting application of double jeopardy denied God's judging activity "here" in history and delayed it until the Last Judgment. The entire Louisiana Purchase was open to slavery from 1804 to 1820.[4]

A more alarming debate (1819-1821) erupted when Missouri asked for admission as a state. Another Federalist amendment for post-nati emancipation (as a condition for admission) was passed by the House, but the Senate defeated it. Congress was deadlocked. Southerners threatened secession. Jefferson called "this momentous question . . . a fire bell in the night [that] awakened and filled me with terror." The Missouri Compromise admitted free Maine, too, and excluded slavery from the Louisiana Purchase north of 36°30' latitude. It was not a true compromise: Northerners did not vote for what the South wanted, or vice versa. Split into two parts, one majority passed the part Northerners wanted, while a different majority passed the South's part. When Missouri drafted a provision preventing free blacks from entering the state, "a deliberately ambiguous resolution" was passed to declare that this "should never be construed so as to violate" the rights of citizens of other states—but it clearly did.[5]

National unity was restored, but the dividing line between free and slave areas was extended westward. God sifted out, but not to a premature, curtain-dropping crisis: President Monroe, a Virginian, would likely not have opposed secession with military force and likely would have failed if he tried—the two sides were more evenly matched than forty years later—leaving slavery safe in an independent Southern nation. The crisis was delayed. The two political parties tried to exclude the slavery issue from Congress. Southern states-rights men and Northerners like Martin Van Buren in the Democratic party ran war hero Andrew Jackson for president and changed the subject to banks, taxes, paper money and local control. An anti-Jackson coalition, the Whigs also recruited Southern support to compete for the presidency. The price for Southern votes was silence or ambiguity on slavery. Democrats sought a common ambiguous

---

[4]Fehrenbacher, *Slaveholding Republic*, pp. 260-61; Roger G. Kennedy, *Mr. Jefferson's Lost Cause: Land, Farmers, Slavery and the Louisiana Purchase* (New York: Oxford University Press, 2003), pp. 210-13 (quoting Robert White of Delaware on p. 213); Rothman, *Slave Country*, p. 34; see pp. 27-34. Hillhouse obtained restrictions on slave imports, but they proved "ineffectual."

[5]Fehrenbacher, *Slaveholding Republic*, pp. 263-65; William W. Freehling, *The Road to Disunion: Secessionists at Bay 1776-1854* (New York: Oxford University Press, 1990), pp. 144-56; *Thomas Jefferson: Writings* (New York: Library of America, 1984), p. 1434; Merrill D. Peterson, *The Great Triumvirate: Webster, Clay and Calhoun* (New York: Oxford University Press, 1987), pp. 59-65; Howard R. Lamar, ed., *The New Encyclopedia of the American West* (New Haven, Conn.: Yale University Press, 1998), p. 722.

policy, while Whigs also ran war heroes for president, adopted no platform and let Northern Whigs say one thing and Southern Whigs, the opposite.[6]

The Second Great Awakening Sifts Out A More Radical Anti-Slavery Movement

Revivals helped to renew and radicalize the anti-slavery movement, which hardened Southern attitudes. God's sifting-out process focused on religious beliefs more than on politics and the halls of Congress, for two decades, but the former barged into the latter. Before 1830, anti-slavery advocates united around gradual emancipation: post-nati freedom at a set age followed ideally by colonization to Africa or elsewhere, with slavery ended in an area in forty years, aided by manumissions. Preferring that plan, Southerners like Jefferson professed, philosophically, that slavery was dysfunctional, ought to be ended by "natural means" and would be in time. This unity grew ambiguous by sheltering too many differing persons under its umbrella concept. The American Colonization Society included slaveholders who wanted to colonize free blacks only, politicians like Henry Clay who wanted Northern and Southern votes for president and sincere anti-slavery activists who saw gradual emancipation as the only responsible means to end slavery. Which of these did the concept call for? Yet this consensus on gradualism was not bound inevitably to collapse or to be attacked by a new group of immediate emancipationists or abolitionists.

Using the Awakening (among other things), God brought about this divisive attack and this collapse of ideological ambiguity in the 1830s. The key concepts forming abolitionism paralleled revival themes: slavery was a sin; sinners must repent and stop immediately, not gradually; God's judgment fell on those who refused. In an 1837 sermon, revivalist Charles Finney undercut ambiguity: "But the man who has doubts is condemned if he eats, because his eating is not from faith; and everything that does not come from faith is sin" (Romans 14:23). The New Testament did not condemn slavery per se, but Northerners and Southerners had doubts about its morality—as shown by Southern sensitivity about abolitionist criticism. Yet the nation "shelter[ed] itself behind its doubts whether slavery is a sin." Doubts could not shield people from God. If slaveowners "doubt its lawfulness, they are condemned be-

---

[6]Michael F. Holt, *The Rise and Fall of the American Whig Party: Jacksonian Politics and the Onset of the Civil War* (New York: Oxford University Press, 1999), pp. 4-9, 25-32, 44, 94-95, 116-17, 319; 356-57; David M. Potter, *The Impending Crisis 1848-1861* (New York: Harper & Row, 1976), p. 81; Richard J. Carwardine, *Evangelicals and Politics in Antebellum America* (New Haven, Conn.: Yale University Press, 1993), p. 134.

fore God, and . . . their sin will find them out, and God will let them know how He regards it."[7]

In God's sifting out, minuscule factions can cause huge impacts. William Lloyd Garrison and his *The Liberator* began the move to immediate abolition in 1831. Dropping faith in a God who judges in history, he installed morally enlightened critics (himself) as judges who condemned churches for hypocrisy, rejected the Constitution as a "Covenant with Death, an Agreement with Hell" that compromised with slavery, spurned corrupt party politics and called for the North to secede from a slavery-stained Union.[8] Garrisonians were an extreme, tiny, left wing that was harshly critical of America. Many anti-slavery evangelicals split from Garrison and formed their own anti-slavery society. Some joined the new come-outer Liberty Party, a minuscule big-tent coalition only because it met under a big tent under a banner, "Holiness to the Lord"— yet it had a huge impact (it may have cost Clay the 1844 election, and that led to further westward expansion and the Mexican War). Most evangelicals never embraced abolitionism.[9] Fragmented in denominations, Christ's church did not end slavery. As a group of redeemed sinners, it lacked the unified will and the means.

As tactics, the Garrisonians' ideas alienated most everyone and served as self-judgments cutting them off from society. Yet their ideas had a huge impact. They offended Southerners into open, strident defenses of slavery—thus hardening the South. Scripture teaches that God acts to harden sinners who refuse to repent. Southerners refused Whitefield's words and evangelicals' calls in the 1790s—even threatening anti-slavery preachers with violence—so God sent a

---

[7]David Brion Davis, "The Emergence of Immediatism in British and American Antislavery Thought," *Mississippi Valley Historical Review* 49 (September 1962): 228-29; John R. McKivigan, *The War Against Proslavery Religion: Abolitionism and the Northern Churches, 1830-1865* (Ithaca, N.Y.: Cornell University Press, 1984), pp. 19-21; David B. Chesebrough, ed., *"God Ordained This War": Sermons on the Sectional Crisis, 1830-1865* (Columbia: University of South Carolina Press, 1991), pp. 34-35. Davis gives several examples of anti-slavery activists fearing God's judgment if slavery was not abolished (see pp. 218, 219, 221, 222, 223).

[8]Bertram Wyatt-Brown, *Lewis Tappan and the Evangelical War Against Slavery* (Cleveland: The Press of Case Western Reserve University, 1969), pp. 79, 185-89; McKivigan, *War Against Proslavery Religion*, pp. 58-64; Robert P. Forbes, "Slavery and the Evangelical Enlightenment," p. 74, in *Religion and the Antebellum Debate over Slavery*, ed. John R. McKivigan and Mitchell Snay (Athens: University of Georgia Press, 1998), pp. 68, 72-74, 84-86.

[9]Wyatt-Brown, *Lewis Tappan*, pp. 191-99; McKivigan, *War Against Proslavery Religion*, pp. 48, 58-61, 144-48; Carwardine, *Evangelicals and Politics*, pp. 89, 134-39; Holt, *Rise and Fall*, pp. 195, 206, 218; Douglas M. Strong, *Perfectionist Politics: Abolitionism and the Religious Tensions of American Democracy* (Syracuse, N.Y.: Syracuse University Press, 1999), pp. 66-67. Holt argues that it was new Democratic voters who mainly defeated Clay in the 1844 election.

message as judgment, as hardening, not as a means to repentance.[10]

In *The Civil War as a Theological Crisis*, historian Mark Noll traces how the Scriptures read by a largely Protestant nation did not unite it around one clear, biblical position on slavery—partly because Americans had added "corollary beliefs about the Bible," that "it also promoted republican political theory, . . . defined the glories of liberty, . . . [and] forecast the providential destiny of the United States." Americans partly defined God ("providence") according to "republican, covenantal, commonsensical, Enlightenment, and—above all—nationalistic categories."[11] We might not be distorting his interpretation too much to say that they sought in Scripture a worldview addressing political and economic issues, such as slavery—or brought their American-republican worldview to Scripture, in a way similar to the elites Rick Kennedy identifies who sought to go beyond a testimony of judgment and salvation through Christ. Southerners and Northerners differed on what worldview was there. None was there, but instead a historical narrative of God's dealings and his promises that gave certainty to believers on necessary matters but uncertainty to political, social and economic systems that an active God would sift out in an ongoing *mishpat*. No scriptural proof text existed to prevent a righteous God from judging! Certain New Testament passages may indicate that a humane, morality-upholding (and hypothetical, given human sinfulness) kind of slavery would not be overturned by God; however, those passages gave the South's racial, marriage-preventing and family-breaking slavery no guaranteed safety from *mishpat*.

Garrison's dismissive approach to Scripture alienated believers North and South and weakened the impact of anti-slavery arguments from Scripture.[12] His abolitionist politics had a similar alienating effect. Extreme pro-slavery Southerners quoted Garrison's extreme words to persuade moderate Southerners that he spoke for the real North. Southern clergy had called for serious reform to end family breakups, legalize marriage, teach literacy and apply church discipline to abusive masters. These Southern critics pulled back a bit now, lest they

---

[10]For God's hardening of the unrepentant, see, e.g., Exodus 4:21; 10:20, Romans 9:18; 11:25; 2 Thessalonians 2:10-12. Mark Noll points out the strength of the Southern biblical defense of slavery, so that confidence in a pro-slavery Scripture must also be taken into account; Mark A. Noll, *The Civil War as a Theological Crisis* (Chapel Hill: University of North Carolina Press, 2006), pp. 33-36.

[11]Ibid., pp. 22, 94; see pp. 31-50. The following sentences present my view and not Noll's, for he turns to European Protestant and Catholic exegesis of Scripture in order to posit an alternative to the republican, Enlightenment, common-sense American exegesis. Noll addresses this "Christian republican" synthesis at greater length in *America's God: From Jonathan Edwards to Abraham Lincoln* (New York: Oxford University Press, 2002).

[12]Noll, *Theological Crisis*, pp. 31-32.

be seen as encouraging Northern abolitionist critics. Honor was a key Southern value; Northern assaults on slavery insulted Southern honor; the South must respond to restore its honor; Northerners condemned Southern responses as acts of aggression; Southerners saw this as a new insult—a chain reaction began.[13] A chain of human, voluntary actions was God's *mishpat*, too. He used each side as a tool to sift out the other toward a more extreme stance.

Northern mobs attacked abolitionists' printing offices, meetings and leaders; Southern mobs broke into a post office to seize their literature. In 1836 the House voted not to receive anti-slavery petitions. The aim was to suppress pro-abolition speech.[14] Forcing unity by stopping the polarizing rhetoric of abolitionists failed, providentially, due to another round of westward expansion.

By the 1850s, some Garrisonians had lost faith that God or peaceful, democratic means could end slavery. They countenanced violent means, mainly slave revolts—which would bring death and destruction to Southern whites, with Northerners escaping these consequences while the slaves did the violent work for them.[15] Violence meant sin: dropping faith in God, individuals taking up the sword in defiance of government, encouraging Christian slaves to violate their Lord's commands and wishing destruction on Southern whites. The North was not a righteous, innocent party: some Northerners profited from slavery, others acquiesced in it, and a few hoped to end it by violent means. In 1835, Finney wrote to abolitionist Theodore Weld, "Will not our present movements in abolition result in [civil war]? Have you no fear of this?"[16] Yet mobs storming post offices would not cause a civil war. The nation's political system still stood, and the two parties still upheld it.

Old Debates Over New Western Territories Recreate Old Divisions: Part 2

How it was split is a complex story. God's sifting out never produced a simple black-and-white alignment with no gray areas, just enough clarity to cause a slavery-ending war. To focus on trees might blur the forest. Each event had discernible, natural causes; none was miraculous. Believers may see God's hand in

---

[13]Eugene D. Genovese, *A Consuming Fire: The Fall of the Confederacy in the Mind of the White South* (Athens: University of Georgia Press, 1998), pp. 5-33. Carwardine describes this chain reaction in *Evangelicals and Politics*, p. 142. Steven J. Keillor, *This Rebellious House: American History and the Truth of Christianity* (Downers Grove, Ill: InterVarsity Press, 1996).

[14]Wyatt-Brown, *Lewis Tappan*, pp. 143-45, 149-57, 160-63; Fehrenbacher, *Slaveholding Republic*, pp. 73-76, 302.

[15]John Demos, "The Antislavery Movement and the Problem of Violent 'Means,' " *New England Quarterly* 36 (1964): 501-26.

[16]Quoted in Benjamin P. Thomas, *Theodore Weld: Crusader for Freedom* (New Brunswick, N.J.: Rutgers University Press, 1950), pp. 108-9.

a president's untimely death or an election result, but some events benefited compromisers and some, polarizers. When we look at the entire sequence, we may see the divine Prosecutor coming back to slavery when the nation on trial tried to change the subject, stuck to a story that omitted that issue, gave evasive answers or invented false stories.

The Missouri Compromise laid down two parallel tracks headed west: slaveholders could go on the track south of 36°30'; free migrants, north of that line. All U.S. territory fell under the parallel track solution: that line and the prior Ohio River and Mason-Dixon lines. When American settlers in Texas won their independence from Mexico in 1836 and asked to be annexed by the United States, Presidents Jackson and Van Buren refused, fearing that to add this slave area was to reignite the dormant slavery issue. This attempt to stifle it failed after Van Buren's successor, William H. Harrison, died after one month in office, and "His Accidency" John Tyler turned into a renegade Whig who belonged in neither party and ignored both parties' desire to keep Texas and slavery out of national politics. Tyler made Texas an issue in the 1844 election, a crucial link in the sifting-out process. The tiny Liberty Party took just enough votes from Henry Clay in New York State to toss the election to the pro-annexationist James K. Polk (there were other factors). The results led Congress to annex Texas in March 1845.[17] Like the first falling domino, Texas set off further acquisitions of new territory. War with Mexico was nearly inevitable after U.S. annexation of the former Mexican state. U.S. victory in the war brought the Mexican Cession: the future states of California, Nevada and Utah, and parts of Arizona, New Mexico, Colorado, Wyoming, Kansas and Oklahoma. The question of slavery's status here reignited the debate that endangered the Union.[18] Westward expansion pushed Americans beyond the old compromises, the old lines.

There were four possible solutions to slavery's status in Western territories. One was to bar it from them—an unambiguous victory for the North. Called the Wilmot Proviso, this plan passed the House but never the Senate, the South's bastion of last resort. Also unambiguous was the second—extending the 36°30' line to the Pacific—but Polk endorsed it too late. Its clarity was a disadvantage to devious politicians for "it did not offer either side the hope of gaining ground

[17]Freehling, *Road to Disunion*, pp. 363, 372-425, 428-30, 440-48, 353, 355; Holt, *Rise and Fall*, pp. 127, 168-70, 172-73, 218-19, 221-22; Potter, *Impending Crisis*, pp. 23-25; Fehrenbacher, *Slaveholding Republic*, pp. 266, 267. For the concept of "parallel tracks," I am indebted to Robert H. Wiebe, *The Opening of American Society: From the Adoption of the Constitution to the Eve of Disunion*. (New York: Random House, 1985), pp. 287-88, 291.
[18]Freehling, *Road to Disunion*, pp. 455-56 (and map on p. 366); Potter, *Impending Crisis*, pp. 24-26; Fehrenbacher, *Slaveholding Republic*, p. 267.

by favorable construction of ambiguous language." That hope came with the third idea: "popular sovereignty" let citizens of a new area decide for or against slavery, but could they do so at the formation of their territory (as the North hoped) or when they later applied for statehood (as the South hoped)? That was unclear. Democrats adopted this idea, selling it in the North as anti-slavery and in the South as pro-slavery. The unambiguous pro-slavery idea was the fourth: slavery could not be kept out of any territory.[19]

Whigs and Democrats could not keep the issue out of the 1848 campaign. Democrats used popular sovereignty's ambiguities. Whigs ran Zachary Taylor, "a [Mexican War] hero who had never voted" or belonged to either party. "While the Democrats had adopted a platform whose meaning no one could be sure about, the Whigs . . . adopted no platform at all." Whig campaign managers told the South one thing about him and the North, the exact opposite.[20] The words *Whig* and *Democrat* meant different things regarding slavery in the West in different states.

To add to the confusion, the slaveholder Taylor won but turned out not to be pro-slavery. To solve the impasse over the Mexican Cession, he proposed to fast-forward those areas past the territorial stage and directly to statehood—as free states, to satisfy the North, but with popular sovereignty and without stigmatizing slavery, to mollify the South. He tried to resolve the issue so quickly that a sifting-out quarrel could not develop, but he failed. Clay pushed a compromise bill that also addressed fugitive slaves and the slave trade in the nation's capital. A "grave sectional crisis over the territories" gripped the capital from December 1849 to August 1850, as Taylor and Clay each had the strength to block the other's plan and, thus, create a stalemate.[21]

Here the plot thickens. A border dispute between Texas and New Mexico threatened to erupt in violence; Texas was set to send its militia to seize Santa Fe; U.S. army troops there might resist with force, setting off a civil war if the stalemate was not ended. Providence intervened. Taylor died of gastroenteritis on July 9, 1850, and his successor, Millard Fillmore, decided to support Clay's bill. Opponents split apart Clay's one bill, but its components were passed, one by one, under Stephen Douglas's leadership. Like the Missouri Compromise, the Compromise of 1850 was not one. Northerners did not give in and support the parts Southerners favored, or vice versa. Most Northerners voted against pro-

---

[19] I am indebted to Potter's excellent analysis in *Impending Crisis*, pp. 54-60, 69-73, 77-81.
[20] Potter, *Impending Crisis*, p. 81; see also p. 77; Holt, *Rise and Fall*, p. 357.
[21] Holt, *Rise and Fall*, p. 459; see pp. 461-63, 474-75, 478-79, 481, 487; Potter, *Impending Crisis*, pp. 91, 94-100, 103. Mexican anti-slavery laws would keep slavery out prior to statehood, without divisive Congressional legislation, under Taylor's plan.

slavery parts, and vice versa. Douglas got them all passed with the aid of "small blocs of advocates of compromise" who were the swing votes. "North and South did not consent to each other's terms . . . and there was really no compromise—a truce perhaps, an armistice, certainly a settlement, but not a true compromise."[22]

It seemed a final settlement. The compromises had now reached the Pacific Ocean, with no more West to argue over. Both parties accepted the finality of this deal. A praying slave must have found late September 1850 the moment of darkest despair. Dealmakers had solved slavery in the territories, and few Americans wanted to interfere with it in the South.[23] Before a holy God, on the issue of Southern slavery with its family breakups and without legal slave marriages, the nation was both strongly opposed to it (in the North) and determined to defend it (in the South). The nation was anti- and pro-slavery, but that did not confuse God.

The Kansas-Nebraska Act (1854): Destroying Two-Party, Whig-Democrat Ambiguity

In January 1854, Douglas introduced "one of the most fateful measures ever approved by Congress," the Kansas-Nebraska Act organizing Kansas and Nebraska territories. "Seldom was the irresponsibility of politicians more glaring," William Gienapp concludes, "than in their reckless agitation of this issue, heedless of long-term national consequences, for personal and factional advantages."[24] Recklessly, it repealed the Missouri Compromise, with respect to these two territories, and allowed slavery north of the 36°30' line—doing so in the name of the 1850 Compromise, but undoing its finality by reopening the slavery issue. That was not Douglas's intention; we can discern a *mishpat* at work. He had introduced similar bills (without the repeal provision) in 1844 and 1848, but they were not acted on, and his 1853 bill (without repeal) was defeated at the last moment by four Northern senators and by its entanglement in a debate over a southern versus a central route for a railroad to the Pacific. Douglas mainly wanted to organize Kansas-Nebraska to make possible his preferred central route. A deal was possible—a southern route in exchange for a free Kansas-

---

[22]Holt, *Rise and Fall,* pp. 459, 463, 497, 518-19, 520, 521-22, 529-30, 531, 534-43; Potter, *Impending Crisis,* p. 113; see pp. 106-16.

[23]Historians debate whether the deal was ambiguous on slavery in Utah and New Mexico territories. Potter (pp. 116-17 n. 45) argues it was ambiguous; Holt (p. 541) argues it was not. It did leave the Constitution's national ambiguity on slavery intact.

[24]William E. Gienapp, *The Origins of the Republican Party 1852-1856* (New York: Oxford University Press, 1987), pp. 81-82.

Nebraska—but Douglas would not surrender his central route. When he reintroduced the bill in 1854, Southern senators pressed him to allow slavery in the area, although it was north of 36°30'. He did not have to give in to them: he knew the dangerous "national consequences" of reopening the slavery issue; excluding that option as unthinkable would postpone a solution to the railroad-Nebraska issue, but mounting pressures might force a solution ultimately.[25]

Douglas realized the dangers. He told one senator that "no man was so wild as to think of repealing the Missouri Compromise." Yet he did it. Why? A reckless, impetuous, darting quickness marked his oratory and his personality. His biographer notes "his often frenzied, pragmatic efforts to secure the passage of western legislation." Practical barriers to his goals led him to risk all: Southern senators refused to support the bill unless he did so; some Northern senators opposed him anyway. He had faith in ambiguity: When did popular sovereignty let settlers outlaw slavery? What had the 1850 Compromise meant for slavery in New Mexico and Utah? Hadn't the 1850 deal superseded the Missouri one without saying so? Couldn't he render the 36°30' line inapplicable without saying so? He started down this road believing he could escape dangers through ambiguity. When both sides insisted on a clear statement of whether the line was applicable or not in Kansas-Nebraska, he had either to embarrass himself by dropping the matter or satisfy Southerners by declaring the line "inoperative" in those territories. He chose the latter. We can discern an individual sifting out here, as earlier defeats of the bill and new barriers exposed the recklessness that was in Douglas. For the nation, the bill led to a fateful sifting-out, clarifying uproar. We can discern here God the active Judge "ending the irresolution of public ambiguity."[26]

After the bill passed, the Congregationalist journal, *The Independent,* prophetically headlined its summarizing editorial paragraph, *"What divine Providence will do."* America had shown it would do nothing to end slavery. "The time for the peaceable solution of that question has gone by forever. Do what we will, we can not now get rid of slavery without *suffering.*" The editors mistakenly saw a national pro-slavery decision as the sign of divine judgment, when an intensifying national disunity marked God's sifting out prior to a judg-

---

[25]Potter, *Impending Crisis,* pp. 146-53; Robert W. Johannsen, *Stephen A. Douglas* (New York: Oxford University Press, 1973), pp. 390-95, 397-98; Holt, *Rise and Fall,* p. 806. Southern opposition in 1853 is sometimes stressed, but the bill would have passed if the four Northern senators had joined the two Missouri senators who voted for it.

[26]Johannsen, *Douglas,* p. 408; see pp. 403-7, 409-10, 411 (quoting Douglas), 412-14, 498-99 (on his speaking style). See also Potter, *Impending Crisis,* pp. 58-62; Gienapp, *Origins,* pp. 70-71; Freehling, *Road to Disunion,* pp. 550-57; and Fehrenbacher, *Slaveholding Republic,* pp. 273-76.

ing war. Yet they were largely correct in noting, "Slavery will go down. The Providence of God is against it. But the law of divine retribution is now arrayed against Us, and will work itself out." The prayers of the righteous could not avert judgment, for the nation no longer had a righteous standing before God "as did our Pilgrim Fathers." No, "Egypt, Babylon, Assyria, Tyre [all targets of the oracles against the nations], Rome—these are now our prototypes, and the judgments that smote them for their oppressions, awake again from the slumber of the ages, and will not linger."[27] His judgments on nations had not slumbered for ages, but they were not long in reaching America.

Like a loose cannon slamming from one side to the other of a tossing ship, the Kansas-Nebraska Act gradually demolished the two parties that had kept slavery out of national politics and ambiguously obfuscated it when it could not be kept out. It first helped to destroy the Whigs, weakened by a free-soil movement of Northerners angry over Texas, the Mexican War and slavery in the territories. A bigger-tent coalition than the Liberty Party, the Free-Soil Party, ran a presidential candidate in 1848 and captured 5 percent of the votes.[28] God was not sifting out a simon-pure anti-slavery faction. This impure, watered-down Free-Soil Party had no quarrel with slavery in the South and only sought to exclude blacks, free or slave, from the white man's West. God was gradually sifting out a faction that was anti-slavery enough (barely) and had enough popular support in the North to provoke a slavery-ending war— the Free-Soil Party was a key step. It was key that Free-Soil congressman took the initiative in attacking Douglas's bill—conservative Whigs might have revived their party by framing the issue as Douglas's Democratic folly, but Free-Soilers aroused the North by framing it as a pro-slavery conspiracy. The more the issue aroused the North, the worse it was for Whigs. An anti-Nebraska coalition of free-soil Whigs and Democrats and (confusingly) Free-Soilers ended the Whig party and created the Republican party (though only the *free-soil* Democrats joined it).[29]

Conservative Whigs tried to survive and to maintain ambiguity by seizing the rapidly growing, nativist Know-Nothings, who were changing the subject from slavery to immigrants. What caused the corruption of American politics? The anti-Nebraska group said it was a "Slave-Power Conspiracy" that controlled the federal government. The Know-Nothings said, millions of new im-

---

[27] *The Independent* 6, no. 288 (June 8, 1854): 180.
[28] Potter, *Impending Crisis,* pp. 72, 75, 79, 80, 82; Carwardine, *Evangelicals and Politics,* pp. 147-52.
[29] Holt, *Rise and Fall,* pp. 815-17, 822, 825-30; Gienapp, *Origins,* pp. 72-78; Johannsen, *Douglas,* p. 418.

migrants, Irish Catholics, who voted as their priests and saloon keepers ordered, in "a papal plot to destroy republicanism in America." Know-Nothings would sift the United States into a native-born, Protestant, virtuous faction and a foreign-born, Catholic, immoral faction. The first Know-Nothings did not deceitfully use the immigrant issue to change the subject away from slavery. In 1855-1856, conservative Whigs used the movement to do so, and they might have succeeded.[30]

In April 1856, it was unclear if the Know-Nothings' American party or the Republican Party would replace the Whigs as the main rival to the Democrats. But that loose cannon—the working out of popular sovereignty in Kansas—kept careening back and forth. Missourians crossed the border to vote in Kansas; New England anti-slavery groups sent abolitionists to settle in Kansas; vote frauds abounded; two legislatures met in two territorial capitals; on May 21, a pro-slavery mob vandalized the anti-slavery capital, Lawrence; Republican newspapers cried, "Sack of Lawrence"; on May 22 a South Carolina congressman caned a Massachusetts senator in the Senate chamber after he had made "scathing personal attacks" on Southern leaders in a speech on Kansas. Here was "the turning point in the Republican party's struggle for political survival." The sifting out would come over slavery, not immigrants or Catholicism. Getting only Northern votes, Republicans won 33 percent of the votes that fall; the American party, only 21.6 percent.[31]

Democrat James Buchanan won but came to regret it. The careening cannon of popular sovereignty in action in Kansas demolished its ambiguity, so appealing to both Northern and Southern Democrats. They were now sifted out into pro-slavery Southerners and their allies (Buchanan) who accepted the chaotic, fraudulent pro-slavery outcome in Kansas—and Douglas and his fellow Northerners who rejected it. When the former pushed through their Kansas bill, the two wings headed to a split in 1860, when they ran separate presidential candidates. The loose cannon of Kansas-Nebraska had demolished the Democrats too.[32]

Who Caused This Divisive Judgment? Chance? Those Who Warned of It? Or God?

How could this collapse of the Union's two pillars occur just ten years after they

---

[30]Gienapp, *Origins*, p. 96; see pp. 92-102, 179-81, 185-86, 260-63, 273; Holt, *Rise and Fall*, pp. 914-15, 926, 929-31, 964-65. Fillmore based his 1856 campaign on Know-Nothings.
[31]Gienapp, *Origins*, pp. 296, 299; see pp. 297-98, 300-303; Holt, *Rise and Fall*, pp. 966-67.
[32]Potter, *Impending Crisis*, pp. 314-26, 407-15.

had solved the issue? Thousands of party activists, the nation's economic elites and its political leaders were committed to the continued dominance of these parties as a bulwark against civil war. Until 1854, those who threatened the parties were minuscule in number, impractical in their zeal for purity over victory and vilified by many Americans. The political system encouraged parties' fragmented ambiguity: Whigs and Democrats were state-level parties needing only to unite on one national candidate every four years; the presidential contest was thirty state elections with Whigs and Democrats free to say contradictory things in different states. A move to a new, third party faced obstacles: politicians not wanting to risk their careers or voters to waste their vote. Nearly everyone agreed the Constitution protected slavery in the Southern states. The territorial controversy appeared to be laid to rest in 1850. If this were a natural phenomenon, we might calculate the odds against a sequence of events leading to party dissolution, secession, civil war and emancipation—and conclude they demonstrate intelligent design of the sequence.

Some observers blamed uncompromising evangelicals in ways reminiscent of our current debates over religion in politics. One New York editor wrote, "*You*, Protestant religionists were the very first to begin this game of disunion." "The fundamental curse of the Republican party [is] its irrepressible disposition to *meddle* with other people's business, and to impose its notions, and its will, on people who do not freely accept them." Reacting to a flood of political sermons and clergy petitions aimed at him in early 1854, Douglas accused clergy of aiming at "theocracy" and dictating to a democracy: they claimed "a divine power in the clergy . . . higher than the . . . Constitution, and above the sovereignty of the people and of the States—to command the senators by the authority of Heaven and under the penalty of exposing them 'to the righteous judgment of the Almighty,' to vote in a particular way upon a given question." The Reverend Leonard Bacon replied that they charged the bill with "'exposing *us*'—not the Senate or the Senators, but the great republic of which we are citizens—" to God's judgment. "Every citizen" should know that "there is such a thing as national responsibility to God for national sins. The government of God, in this world, deals not with individuals only, but also with communities and nations."[33]

Interestingly, Senator Douglas compared the clergy's alleged theocratic

---

[33]Carwardine, *Evangelicals and Politics*, pp. 319-20 (quoting New York editor); Robert W. Johannsen, ed., *The Letters of Stephen A. Douglas* (Urbana: University of Illinois Press, 1961), pp. 308-9; [Leonard Bacon], "Morality of the Nebraska Bill," *New Englander* (May 1854), pp. 305, 331; see pp. 329, 332 (quoting Douglas), 334-35.

claims to those of Islamic mullahs. He had returned from a trip that included stops in Constantinople and Smyrna in Turkey, "where the successor of Mahomet proclaimed and enforced God's will on earth according to" the Quran. When "surrounded by [the Ottoman Emperor's] bayonets," he had not argued over these Islamic decrees, but "when I set foot on the shores of my native land," then clerical decrees in God's name seemed unacceptable.[34]

One American warned of judgment and, like an Islamic jihadist, tried to execute it himself. Financed and supported by Boston abolitionists who had lost faith in peaceful means, John Brown and sixteen followers seized the federal arsenal at Harpers Ferry on October 16, 1859, in hopes of sparking a slave revolt. Brown's backers did not share his conservative, Calvinist theology but were equally willing to spark a revolt that might lead to the deaths of hundreds or thousands of white Southerners. Brown's path was not that of the Son of Man he claimed to follow (nor did Christian slaves follow Brown): to defy government, not passively, but by seizing its arsenal; to recruit slaves to violent deeds; to form a freedmen's republic in the mountains—all on his own initiative, without waiting for the Father's timing. "Am I leading a rebellion, that you have come with swords and clubs?" Jesus asked those who arrested him (Luke 22:52), and the answer was clearly no. Brown's answer was yes.[35]

God did not choose to use slave revolts to judge the nation and end slavery, or even to cause the war that did both. Lincoln's election in 1860 caused secession and war. Republicans' stance on slavery was a bit ambiguous but clear enough to make them a North-only party. A Southern secession faction would leave the Union if a Republican was elected president. This North-only party provided the crucial base of popular support needed if a Republican president was to wage a Union-saving war. Democrats' split and Republicans' rise were well-advanced by October 1859 on a track separate from Brown's plans. His raid caused some additional Southerners to convert to the cause of secession, but it would have come anyway. His raid led to increased judgment on the North by augmenting Southern strength and, thus, Northern casualties. John

---

[34]Johannsen, *Letters of Douglas,* p. 312.
[35]Potter, *Impending Crisis,* pp. 359-80; Louis A. DeCaro Jr., *"Fire from the Midst of You": A Religious Life of John Brown* (New York: New York University Press, 2002), pp. 138-39, 253-54, 261-63, 264-65, 270-72, 278; Edward J. Renehan Jr., *The Secret Six: The True Tale of the Men Who Conspired with John Brown* (New York: Crown, 1995), pp. 110-15, 136-39, 143-47. DeCaro rebuts the exaggeration that Brown believed only in the Old Testament God of wrath; he is too sympathetic to Brown (whose drift into violence may have been partly caused by his withdrawal from organized churches, p. 138) and does not adequately address the contradiction of Christ's follower plotting a slave revolt.

Brown and his Boston backers were not rewarded for taking God's judgment into their hands.[36]

God himself, in his long-term sifting-out *mishpat,* caused the final, negative consequence, the Civil War—the judgment for slavery in our narrow sense of that word. That Northern elites would finance and cheer slave revolts showed that they had been sifted out—not as a righteous remnant but as an unrighteous faction doubting God's ability to end slavery. God is merciful, and a revival in 1857-1858 preceded the war. Abolitionists, evangelical and nonevangelical, criticized this revival for focusing on individual conversions and neglecting anti-slavery reform. To them, and to some later historians, it marked "the failure of New England revivalism to resolve the divisive issue of slavery."[37] Yet, it was then too late to resolve that issue short of war—the Republican rise and Democratic fall were well advanced toward Lincoln and secession—and clergymen warned that God's judgment was one possible resolution. If God acted when Americans had not, that was not failure. The 1820s revivals helped sift out a Northern anti-slavery faction, but that process was complete by 1857-1858, and that revival only, but mercifully, saved souls before the final cataclysm. Paradoxically, an event (Civil War) can be a condemning catastrophe for the unbeliever and a chastening, refining deliverance for the believer. God uses the same event as salvation to some and judgment to others. Diaries and letters of Christian soldiers in both armies indicate they "endure[d] hardship as discipline" from their Father (Hebrews 12:7).[38]

In *Theological Crisis,* Noll describes how the Civil War provoked a crisis of confidence in Americans' ability to discern what Providence's purpose was in events. People reading the same Bible with similar beliefs came to very different conclusions, and some concluded that God had acted in surprising ways, perhaps contrary to his previous ways.[39] It would be a worldview approach to expect one, uniform divine purpose in the war—a unitary divine foreign policy as it were—when judgment involves different verdicts for different people: freedom for slaves but responsibilities accompanying freedom; chastening hard-

---

[36]Potter, *Impending Crisis,* pp. 380-84; Carwardine, *Evangelicals and Politics,* pp. 283, 284-85. Interestingly, DeCaro notes, "Brown correctly predicted that the South would secede from the Union in 1860 if the Republicans won the presidential election" (p. 252). For the final moves toward secession and war, see, e.g., *Impending Crisis,* chaps. 16-20.

[37]Kathryn Teresa Long, *The Revival of 1857-58: Interpreting an American Religious Awakening* (New York: Oxford University Press, 1998), p. 95; see pp. 93-94, 96-104, 110-14, 118.

[38]Kevin Carr and Steven J. Keillor, "More Than Conquerors (Through Him Who Loved Us)," ms. in author's possession, based on diaries and letters of the prayer group, Company F, First Minnesota Regiment.

[39]Noll, *Theological Crisis,* pp. 75-81, 84-86, 93-94.

ships for Northern believers; perhaps a push toward victory's arrogance for Northern unbelievers, who already had the pride of unbelief; a sure punishment for Southern slaveholders; for Southern believers, a nudge toward undivided faith instead of faith in God *and* Southern wealth. An omniscient God can use the same war for an almost infinite number of purposes. Varying, contradictory notions of God's purposes point to the danger of assessing God's will during a crisis, from a partisan stance or with false certainty.

"This Mighty Scourge of War": The Civil War Perceived as God's Punishment

We Americans have often romanticized our Civil War, but those who experienced it knew it as a terrible cataclysm. About 620,000 soldiers died; the injured, maimed, orphans and widows added to an incalculable toll of human misery.[40] There was nothing romantic about getting your head taken off by a cannon ball. Harry S. Stout's *Moral History* of the war forces us to examine the war itself as *mishpat*. The start of hostilities in April 1861 dropped the curtain on decades of political ambiguity that we surveyed and began a terrible sifting out as the horrendous losses, huge stakes and fears of enemy victory tempted and pressured leaders toward immoral and brutal war-making tactics. Some leaders gave in; others did not. Detailing the brutality but not the sifting-out pressures, Stout's book lacks this sense of divine *mishpat* and examplifies what our analysis seeks to avoid. To use Old Testament figurative language, we analyzed the Civil War as a terrible cup that God made the nation drink; the romanticizers picture the cup as not so terrible since it was full of military glory, too; Stout correctly restores its terribleness but sees it as a cup Americans gave to themselves to drink, due to their zealous patriotism, religious thirst for blood sacrifice and inability to be morally self-critical or to follow just-war principles.[41] The result is a lack of empathy and compassion, of a sense that but for the grace of God there go we. Stout's book of human "moral judgments" is far different from this book on divine judgment, which encourages humility and compassion, for if they were given the cup, so may we.[42]

Stout's "moral history" represents a leftist anti-war political worldview imposed on Yankees and Confederates after the fact. A critical look at attacks on civilian populations contrary to codes of military conduct well understood at the

---

[40]Davidson et al., *Nation of Nations*, pp. 598-99. Some $20 billion was spent on both sides to prosecute the war; about $1.5 billion in property was destroyed.

[41]For the cup of the Lord's anger, see, e.g., Isaiah 51:17-23.

[42]Harry S. Stout, *Upon the Altar of the Nation: A Moral History of the Civil War* (New York: Viking, 2006), pp. xii, 459.

time is fully justified—and his "moral history" is partly that—yet the bulk of it goes beyond that to skewer and ridicule the clergy's patriotic and providentialist sermons, the people's patriotic enthusiasm for the flag, the religious newspapers' war coverage and even the joy over revivals in the Confederate armies. Much of the patriotic speech criticized did not involve calls for violating just-war principles but commemorations of the courage (or courageous deaths) of soldiers fighting other soldiers. References to "preemptive war" and patriotic flags flying "in 2005 no less than in 1861"—and the steady drumbeat of criticism of pro-war patriotism—make this sound like an anti-war tract aimed at the Civil War but meant to hit the Iraq war, too, with Lincoln criticized, often unfairly, as a stand-in for the current Republican president.[43] Stout's book shows the need to try to restore divine judgment as a real category, difficult as that is, lest we have only partisans' moral judgments.

The war's costly duration surprised Americans on both sides: "each looked for an easier triumph," Lincoln concluded. He noted that God "could give the final victory to either side any day. Yet the contest proceeds." Providential events prevented a Confederate victory prolonging slavery—Lee's lost orders, Stonewall Jackson's death, delay in permitting Gordon's flank attack at the Wilderness. Others prevented an earlier Union victory that might have ended the war without ending slavery—McClellan's wild overestimation of Confederate strength, for example. War-prolonging events meant a shift from the North's original purpose—preserving the Union—to one that Lincoln could not have proclaimed at the start—ending slavery.

Nicholas Parrillo traces the shift in Lincoln's thinking about God, war and slavery. Lincoln played a crucial role: the Emancipation Proclamation was an executive order; the second inaugural address was Lincoln's personal statement; another Republican president might have acted and thought differently. Before the war, Parrillo argues, "Lincoln's God lacked any palpable motive force or determinative power." American republicanism and Jefferson's Declaration "had the force and weight of sacred doctrines." In 1852, Lincoln shared Jefferson's and Clay's sunny philosophical optimism that colonization and voluntary eman-

---

[43]Ibid., pp. 79, xiv; see pp. xi-xxii, 28-29, 37-46, 47, 51-52, 53-55, 73 (ridiculing Stonewall Jackson), 77-81, 100-103, 137 ("Lincoln's taste for blood"), 187, 188, 242 ("Lincoln's grim appetite for greater short-term casualties"), 248-50, 268-69, 287-88, 290-92 ("Civil War apologists now praised war as a converting institution for white soldiers"), 386-89, 432-33. Often, the statements come as seeming summaries after a long quotation, which does not support the statement. For example, on p. 242, where Lincoln's rebuke (never sent) of Meade for not pursuing Lee after Gettysburg is followed by "Lincoln's grim appetite for short-term casualties," although the quote mentioned no such thing, and a rapid pursuit of a defeated, worn-out foe might decrease casualties.

cipation of slaves would proceed "so gradually that neither races nor individuals shall have suffered by the change." Suffering as a wartime president caused Lincoln to change his views. By summer 1862, the war caused him to look for a sign from a sovereign God as to what he should do. After the Union quasi-victory at Antietam, he told his cabinet, "God had decided this question in favor of the slaves." He issued the proclamation and stuck to it. By April 1864, he could see that "God now wills the removal of a great wrong," slavery. That spring and summer, he stuck by his commander, Grant, despite horrendous casualties and an upcoming, decisive presidential election. Providentially, Sherman's capture of Atlanta and the Democrats' platform gave him the victory. By March 1865, he knew the "Almighty has his own purposes"—to end slavery and punish North and South for it. The witness closest to events had learned to discern a divine Judge. The second inaugural address "contains no references to American republicanism," and "Lincoln wrote himself out of the speech completely." God was fully sovereign. It was as if a U.S. president had said the first, the repentance, part of the sinner's prayer—we have sinned, you are just to judge us—on behalf of the nation; it was as if a president had finally admitted, "He must increase, I must decrease."[44]

Lincoln's Second Inaugural works as our summary. "Both parties deprecated war" and tried to avoid it. Yet "the war came"—the speech strongly implied that God caused it. Slavery was "somehow, the cause of the war." Both sides "read the same Bible, and pray to the same God," yet faced each other in a deadly war far more protracted than expected. "The Almighty has his own purposes," and judgment for slavery was almost certainly one of them. Yet Lincoln on judgment was followed immediately by Lincoln on "Malice to none" and "charity, for all." God gave them the cup to drink—neither side forced it on the other or on the nation—so Northerners could show mercy to the South. Not Lincoln's moral judgment, this was his confession of divine judgment.

---

[44]Nicholas Parrillo, "Lincoln's Calvinist Transformation: Emancipation and War," *Civil War History* 46, no. 3 (2000): pp. 228, 229, 232, 242, 247, 249; see pp. 227-53; David E. Long, *The Jewel of Liberty: Abraham Lincoln's Re-election and the End of Slavery* (New York: Da Capo Press, 1997), pp. 235-36.

10

Why Has Lincoln's Biblical Language of Judgment Become Incomprehensible to Us?

As Walter Sundberg noted after September 11, "the theological ideas that inspired Lincoln" in his second inaugural address "are alien to us, impossible for us to employ." His central idea, that the war was God's judgment on the nation for slavery, has become nearly impossible for some analysts even to identify as the central idea. At the very least, we need to recover judgment as a real category in order to recover Lincoln's speech. Garry Wills sidestepped God as an actor in history by arguing that "the Second Inaugural was meant, with great daring, to spell out a principle of not acting on principle." As presidential actor, Lincoln sought flexibility to improvise a Reconstruction policy, Wills claimed. That is an argument from Lincoln's unexpected silence about the pressing issue of Reconstruction. It avoids the central idea of God's acting on the principle of judgment. Lincoln had come to realize that it did not matter whether people acted on principle or did not. God's acts would determine the outcome.[1]

Partly, Lincoln's statement of God's retributive justice ("every drop of blood drawn with the lash, shall be paid with another drawn by the sword") is incomprehensible to us because it ignores the Son of Man's atoning work on the cross.[2] There is another way for sin's guilt to be paid for. Yet our main problem with Lincoln's speech is the many nonscriptural ideas superimposed on our national consciousness, rendering "alien" the idea of God judging the nation. We will peel back these layers, because these ideas are incorrect and the Son of Man's testimony shows that his descent and ascent are history's meaning and

---

[1]Walter Sundberg, "'Evil' After 9/11: The Alien Work of God," *Word & World* (spring 2004): 206; Garry Wills, "Lincoln's Greatest Speech?" *Atlantic Monthly*, September 1999, p. 64.
[2]Allen C. Guelzo emphasizes Lincoln's difficulty in perceiving God as Savior in *Abraham Lincoln: Redeemer President* (Grand Rapids: Eerdmans, 1999).

do not end divine judgment. No ideological shift in one nation's history can render obsolete his enduring the divine judgment on the cross or his executing the divine judgment at his return. If it could, that ideology or nation would take over as history's meaning and the Son of Man would prove a false witness. "May God forbid," the apostle Paul would say.

No one has traced out the path whereby Americans departed from the idea of God's judgment on the nation in order to restore that idea. Specific biases have caused some would-be prophets incorrectly to proclaim judgment, but the general human bias is against the idea, and that hinders any restoration of it. Historians share that general bias, often believe nonscriptural ideas, write histories that celebrate them and are very unlikely to examine the past to strip them away. Historians' accounts of past events' causes and consequences tend to set the parameters for what we see as possible causes and consequences of current and future ones: no judgment in the past, then none in the present or foreseeable future. Yet, history writing can give no such guarantee. We historians write for audiences that do not demand the return to history of a divine judge. I wrote a narrative of the Grand Excursion (1854) for readers participating in its sesquicentennial. The trip occurred days after the Kansas-Nebraska Act was signed into law, amid portents of the impending crisis. Yet I did not offer the analysis given in the preceding two chapters; my audience did not want that.[3]

Fortunately, someone has traced out the path whereby Americans (and others) have departed from the idea of God, in order to restore that idea. As our main guide, we will use Craig M. Gay's comprehensive analysis in *The Way of the (Modern) World: Or, Why It's Tempting to Live As If God Doesn't Exist* to explain why Americans live as if God's judgments do not exist.[4] We revisit the deficiencies of a worldview apologetic that fails to mention God's judgments, for in Gay's book even the best apologetic cannot deal with the "practical atheism" it deplores. Even Christian apologetics contributes to our present incomprehension about judgment.

In peeling back these nonscriptural ideas that erroneously exclude divine judgment, we have to violate the grammarians' rule against using double nega-

---

[3]Steven J. Keillor, *Grand Excursion: Antebellum America Discovers the Upper Mississippi* (Afton, Minn.: Afton Historical Society Press, 2004). Yet I was thinking to myself that these celebrity travelers were heading toward the divine judgment Lincoln described; however, a celebration (in 2004) did not seem like the appropriate time to bring the subject up.

[4]Craig M. Gay, *The Way of the (Modern) World: Or, Why It's Tempting to Live As If God Doesn't Exist* (Grand Rapids: Eerdmans, 1998), esp. pp. 2-3, giving Gay's main theme and defining the concept of "practical atheism."

tives. In the chapters on Scripture, we examined the simple, single affirmative. We now disprove the nonscriptural ideas that purport to disprove judgment. We must be brief and incomplete, for it would take a book to unravel fully the mystery of judgment's disappearance.

The New England Jeremiad, the Fear of a Republic's Decline and the Social Contract

We must first examine an American form of judgment talk, the Puritan jeremiad. Their fears that God was about to judge England for its corruption, impiety and return to Catholic practices led the Puritans to flee to the New World in 1630. Their success in settling New England they saw as a sign that God had sealed a covenant with them as a people set apart for blessing, a "city upon a hill," in the famous passage from John Winthrop's sermon on the *Arbella*. They saw themselves as a new Israel. What is not always remembered is that the city's visibility meant disobedience would yield open disgrace: ". . . if we shall deal falsely with our God in this work we have undertaken and so cause him to withdraw his present help from us, we shall be made a story and a by-word through the world . . . till we be consumed out of the good land whither we are going." If New England's Puritans broke the covenant, Winthrop warned, "the Lord will surely break out in wrath against us [and] be revenged of such a perjured people." For the next century, in election-day and fast-day sermons, New England preachers pointed to natural or military calamities as God's judgments and warned the people that covenant breaking brought God's judgment.[5]

This postbiblical concept of a covenant made in 1630 with the God who helped them settle New England may have had its validity for them. Certain events may have been God's judgments on them for violating it. Yet, it was too narrowly New England's idea to apply it to colonies without covenant promises in their founding. Arguably, the Puritan jeremiad did not apply to the new nation that was founded not by an act of emigration but by an act of revolution. That did not nullify the broad biblical concept of God's judgments. The removal by obsolescence of a specific basis for judgment returned Americans to the general basis as given in Scripture. God judges all nations,

---

[5]James G. Moseley, *John Winthrop's World: History as a Story; the Story as History* (Madison: University of Wisconsin Press, 1992), pp. 31-36; Harry S. Stout, *The New England Soul: Preaching and Religious Culture in Colonial New England* (New York: Oxford University Press, 1986), pp. 69-85. I have modernized the spelling of Winthrop's words, as taken from Giles Gunn, ed., *Early American Writing* (New York: Penguin, 1994), pp. 111, 112. The classic study is Sacvan Bercovitch, *The American Jeremiad* (Madison: University of Wisconsin Press, 1978).

not just a chosen people like Israel or peoples who see themselves as new Israels.

A decade of protests against British policy culminating in the American Revolution resulted from and reinforced ideologies of republicanism and liberalism that weakened Americans' sense of the biblical doctrine of divine judgment. Cromwell's Puritan Commonwealth (1649-1653) gave some Protestant connotations to "republic," and republicanism used moral terms like "virtue"— yet without always stressing a God who judged vice. In *America's God*, Mark Noll persuasively describes how, to Europeans, the term "Christian republicanism" seemed self-contradictory (republicans often being unorthodox, Deists or atheists), while, to Americans, the two terms seemed highly compatible. As we saw, Americans brought their republican-commonsensical-national worldview to their interpretation of the Bible. They would not have done so if that worldview had openly contradicted the scriptural testimony about judgment and salvation. Their version of it did not. However, it tended subtly to erode the public dimension of that testimony: a republic's citizens must and could possess virtue (mainly, independence and good sense) to battle conspiracies of would-be tyrants; lacking it brought a decline into corruption and despotism, not divine judgment. Partly, Americans sought independence because they feared that Britain was already in decline. Republicanism highlighted a separate realm for politics, apart from religion, and thereby implied that God's judgment—in the sense of a curtain-dropping punishment—on a republic was unlikely, if not inappropriate. God might chasten a republic, however. Ministers in their sermons in church still preached on judgment, even judgment on the nation, but their citizen-hearers now had another narrative of vice-corruption-tyranny.[6]

The new American republic was virtually alone amid European monarchies, so its ideology of republicanism (later, it added liberalism and democracy) gave it a historic, nearly global, mission as a city on a hill lighting the way to liberty for all peoples. A redeemer nation, the United States took on attributes of Christ's

---

[6]Mark A. Noll, *America's God: From Jonathan Edwards to Abraham Lincoln* (New York: Oxford University Press, 2002), pp. 53-70, 73-75, 82-92 (see especially his quote from Jonathan Clark on p. 62). Noll does not examine Christian republicanism and judgment, that I can see, so I am extrapolating from his work. My thinking about republicanism and the Revolution has been greatly influenced by Bernard Bailyn, *The Ideological Origins of the American Revolution* (Cambridge, Mass.: Belknap Press, 1967); Gordon S. Wood, *The Creation of the American Republic, 1776-1787* (New York: Norton, 1969); and Gordon S. Wood, *The Radicalism of the American Revolution* (New York: Knopf, 1992). For a fuller discussion, see Steven J. Keillor, *This Rebellious House: American History and the Truth of Christianity* (Downers Grove, Ill: InterVarsity Press, 1996).

church: people of many races and ethnicities came to it for liberty; it shaped them into one new humanity; it modeled what their home nations should become. American Christians participated in the church's global mission of proclaiming the gospel, but this republican-democratic mission defined the nation and made it problematic to invoke divine judgment on the redeemer nation if it failed in a political mission nowhere mentioned in Scripture. Advocates of this mission, even atheist Tom Paine, tried to motivate Americans to greater striving by using scriptural analogies—"a fallen Old World (harboring Romish Antichrist), an Egyptian England (in bondage to a 'hardened, sullen-tempered pharaoh' [King George III], and a New Canaan charged 'by the design of Heaven' with 'the cause of all mankind.'" Yet, as Noll argues, "a religious language put to political use took on political values that altered the substance of religion."[7]

We need not address the ongoing debate over whether republicanism or liberalism was more predominant in the Revolutionary era, but liberalism also had a key role in gradually removing the concept of God's judgments from the public sphere. By liberalism we mean the ideas of John Locke and his successors that human beings were once in a state of nature without government but entered into a social contract with each other that created government to protect individuals' rights to life, liberty and property. The Declaration of Independence's "self-evident" truth that people have "inalienable rights" to "life, liberty, and the pursuit of happiness" and that governments are created by "the consent of the governed" in order "to secure these rights"—this language, as political scientist David T. Koyzis observes, "reads like a paraphrase" of Locke. Note that Puritans' covenant between God and the colonists is here replaced by a contract between individuals, a contract that presumably God cannot enforce by his judgments since he is not a party to it. In fact, the penalty inflicted on government for "becom[ing] destructive of these ends" is not divine judgment but popular revolution. In the Declaration's opening, the watchmaker God "endow[s]" individuals with rights, but then they become the only actors, creating and throwing off governments to maintain these rights. In its ending, its signers are "appealing to the supreme judge of the world," but only so that he can attest to "the rectitude of our intentions," and the American people are pictured acting alone to end the king's "abuses and usurpations."[8]

---

[7]Bercovitch analyzes the secularizing and politicizing of the jeremiad during and after the American Revolution; *American Jeremiad*, p. 121; see pp. 93-94, 118-24, 142-43. Noll analyzes Paine's skillful use of Scripture for republican purposes; *America's God*, p. 85; see pp. 83-85.
[8]*Thomas Jefferson: Writings* (New York: Library of America, 1984), pp. 19, 23; David T. Koyzis, *Political Visions and Illusions: A Survey and Christian Critique of Contemporary Ideologies*

Liberalism Changes Shape in Our History to Evade a Pursuing Divine Judge

Confusingly, liberalism has changed shape since 1776, as Americans reacted to various threats (after the threatening king) to the "sovereign individual," who lies at the heart of this ideology as the knowing self lies at the heart of worldview. Koyzis argues that "the first and most basic principle of liberalism" is that "everyone possesses property in their own person and must therefore be free to govern themselves in accordance with their own choices, provided that these choices do not infringe on the equal rights of others to do the same." This principle can be used to undercut God's right to judge individuals for their choices or to judge the government, for its duties are to the individual(s), not to God. David Koyzis identifies four stages of liberalism's development: (1), "the *night watchman state*" defending private property, especially against possible governmental interference with its uses; (2) "the *regulatory state*," defending ordinary individuals against the wealth and power gained by some individuals and corporations during the first stage; (3) "the *equal opportunity state*" that does not just prevent interference but gives compensatory advantages to individuals handicapped in the competitive race; (4) "the *choice enhancement state*," defending individuals against a fixed definition of what constitutes victory in the race, so they can define reality, and the state shelters them from negative consequences of that choice. Many Americans oppose the second, third and fourth stages. We call them conservatives, although they are classic liberals who support the sovereign individual's property rights and "the *night watchman state.*"[9]

Later stages did not restore divine judgment to the public sphere, nor have conservatives restored it. Partly, the later stages revised the ideology to compensate for historical events that we might interpret as God's judgments on it. Liberalism adapts to evade judgment (in vain) and to make that idea ever more unintelligible to its adherents. As Koyzis notes, ideologies grow out of forms of idolatry, and liberalism makes an idol of the sovereign individual, with his or her rights and freedoms.[10] We can regard the subsequent acquisition of god-like wealth and power by some sovereign individuals or their social-contract corporations as God's judgment on this idolatry, but liberalism tried to evade judgment by enlisting the state to regulate these gods and to give others an equal start in the race. The "*choice enhancement state*" protects individuals against

---

(Downers Grove, Ill.: InterVarsity Press, 2003), p. 46. I am generally indebted to Koyzis, *Political Visions*, pp. 42-71, for his analysis of liberalism.
[9]Koyzis, *Political Visions*, pp. 53, 58, 59, 61; see pp. 51-64.
[10]Ibid., pp. 27, 42-43, 47-48, 49-50.

judgment, for it "denies that there is a substantive good which human beings or their political leaders are obliged by their nature to follow."[11] Without obligations to follow a fixed good, there can be no judgments for not doing so. In their private sphere of influence, pastors may preach judgment, but liberalism undercuts any public application of that doctrine.

The Ideology of Democracy Is Used to Shelter People from Divine Judgment

Craig Gay critiques ideology as "a definition of reality" that claims to "comprehend and explain the world" and "promises power over the world and legitimates the use of this power." The United States is part of a modernizing Western civilization that stresses "human agency" and minimizes divine agency to the point where people assume "that even if God exists he is largely irrelevant to the real business of life." Ideology is one tool whereby human control can attempt to replace divine control. He analyzes how this "practical atheism" developed in various sectors of Western life and thought. It began in politics and government, he argues, as the "myth of democracy" and a "faith in the political process" verging on "a veritable apotheosis of the modern state" diminished personhood and caused "the collapse of genuine individuality into mass conformism." True, a reliance on the state as the actor in solving human problems has diminished a sense of God as actor.[12] Yet ordinary twenty-first-century Americans hardly exhibit a sterling faith in politics. American governments (before 9/11) provided relative security from foreign foes, most natural disasters and depressions—hence, by implication, from God's judgments. Sheltered by democracy, average citizens retreat to private life, individualism and an inflated democracy as worldview in which each citizen constructs his or her view of the universe, free of negative consequences. Making democratic choices, collectively or individually, sanctifies the choices and forestalls consequences. No vice exists where the virtuous method of democratic decision-making is used. Democratic deeds are not even fate-effecting. In *What's Wrong with Democracy?* Loren J. Samons focuses on democracy as a religion that makes freedom of choice an absolute. Democracy used to be judged on whether it achieved certain ends, but now it is an end in itself and a standard by which programs are judged. "Moral judgments" that limit choice "are often treated as potentially harmful, if not evil"—and Samons is dealing only with

---

[11]Ibid., p. 61.
[12]Here and above, Gay, *The Way of the (Modern) World*, pp. 31, 42; see also pp. 29-30, 32-35. The term "myth of democracy" is Tage Lindbom's term.

citizens' moral "judgments," not God's.[13]

Koyzis distinguishes "between *democracy as structure*" (rules for voting, campaigning and legislating) "and *democracy as creed*," that is, "a belief in the near infallibility of the vox populi—the voice of the people." People use the creed to shelter and justify their retreat into private individualism. The *vox populi* may shout, "The Weekend!" more than, "Smith for Congress!" Democracy is the best structure available for governmental and political purposes, Koyzis notes, but it is questionable "to extend the democratic principle . . . into the whole of life, including an array of spheres [education, religion, family, etc.] where for various reasons it is simply not appropriate." He charges that "democracy attempts to subject the whole of life to its chosen divinity," the people. In our terms, it promises humans a control that properly belongs to the judging God alone. The democratic motto— *vox populi, vox dei*—thus takes on a literal, idolatrous meaning.[14]

To use an overarching term like "democracy" is to risk minimizing our deep partisan split. Republicans and Democrats are so bitterly divided they hardly admit they participate in one democratic process. We Americans implicitly use our partisan divisions to render the idea of judgment more incomprehensible. If God used environmental problems like global warming as a judgment on the materialistic excess of free-market economies, then he would be acting in a biased, inappropriate manner as a liberal Democrat. If he judged the nation for allowing abortion on demand, then he would be acting inappropriately as a conservative Republican. Thus, he cannot judge at all. Or so we think. The correct answer to the multiple-choice question—what does God judge? (a) materialism or (b) abortion—may actually be (d) all of the above—and not the answer we prefer: (c) none of the above. God can use Republican victories to judge Democrats, and vice versa. He is not stymied by our split.

This democratic, partisan debate discourages warnings of God's judgments—understandably so. Fundamentalists and partisans have incorrectly used warnings to combat policies or ideas they opposed but that Scripture did not condemn. Yet an incorrect use does not disprove a valid doctrine. As Sundberg notes, judgment theology is "rejected" because it has been "misused." Yet "every theology across the centuries has been misused. Why single out this one?"[15] A political partisan may be disqualified from acting as the person who identifies an event as God's judgment, but that does not mean such judgments do not exist.

---

[13]Loren J. Samons II, *What's Wrong with Democracy? From Athenian Practice to American Worship* (Berkeley: University of California Press, 2004), p. 182; see pp. 175-86.

[14]Koyzis, *Political Visions*, pp. 124, 125, 138, 143 (all quoted); Gay, *The Way of the (Modern) World*, pp. 49-50.

[15]Sundberg, " 'Evil' After 9/11," p. 206.

Church-State Separation, Denominationalism, Theological Drift Quiet Judgment Talk

Church division renders one denomination's warning of judgment suspect. The Constitution's First-Amendment prohibition of any established church, and the later disestablishment of state tax-supported churches such as the Congregationalist (Connecticut) and Anglican (Virginia) ones represented a break with Christendom. Gradually, a "wall of separation" (Jefferson's words, not the Constitution's) between church and state became the accepted norm, enforced by a vigilant Supreme Court. That separation rendered problematic any attempt by a pastor or religious prophet to warn the nation's government of divine judgment if it pursued a certain policy.[16] Stephen A. Douglas protested vigorously against such warnings. He lost on slavery, but he won the long-term battle on the inappropriateness of citizens using God's name and judgments to oppose a democracy's policies.

The fragmentation of American Protestantism both necessitated disestablishment and was accelerated by it. The arrival of millions of Catholic immigrants in the nineteenth century created more religious fragmentation, which now has gone far beyond Christian denominationalism to include Islam, Judaism, Buddhism and a plethora of religions. This pluralism may make judgment impossibly complicated for us, but not for God. Yet who can authoritatively warn Americans of God's coming judgments? If a Baptist warns of judgment, then a Methodist might openly dispute the accuracy of the warning. A religious competition for market share discourages the preaching of unpopular doctrines like divine judgment.[17] A church that caters, even subtly, to the general human bias against the idea gains a competitive advantage.

Theological drift also quiets judgment talk and makes it incomprehensible. On the popular level, in the nineteenth century, the prototypical evangelical conversion shifted from one produced by warnings of judgment at a camp meeting to one produced in the child on a mother's knee or at a Sunday school that stressed God's love more than his judgment. Biblically and theologically, this is a false dichotomy, as John Stott reminds us in *The Cross of Christ*: ". . . it is the Judge himself who in holy love assumed the role of the innocent victim, for in and through the person of his Son he himself bore the penalty which he himself inflicted."[18] In an analysis of recent sermons, Marsha Witten shows how the drift

---

[16]The best single account of the doctrine of separation erroneously thought to be contained in the First Amendment is Philip Hamburger, *Separation of Church and State* (Cambridge, Mass.: Harvard University Press, 2002).

[17]David F. Wells indicts this marketing frenzy in *Above All Earthly Pow'rs: Christ in a Postmodern World* (Grand Rapids: Eerdmans, 2005).

[18]John R. W. Stott, *The Cross of Christ* (Downers Grove, Ill.: InterVarsity Press, 1986), p. 159.

has resulted in pastors "draw[ing] more dominantly on images of God as daddy or as sufferer, and tend[ing] to underplay aspects of God's judgmental characteristics even as they discuss them."[19]

At the theologians' level, James P. Martin traced the disappearance of the Last Judgment (or its importance) in Protestant thinking. Partly, the idea declined due to the lack of a "Christian interpretation of history" that could recognize "previous judgments in history" and link them to the coming Last Judgment in one "historical process." That lack is what we are trying to address. If God did not judge in current or past history, then his final judgment became "spiritualized and individualized"—and, since justification by faith already indicated the final verdict for the individual believer, the soul's immortality was highlighted and a stress on individual ethics came to replace the Judge's verdict. The well-meaning work of Christian apologists who used natural theology (general revelation) to meet new scientific arguments also undercut the notion of a unique, unparalleled event like the Last Judgment.[20] Gay is a recent apologist who also sidesteps divine judgment. By ignoring evangelicals' warnings about it, Gay exaggerates Protestants' role in starting secularization and a "disenchantment" of the world by their critique of medieval Catholic "mystery, miracle, and magic."[21] A sense of the supernatural is evident in evangelicals' proclamation of the gospel, their warnings of divine judgment and their urgent pleas to seek shelter by faith in the Savior's atoning work. Rejection of divine agency was partly caused by unbelievers' (especially intellectuals') dislike of warnings of judgment. By sidestepping this fact, Gay offers a solution (personhood with personal responsibility, unlike a depersonalizing secularism) that includes the very accountability that many secularizers rebelled against.[22]

Science, Technology and the Economy Enhance Human and Minimize Divine Agency

Gay asserts that "the plausibility—and indeed the attraction—of practical atheism in contemporary culture owes much to the impact that science and technology have had upon the modern imagination." They offer humanity a mastery over nature that enhances human agency and minimizes divine agency. To ob-

---

[19]Marsha G. Witten, *All Is Forgiven: The Secular Message in American Protestantism* (Princeton, N.J.: Princeton University Press, 1993), p. 49; see pp. 48-52.
[20]James P. Martin, *The Last Judgment in Protestant Theology from Orthodoxy to Ritschl* (Grand Rapids: Eerdmans, 1963), pp. 23, 24, 25, 27; see pp. 23-27, 41-46, 99, 103, 105.
[21]Gay, *The Way of the (Modern) World*, pp. 21, 23; see pp. 22-24, 65-72, 265-66. Gay draws on the work of Peter Berger here but accepts Berger's conclusions as his own.
[22]Ibid., pp. 279, 294.

tain practical knowledge and mastery, they focus on observable phenomena that can be "weighed, measured, or counted," utilize mathematics when possible and employ hypotheses and experimentation to determine laws that predict events in nature. As the realm of human knowledge and control is extended, the realm of divine action shrinks or disappears, people believe. This scientific and technological mindset "is at once highly practical" in stressing usable means at hand rather than final goals "and deeply skeptical" in rejecting authority and past testimony about the universe in favor of its own quantitative, observable and replicable knowledge. When it yields impressive new tools like computers or satellites, its skepticism about divinity and authority seems validated.[23]

Thus, natural disasters are no longer seen as "acts of God" and possibly God's judgments, although the insurance industry has retained that phrase. Science's "interpretive grid" sees the event as an effect caused by measurable changes in temperature, or barometric pressure or seismic activity.[24] Science's naturalistic presupposition is that only natural processes can be at work, for supernatural ones would cast uncertainty on scientific research. Yet, to conclude that natural causes eliminate divine action is to cast God as a magician who achieves his effects only if the audience cannot see his means. Visible means and observable (secondary) causes do not remove an invisible actor. When science goes beyond currently observable phenomena to offer explanations of origins, then the idea of divine judgment is undercut. God as Creator is foundational for God as Judge.

The market economy, now global, "provides the institutional context within which science, technology, and even political life operates today." Market incentives drive rapid conversion of scientific knowledge into usable and affordable technological products, the icons proving the scientific worldview. This economy "underwrites much of the plausibility of practical atheism." How does it undercut the idea of divine judgment? He does not address this issue. Certainly, "the market system" does not "reward virtue," and its division of labor complicates reality so that moralists (but not God) cannot sort out economic right from wrong.[25] Adam Smith's *Wealth of Nations* (1776) argued that the Invisible Hand of the market allocates goods and services and determines prices far more efficiently than any church or government could. Peter Minowitz notes that Smith's project was to liberate the economy from both church and state.[26] There was no need for either to regulate the economy, because

---

[23]Ibid., pp. 80, 88; see also pp. 84-86 (quoting Lewis Mumford on p. 85).
[24]Ibid., p. 80.
[25]Ibid., pp. 132, 152; see pp. 133-35, 158.

self-seeking behavior in the market worked out for the public good. The *"night watchman state"* only guarded profit seekers' property. The profit seeker supplied goods or services that were scarcest, most needed and, thus, most profitable. The medieval church helped to set a "just price" for goods and services, but that was no longer wise, said Smith. "In *Wealth of Nations,* Smith never mentions God or Providence," and nowhere in his "writings (including his correspondence) does 'Jesus,' 'Christ,' or 'the Son' appear." Smith presented a four-stage economic history (hunting and gathering, pasturage, agriculture, then commerce) that ignores the Son of Man's transcending historical role.[27]

Indirectly, in the long term, free-market economics weakened the idea of God's judgments by seeming to remove from the divine Judge a whole class of economic activities, for which people could supposedly not be judged. Free-market capitalism produces benefits, including unprecedented prosperity in America and rapid technological advances. Yet, like any human system, it is sifted out, tested and judged by God over time. No "very desirable alternatives" to free markets exist, yet a lack of good *human* alternatives does not mean an absence of *divine* judgment.[28]

Living before democracies, Smith stressed producer and retailer, but democracy contributed to a new stress on the consumer, whose role combined the democratic ethos of the citizen's liberties with the customer's price-lowering, quality-maximizing strategies of shopping around. We are prone to expand a role we find liberating and appealing (especially if it undercuts the unpopular idea of God's judgments), so the idea of consumer choice expanded beyond selecting a Ford or a Chevrolet, a Smith or Jones for Congress, to selecting preferred lifestyles, worldviews or religions—and the latter choices were considered just as immune from divine judgment as the former. Marketers' appeal to the individual's sovereignty of choice contributed to this subtle redefinition of a modern self free to construct its own personality and worldview apart from consequences imposed externally, whether by government, family or God. The *"choice enhancement state"* tries to validate this right to redefine reality.[29] This redefinition makes it seem absurd to suggest God judges individuals for choices of lifestyle, worldview or faith. For those who still see marketing and preaching as separate compartments, our critique may seem leftist; however, as an increas-

[26]Peter Minowitz, *Profits, Priests and Princes: Adam Smith's Emancipation of Economics from Politics and Religion* (Stanford, Calif.: Stanford University Press, 1993).
[27]Ibid., p. 141; Koyzis, *Political Visions,* pp. 53-58.
[28]Gay, *The Way of the (Modern) World,* p. 132. The rest of the analysis here is my own.
[29]Koyzis, *Political Visions,* pp. 61-63. Wells deals with this at length in *Above All Earthly Pow'rs.*

ingly market-driven evangelicalism subtly alters the gospel to adapt to consumer tastes that find God's judgments distasteful, defenders of orthodoxy like David Wells attack this "false premise upon which this marketing of the Church is based," that "treat[s] sinners as consumers," each of whom "defines his or her own wants. . . . In the biblical world, however, consumers are not left to define their own needs because as sinners they always misunderstand themselves."[30]

Psychology's Therapeutic Worldview Excludes the Idea of Divine Judgment

Psychology—mainly the popular versions, but these flow out of academic research—combines these secularizing forces: this science yields various technologies for healing or improving the self; prescribing and applying such technologies is a lucrative business; client-consumers utilize these services in "the project of self-construction-by-consumption," with the chosen therapy another identity-forging product along side consumer goods, sexual preference or political ideology. Religion may be added, not to escape judgment, for that is inconceivable in this self-referential project. Philip Rieff noted, "Religious man was born to be saved; psychological man is born to be pleased." (And what does "saved" mean except to be saved from judgment?) Gay criticizes this "commitment to autonomous self-creation," but not on grounds that the Creator judges self-willed rebellion. He sees self-creation producing despair and offers a modern practical atheist "a theology of personhood": "we become persons only in relation to other persons" and a personal God. This apologetic caters to modern secularism by offering it a self-construction by faith and confirms the "gravedigger hypothesis" that Protestants helped to undermine faith by using apologetics that catered to modernity. The "plasticity and absorptive capacity of contemporary Western culture" utilizes "virtually any idea," even critical ones, "in the ongoing construction and management of self." His theology of personhood will be so used.[31]

Does Evangelical Apologetics Find the Idea of God's Judgment Incomprehensible?

Our brief tour through Gay's comprehensive and learned analysis is not meant as an uncharitable criticism. Yet, if the best evangelical apologetics does not ad-

---

[30]Wells, *Above All Earthly Pow'rs*, p. 302.

[31]Gay, *The Way of the (Modern) World*, pp. 191, 214-15, 279; see also pp. 11, 71, 103, 184, 186 (quoting Rieff), 231-33, 248, 271-313. He does refer to the Last Judgment in two sentences on p. 305, but in such a way as to imply there is no judgment before "the end of history." The "gravedigger" idea is explored most fully in Os Guinness, *The Gravedigger File: Papers on the Subversion of the Modern Church* (Downers Grove, Ill.: InterVarsity Press, 1983).

dress this scriptural truth, will lesser works do so? If evangelicals steeped in a gospel of salvation from judgment by means of faith in a substitutionary atonement do not address it, who will? Not religious liberals, whose faith in Scripture was undercut by German higher criticism, the theory of evolution, and other ideas. If they rejected supernatural events while retaining ethics, will they restore divine judgment? Gay's book is a jeremiad against modern "practical atheism," but if a jeremiad contains no warning of judgment, where can we look for one? Often the Christian apologist acts as the defense attorney for a God who is seen, in C. S. Lewis's words, "in the dock," questioned and judged by modern people, when the real situation is quite the opposite. Gay presents "practical atheism" as a fate-effecting deed or thought, a worldview with logical fallacies and "ironic and unintended consequences" harmful to humanity. Human-centered modernism is "profoundly dehumanizing"; secular liberation from religion might "become at least as repressive as the worst of the traditional religions"; seeking better technology, we "impoverish ourselves"; therapeutic consumerism seeking self-satisfaction is "profoundly unsatisfying"; "the therapeutic quest for self-discovery must end in self-deception and, finally, in self-annihilation."[32] This is the worldview thinker's tactic of identifying self-contradictions in his opponent's argument. It is not a full disclosure. It showcases aspects of the faith most appealing to modern tastes (thus acting as a gravedigger) but does not mention judgment. Yet modernists do not see "practical atheism's" defects as so negative when compared with divine judgment, which they know is in the Christian alternative even when the apologist omits it. The apologist loses the best means of challenging modernism, for a doctrine so offensive to modernist ears is one that modernism cannot co-opt into its program of constructing the autonomous individual. The apologist fails "to assume a truly prophetic stance," for what do prophets do if not warn of judgment?[33]

On the positive side is Wells's recent apologetic addressed to "a postmodern world." He traces the origins of postmodernism and identifies some of its self-contradictions; however, he does stress God's judgments: "All stand under divine judgment. God thunders out his rejection of human pride, arrogance and its fraudulent sense of self-confidence in his presence. This divine No . . . stands as the unyielding barrier . . . to every attempt to forge meaning on our own terms." This judging no is not spoken "only at the end of time" but is "a present reality." Here is more than a fate-effecting deed, more "than simple cause and effect in the moral realm. God, in fact, is *active* in this judgment."[34]

---

[32]Gay, *The Way of the (Modern) World,* pp. 41, 55, 89, 193, 218, 229.
[33]Ibid., 256.

Taking God's judgments off the table places the burdens of history fully on someone else. The scientist must now protect the earth from oncoming comets or global warming. The citizen must stay informed on all threats to the republic, participate in politics to elect officeholders who can meet these threats and write letters to them if they do not. The believer must uphold a church and a faith, stay informed on threats to both, including threats from democracy, and fulfill a citizen's normal duties. The Christian intellectual must identify current challenges to the faith, trace their historical roots and offer antidotes. (By tracing the corruption of the church's thinking while its Head seemingly did nothing to judge it, Gay's book ironically implies the church can act as if its Head did not exist.) These actors' deeds are needed and commendable but will never prove sufficient to their tasks. A divine actor will not delegate his duty to judge and to save.

Yet, these hints about why the doctrine of judgment should be returned to our proclamation of the gospel—that apologetics fails without it, that it alone enables believers to escape modernism's (or postmodernism's) co-opting embrace—are only helpful hints. The real reason, the sufficient one, is that the doctrine is true. The reason why the doctrine is nearly incomprehensible to twenty-first-century Americans is that we dislike it and shelter beneath layers of nonscriptural notions that deny it. Yet, Scripture and the Son of Man in Scripture testify to the truth that God judges humanity, collectively and individually, and that the only shelter from judgment is to be found by faith in the Son of Man who himself bore this judgment on sin on the cross and offers justification to those who believe in him. That faith in that truth is not an ideology falsely promising humanity control over history but a testimony to God's agency, to his control, to a work of redemption he has accomplished. It is not falsely triumphalist, for the believer must follow the Son of Man's path of suffering obedience before glory, must be judged (chastened and disciplined) and will not be exempt from the nation's or the world's collective sufferings and judgments. Yet the Son of Man's real triumph through judgment (through his propitiatory sacrifice and their sanctifying chastening) he graciously gives to his followers, not an illusory denial of divine judgment.

---

[34]Wells, *Above All Earthly Pow'rs,* pp. 200-201.

11

Can We Warn Against Re-engineering Humanity Without Warning of Judgment?

What's done is done. Gravedigger mistakes of the past cannot be undone. If an otherwise excellent analysis of the history of our journey to practical atheism does not address divine judgment, then that handicaps our view of that history, but does it impact the future? If this conceptual, worldview analysis *will* meet twenty-first-century challenges to the Christian faith, then perhaps only historians worried about historical interpretations will care about its drawbacks. Is worldview thinking up to these challenges? To answer that question, we look at biotechnology, human genetic engineering (HGE), and related attempts to redesign human beings. Many worldview and public-policy evangelicals regard this issue as the most serious challenge for the church this century, and they may be right. At a century's start, predictions are hazardous, but Christians who oppose HGE correctly regard it with utmost concern.

We are not questioning their ends but the arguments they use as means. The only alternative is not the quietist means of doing nothing but trusting God to solve the problem without us lifting a finger. Public campaigns against HGE are appropriate in a democracy. On a personal note, I have campaigned for the state senate in Minnesota as an independent advocating a ban on human cloning. A proper goal and the propriety of pursuing it do not dictate the best means. A narrowly tactical approach to means is risky; concepts spill over beyond the issue at stake and can have gravedigger effects. HGE's far-reaching, utopian aspects allow us to examine arguments pushed to their logical conclusions, to extreme tests of their validity. Practical barriers may prevent this revolution from advancing that far, but we will assume that it can in order to assess the underlying nature of this hope and the coherence of arguments used against it.

Worldview apologetics and Christian public-policy advocacy are linked and

are considered together. Both use coherent arguments persuasive to nonbelievers. Both make their cases in the public square: apologetics, partly by defending Christianity on secular campuses; public-policy advocacy, in political
campaigns, before legislatures, courts and government agencies. Both are silent on divine judgment, an unpopular and nearly incomprehensible topic in
those settings. The same leaders and organizations conduct both activities,
which are linked symbiotically: a Christian worldview is often the best rationale for a public policy, and faith-based public policies in the United States increase the plausibility of Christian worldview. In Europe, secular policies mar-
ginalize Christianity and make it seem less plausible to nonbelievers. In the
United States, we are fortunate to have Christians stating the worldview-policy
case. We do not seek to silence them but to assess whether their case is up to
the challenge, especially in regard to their neglect of judgment. In an irenic
spirit, and because their view is a broad consensus, we will not mention individual authors' names.

The Serious Threat Posed by Possible Future Scientific Redesign of Human Beings

"This moment in history is a crucial point for the human race," according to
the introduction to one book; "technologies may prove devastating: promoting
loss or erosion of personal identity," leading to "an ever more powerful technological tyranny, or even contributing to the destruction of our species." Another introduction asserts, "The moral issue at stake in the biotech debate is
no less than what it means to be human." The winner of that debate may determine "the future of humanity." A third book worries that HGE "will inevitably lead to the conclusion that there is no core human nature that is part of
the moral order and that we are obliged to respect."[1] We can only sketch the
scientific advances and potential future ones, but they seem to justify this
alarm. Francis Collins, director of the U.S. Human Genome Project (HGP),
notes, "Some of the scenarios that sound truly scary are actually not scientifi-
cally very likely." Yet, to wait until they are tried in the lab may be to wait too
long; then, effective governmental or professional control may be impossible.

---

[1]John F. Kilner, C. Christopher Hook and Diann B. Uustal, eds., *Cutting-Edge Bioethics: A Chris-
tian Exploration of Technologies and Trends* (Grand Rapids: Eerdmans, 2002), p. ix; Charles W.
Colson and Nigel M. de S. Cameron, eds., *Human Dignity in the Biotech Century: A Christian
Vision for Public Policy* (Downers Grove, Ill.: InterVarsity Press, 2004), pp. 16, 18; Nancy R.
Pearcey, "Technology, History and Worldview," in *Genetic Ethics: Do the Ends Justify the
Genes?* ed. John F. Kilner, Rebecca D. Pentz and Frank E. Young (Grand Rapids: Eerdmans,
1997), pp. 46-47.

Collins finds some scenarios "both realistic and quite troubling."[2] The latter kind of scenarios warrant the alarm and the public campaign. We examine five books, each written from a Christian perspective.[3]

Human cloning and embryonic stem (ES) cell research have received the most publicity. Both involve inserting or removing cellular or subcellular material; cloning produces embryos from which ES cells could be extracted. ES cells are "pluripotent" ones that "can form all of the tissues of the adult body"; they might be placed in a diseased adult body "to become an insulin-secreting cell to treat diabetes, a dopaminergic neuron to treat Parkinson's or a cardiac muscle cell to treat heart disease." Yet extracting ES cells destroys the embryo, which many argue (I agree) is a human being deserving the state's protection. Adult stem cells have shown promise in treating many diseases without destroying a human life. Many who dispute the embryo's human status find human cloning troubling. The most-discussed cloning method is somatic cell nuclear transfer (SNCT): "the nuclear genetic material" from "human somatic (body) cells" is placed in a human egg cell "whose nuclear genetic material has been removed or inactivated, producing a human embryo" nearly identical to the somatic cell donor. That embryo can be put in a womb and brought to birth or used as a source of ES cells, perhaps to heal the donor, whose body might accept them better than alien ES cells.[4]

At the infinitesimal level of the gene, the double helix DNA in each cell contains forty-six chromosomes; "the chromosomes contain around 30,000 genes"; smaller still are the "base pairs" that are "one of four different pairs of nitrogen compounds." In April 2003, the HGP finished "accurately mapping the three billion base pairs of the DNA ladder and of identifying each gene" in these sequences. Identifying genes that cause specific diseases is well underway; others have a more complex causation that will take longer to identify. These advances make possible HGE: normal genes can be inserted into cells to replace disease-

---

[2]Francis S. Collins, "Human Genetics," in *Cutting-Edge Bioethics: A Christian Exploration of Technologies and Trends,* ed. John F. Kilner, C. Christopher Hook and Diann B. Uustal (Grand Rapids: Eerdmans, 2002), p. 3. Also informative on the significant barriers and some present impossibilities in biotechnology is David A. Prentice, "The Biotech Revolution: Major Issues in the Biosciences," in *Human Dignity in the Biotech Century: A Christian Vision for Public Policy,* ed. Charles W. Colson and Nigel M. de S. Cameron (Downers Grove, Ill.: InterVarsity Press, 2004), pp. 40-59.

[3]The other two works are James C. Peterson, *Genetic Turning Points: The Ethics of Human Genetic Intervention* (Grand Rapids: Eerdmans, 2001), and Timothy J. Demy and Gary P. Steward, eds., *Genetic Engineering, A Christian Response: Crucial Considerations in Shaping Life* (Grand Rapids: Kregel, 1999).

[4]Prentice, "Biotech Revolution," pp. 42-51. I am greatly indebted to Prentice's clear explanation of the science involved.

causing ones (or variants). Insertions into somatic (body) cells only affect the individual; changes in germ (egg or sperm) cells affect the offspring, their off-spring, and so on. This "germline genetic engineering" raises troubling scenarios of breeding enhanced individuals, creating an inferior class of unenhanced persons and altering human nature.[5]

There is more. Advances in computers, in miniaturization of silicon chips, in "the creation of neural-silicon junctions" connecting the human brain to the hardware of information technology, in nanotechnology operating at "one-billionth of a meter"—all might greatly enhance human performance by combining the best organic with the best inorganic capabilities. Medical uses abound: in the body itself, drugs might be made and released, monitors implanted, DNA repaired, tumor cells attacked and red blood cells replenished.[6]

Potential uses of these technologies go beyond healing diseases or replacing damaged organs. Pharmaceutical companies may be able to customize drugs to an individual's genetic makeup and create drugs that change his or her personality, blurring the definition of individuality or personality. Implanting ES cells may enable "scientists to regenerate virtually any tissue in the body, such that life expectancies are pushed well above 100 years." If the life span was pushed high enough, immortality might beckon as a goal for science, as it already does for transhumanist utopians. Genetic screening of in vitro embryos before implantation, selection of ones with above-average height or intelligence or HGE adding superhuman capacities to that embryo's genetic code could redefine "human" and create a society whose members are not united by a common humanity. Cybernetics and nano-technologies multiply the options.[7]

Without scientists, entrepreneurs, organizations and governments seeking these uses, they would remain only theoretical possibilities. Worldview, public-

[5]David Stevens, "Promise and Peril: Clinical Implications of the New Genetics," in *Human Dignity in the Biotech Century: A Christian Vision for Public Policy*, ed. Charles W. Colson and Nigel M. de S. Cameron (Downers Grove, Ill.: InterVarsity Press, 2004), pp. 100-101, 102, and Prentice, "Biotech Revolution," pp. 56-59.
[6]C. Christopher Hook, "Techno Sapiens: Nanotechnology, Cybernetics, Transhumanism and the Remaking of Humankind," in *Human Dignity in the Biotech Century: A Christian Vision for Public Policy*, ed. Charles W. Colson and Nigel M. de S. Cameron (Downers Grove, Ill.: InterVarsity Press, 2004), pp. 77-84. See also Hook, "Cybernetics and Nanotechnology," in *Cutting-Edge Bioethics: A Christian Exploration of Technologies and Trends*, ed. John F. Kilner, C. Christopher Hook and Diann B. Uustal (Grand Rapids: Eerdmans, 2002), pp. 52-68; and C. Christopher Hook, "Techno Sapiens: Improving on God's Design?" *Christianity Today* 48 (January 2004): 36-41.
[7]Francis Fukuyama, *Our Posthuman Future: Consequences of the Biotechnology Revolution* (New York: Farrar, Straus and Giroux, 2002), pp. 8-9; Lee M. Silver, *Remaking Eden: Cloning and Beyond in a Brave New World* (New York: Avon, 1997), pp. 227-33; Hook, "Techno Sapiens," pp. 79-95.

policy critics identify rich rewards to cause these actors to seek HGE and to resist any prohibition of it.[8] Scientific prestige, enormous profits and military applications create strong motives to add to the long-standing modern motive of using science to escape the biblical narrative once and for all. Darwin's theory of evolution situated the scientific "case" in distant prehistory, in hypothesized events no modern person witnesses as they occur. The search for extraterrestrial life and for a radical rearranging of the human body are partly searches for a present, visible proof that scientific discovery has defeated the biblical view of humanity for good.

Bart Kosko's *The Fuzzy Future* is one example of a techno-utopian book that exudes an anti-Christian hope. If we can download our brain's contents on to a silicon chip, then "the bit-based digital culture can compete with the old atom-based religions." It could develop its own version of heaven. "Heaven is too wonderful a concept to restrict it to the fearful imaginings of long-dead and pre-scientific men and women." And the old "heavenly deal" of suffering now and glory by and by "may be the greatest sucker strategy of all time . . . one of the most cynical swaps of present and future value: Pay now and collect after you die." If the astounding capacity of a silicon chip wedded by nanotechnology to our physical selves can create a version of heaven, then we have achieved the ultimate autonomy. "Why live in your own heaven and not *be* God?"[9] That was written in the balmy days of the late 1990s' "dot com" boom, but biotech hype has survived the crash of those hopes.

The Worldview, Public-Policy Case Against Re-engineering Humans

We have, then, the basic science, its technological applications and actors with motives and capabilities to develop and market enough of them to pose a real threat. The worldview, public-policy case for prohibiting HGE is tailored to be understandable to a secular audience. It presents scientific facts showing the present risk or future impossibility of certain HGE scenarios. It uses concepts such as "the diagnosis/therapy gap," a period when we can tell people they have a genetic defect but we cannot treat it, and so they may be discriminated against. It draws "a moral boundary" "between *healing* and *enhancement*" that a secular audience can understand. These arguments may be temporary (scien-

---

[8]C. Ben Mitchell points out that scientists are often also entrepreneurs; "The New Genetics and the Dignity of Humankind," in *Human Dignity in the Biotech Century: A Christian Vision for Public Policy,* ed. Charles W. Colson and Nigel M. de S. Cameron (Downers Grove, Ill.: Inter-Varsity Press, 2004), pp. 60, 71-74.

[9]Bart Kosko, *The Fuzzy Future: From Society and Science to Heaven in a Chip* (New York: Harmony Books, 1999), pp. 252-56.

tists may end risks or close gaps), arbitrary or hard to define (biotech proponents try to blur boundaries) or partial (each aims at one scenario, but a movement needs an overarching, integrating case).[10]

The overarching, integrating argument is that we must prohibit HGE to preserve humanity and human nature. "We must resist the new eugenicists if we
are to preserve a truly human future." Implicit in this appeal to a secular audience is the warning that HGE is a fate-effecting deed with a self-contradiction:
in trying to enhance human nature, we would destroy it. To their credit, worldview, public-policy advocates include God in their case: "Only as we respect
God's design and plans for humanity can there be any long-term hope of pro-
tecting and preserving human significance and dignity—in fact the very species
homo sapiens, the bearer of the image of God." The *imago Dei* (Genesis 1:26-
27; 5:1) figures prominently in the five books mentioned above.[11] It is presented
positively, for a secular audience, as a sign of "human significance." That God
holds his image-bearers accountable for their use of their high standing is rarely
made explicit. A Genesis worldview forms part of a broader political strategy,
modeled after the pro-life strategy of enlisting secular allies by "learn[ing] *how
to communicate in a secularized public square*." The goal is to secure majority
support for a ban on human cloning, on germline HGE and on discrimination
based on genetic tests. Advocates frame the issue as a defense of human nature;
appeals to voters' self-interest are felt to be more effective in our democracy
than are appeals based on Scripture.[12]

Assessing the Worldview, Public-Policy Argument Against HGE: Part 1

A recent analysis by sociologist John H. Evans (*Playing God,* 2002) of the HGE
debate from 1959 to 1999 helps us to begin to assess this appeal. The news is not
encouraging. He distinguishes a "thick" debate involving a "substantive rational-

---

[10]Prentice, "Biotech Revolution," pp. 45, 52, 53, 55, 58; C. Ben Mitchell, "The New Genetics,"
pp. 64-65; Hook, "Techno Sapiens," p. 94, all in *Beyond Human Dignity;* Silver, *Remaking
Eden,* p. 229.

[11]Mitchell, "New Genetics," p. 69; *Cutting-Edge Bioethics,* p. x; see also p. ix (implying the self-
contradiction). There are twenty-three page references for "image of God" in the index to *Human Dignity in the Biotech Century* (p. 249); eleven in the index to *Genetic Ethics* (p. 280);
five in *Genetic Turning Points* (p. 362); and twenty-five in *Genetic Engineering* (p. 318). *Cutting-Edge Bioethics* does not index the term, but it is certainly present (e.g., pp. x, 28, 51).

[12]Paige Comstock Cunningham, "Learning from Our Mistakes: The Pro-Life Cause and the New
Bioethics," p. 159; see pp. 136-59; Wesley J. Smith, "Lessons from the Cloning Debate: The
Need For a Secular Approach," pp. 182-99 (see especially p. 183); and "The Sanctity of Life
in a Brave New World: A Manifesto on Biotechnology and Human Dignity," pp. 240-42, all in
Human Dignity in the Biotech Century: A Christian Vision for Public Policy, ed. Charles W.
Colson and Nigel M. de S. Cameron (Downers Grove, Ill.: InterVarsity Press, 2004).

ity" in which ultimate ends (even theological ones) were allowed from a "thin" debate of "formal rationality" in which scientists and bioethicists eliminated all but a few narrow "*assumed* ends" and then further narrowed it to a calculation of which technological means could best accomplish those ends. Evans's sociological analysis is revealing. After utopian scientists proposed ultimate ends for HGE in the 1950s, liberal Protestant theologians objected, from an already "thinned" view, that religion was ethics and HGE was unethical. Their view was further narrowed to four ends: autonomy, beneficence, nonmaleficence (not hurting people) and justice. In the 1970s and 1980s, "push[ing] religion aside" but taking the four ends as givens, a bioethics profession emerged with the government advisory commissions that used bioethics to placate public concern while giving scientists maximum freedom. When attacked, scientists drew a line between healing and enhancement, retreated from the latter and dropped germline HGE. By 1998, the line was blurred, germline HGE was back on the table, and "theologians were no longer seen as serious contributors to the debate" but as "spokespersons" for religious citizens "closely watching the cloning debate."[13]

Even when public concern was at its height in 1997 after news of Dolly the cloned sheep, the resulting National Bioethics Advisory Commission (NBAC) merely listened to religious arguments against human cloning to reassure the public that it was listening. In the end, "the commissioners recommended a temporary moratorium on creating a child through cloning, but the only argument they could agree upon to support this policy was that cloning is not safe."[14] Of course, scientific advances might later make it safer. As Evans describes it, the history of the HGE debate resembles a shell game: public, religious concerns about "playing God" trigger a semantic shuffling of terms and a flurry of professional activity during which theology always loses, religious citizens never find their concerns under any shell or really addressed in any bioethics report and researchers always win their freedom to continue.

By grounding human nature in God's creation of humanity in his image, a worldview, public-policy argument partially avoids the "thinning" Evans identifies. Its evangelical and Catholic proponents do not reduce religion to ethics. Worldview thinking embraces broad approaches to issues. Yet, an argument for preserving an image-of-God-based human nature does thin out theology by including only God's creation ends and avoiding his judging-and-saving ends in history and the Son of

---

[13]John H. Evans, *Playing God? Human Genetic Engineering and the Rationalization of Public Bioethical Debate* (Chicago: University of Chicago Press, 2002), pp. 13, 88, 189; see also pp. 4-5, 14-18, 27, 47-52, 55-69, 73-74, 77, 81-85, 87, 99-101, 129, 135, 141-48, 151, 184-86, 188.
[14]Ibid., p. 191; see pp. 188-91.

Man's judging-and-saving trajectory. That represents less than a full disclosure. Human frailty and mortality are divine judgments (Genesis 3). The informed secularist knows that is the Christian view. God is merciful and may allow any one limitation or cause of death to be ended by science and medicine. Cumulatively, many such breakthroughs might encourage humanity to set a goal of ending limitations and death. To pursue that goal seriously is to seek to undo God's judgments. Only the Judge can defend his own judgments. One person cannot easily persuade another to preserve death as essential to human significance. This case awkwardly tries to persuade the public that judgments are natural to the system, that to evade them is to destroy our humanity, that death safeguards human dignity. This case does not deny human sin but sidesteps divine judgment.[15]

Practically, how can defenders of the Creator's prerogatives draw lines between acceptable and unacceptable science and enforce them against researchers determined to step across the lines? Parents draw a line, but children edge closer to it and then across it, asking "Is this too far? Surely this small step is OK?" The boundary between healing and enhancement will also be pushed and tested by researchers who know the science better than do the enforcers. Only a divine Judge who knows motives and his own plans can decide when enough is enough, when a project's backers seek to create an enhanced person to defy his limits on humanity. We can warn them there is such a Judge and avoid taking on ourselves an impossible task.

Worldview, public-policy arguments do not deny Christ's life and work, and these are shared with other Christians as one more reason to oppose HGE. One piece that addresses frailty and death as consequences of sin, and Christ's work as the one way to overcome these, is Amy Michelle Debaet's article in *Ethics & Medicine* (summer 2005). But the argument is typically based on general revelation, the created order, a natural theology and natural law, which do not require belief in Christ. Special revelation, especially of judgment, is often absent. Yet it is anachronistic to stop with Genesis 1 or Genesis 3 and not tell the later history of Israel and Christ. Special revelation, too, is addressed to nonbelievers, through the Word and not nature, albeit they may not believe it. What other viewpoint censors itself by omitting what its opponents might not accept? Of course, Christians are still free inside the church to warn of judgment, but advocates discourage doing so in the public square. Warnings are thereby trivialized as mere private opinions. Where else would one warn of God's judgment

---

[15]"Death is a very natural part of the ecosystem human beings inhabit"—an argument a secular ecologist can make but one that sidesteps death as divine judgment; Hook, "Techno Sapiens," in *Human Dignity*, p. 95.

on a nation except in the public square? We are ambassadors. Judgment is part of our home government's foreign policy. To talk about it only in church is like embassy staff only holding in-house chats about their government's policy.

Advocates might respond that they accept the reality of this "thin" debate by "thinning" their case from the start and translating it into secular individualistic reasons that can win that debate. Evans shows the other side can play this game, too. Scientists can temporarily limit their ends or means when threatened with public outcry, only to expand these again later with the attractive rhetoric of personal autonomy. Their promised cures for individuals in the near future prove more persuasive in this context than long-term worries about undoing that collective, abstract concept called human nature. What Evans describes is a public-policy machine that reduces substantive concerns to four bioethical ends and calculates what means best achieve those ends. Whether one comes to the machine with "thick" ideas or has already "thinned" out one's own ideas, the result is the same. The machine wins.

Worldview thinking has its own reason to be alarmed about HGE. As a philosophically oriented system, it starts with the given nature of things, which serves as a set of axioms from which moral principles can then be deduced. Transhumanist and posthumanist projects to re-engineer human beings threaten to eliminate these axioms. Genetically unenhanced people could continue to base their worldview on the old nature of things; however, those with enhanced genes and implanted nano-devices might then claim it was rational to assume another worldview, not as a matter of opinion but as a reflection of their different reality. Postmodernists relish this dilemma, as confirmation of their case that the notion of one objective reality that can be accurately represented in one worldview is a mistake. They would applaud the end of old deductive certainties. (That is not my position!) Worldview thinkers displays a distaste for history, for the ongoing stream of events causing unpredictable change. They see their foes, postmodernists, using historical change as an argument for relativism, and they dislike it accordingly. "In postmodernism," one worldview advocate writes, "contingency is understood to mean there is no objective moral order to which we must submit. There is only a constant flux of uninterpreted events, of history, which we are free to master according to our own purposes."[16] The reaction is to try to dam up the stream of

---

[16]Pearcey, "Technology, History and Worldview," in *Genetic Ethics,* p. 45. Pearcey later adds (p. 46) that "the order of the world is open to *re*-ordering—both by God and by human beings, who have the power to inject new events into chains of cause and effect." Yet this line of thought is not further developed to show how God injects new events in order to maintain his moral order, and the worldview stress on an unchanging order is not really surmounted here.

events with a wall of axioms from natural theology.

Yet this is a false choice: a history-distrusting, fixed, objective worldview versus a postmodern history-and-contingency-loving relativism. What guarantees a fixed objective moral order is God's mastery of the flux of events by means of judging events, now and at the Last Judgment (Revelation 20), an event when his moral order is upheld by its serving as the basis for his verdicts. By its silence on God's judgments, worldview thinking conceptually (not really!) deprives God of his major means of upholding moral order and devolves that duty on Christians' apologetics and political advocacy.

A secular writer, Francis Fukuyama, famously announced *The End of History* (1989, 1992): history was the battle of ideologies; free-market, liberal democracy had won that battle; the lack of any realistic rivals ended history. Fukuyama recently wrote *Our Posthuman Future: Consequences of the Biotechnology Revolution* (2002), in which he responds to his "more perceptive critics" who point out that "there can be no end of history without an end of modern natural science and technology," and biotechnology promises to provide governments and individuals with powerful new tools that will reignite ideological quarrels, this time over their proper use or non-use.[17]

One Christian opponent of HGE and cyber-nano enhancements commendably admits that it will prove impossible to construct a dam to halt the biotech revolution: a consensus on "limiting or forbidding certain areas of research" is highly unlikely, and even if we achieved it, "policing such restrictions will be essentially impossible" due to "the force of human curiosity, as well as the stubborn human heart's universal propensity to rebel against restriction." The only hope is to "direct the development" by "prepar[ing] defenses while we create the devices themselves."[18] We cannot know how a battle of defenses versus devices would play out, but this is a more realistic scenario of events in the near future, at least.

Applying God's Judgments and the Son of Man's Triumph to a Christian View of HGE

The ideas we considered in prior chapters—especially the Son of Man as history's meaning—give us an alternative to a fixed, philosophical worldview or a postmodern relativism. They represent a "thick" Christian view that does not limit itself to Genesis 1 but incorporates the later history of salvation: the Fall

---

[17]Francis Fukuyama, *Our Posthuman Future: Consequences of the Biotechnology Revolution* (New York: Farrar, Straus and Giroux, 2002), p. 15.
[18]Hook, "Techno Sapiens," in *Human Dignity*, pp. 90-91.

(Genesis 3), Israel as God's chosen start at redeeming humanity, the Son of Man fulfilling Israel's mission, his descent to the cross, his resurrection, his ascent to God's right hand and his promised return. This is one salvation history. It is anachronistic to halt it at some earlier point and often impossible to subdivide it and only discuss one part of what is one whole plan.

Genesis 3 provides a full disclosure: the limitations, pains and death that we all experience are God's judgments on us, not part of a fixed, original, created order. The *imago Dei* and dominion given to humanity brought accountability; judgment for disobedience came as God had warned (Genesis 1:26; 2:17). Our intense desire to transcend judgments, gain immortality and escape the flesh's frailty is not something unnatural that can be repressed by arguments that dying is essential to our human nature or to a fixed natural order. Desire for eternal life is part of the *imago Dei*: "He has also set eternity in the hearts of men" (Ecclesiastes 3:11) and even the limitation mentioned there—"yet they cannot fathom what God has done from beginning to end" (Ecclesiastes 3:11)—is partly removed in the New Testament. There God graciously placed his judgment for sin on the innocent Son in order to redeem us from judgment and eventually to lavish on us far more than we possessed before the Fall. The Son of Man's path of obedient suffering before victory and vindication at the Father's chosen time is there revealed as the only path to redemption and glory. The end result is all that our desire for transcending judgment could wish: Christ "by the power that enables him to bring everything under his control, will transform our lowly bodies so that they will be like his glorious body"; the lowly body goes from "perishable" to "imperishable," from "dishonor" to "glory," from "weakness" to "power," from "a natural body" to "a spiritual body" (Philippians 3:21; 1 Corinthians 15:42-44).

God desires to fellowship with people who have been redeemed and given imperishable, spiritual bodies necessary for that face-to-face fellowship. Our testimony to our generation must go beyond Genesis 1. It cannot stop there for tactical reasons, for philosophical coherence, not even for a democratic debate. God is more gracious than a natural-theology picture of a system designer makes him appear. When discussing our stewardship over God's created plants and animals, it may be possible to deal only with the Genesis 1 dominion. When we discuss the future of God's image bearers, we distort the issue if we stop with Genesis 1. Judgment and salvation are two sides of one coin, God's righteous activity in history. We cannot mention only salvation to make our message more palatable to a secular audience. It is a salvation from judgment. Judgment has begun in our limitations, frailty and mortality. To be faithful to Scripture, we must tell the full story—creation, fall, judgment, salvation.

This gracious action of God to redeem us from judgment makes the transhumanist and posthumanist project gravely culpable. Thus, the worldview, public-policy case that indicts this project as totalitarian or postmodern or a destroyer of human freedom and human nature vastly understates its guilt. At its heart, this is a project to render the Son of Man's death and resurrection superfluous, to achieve similar humanity-transforming effects apart from Christ and, thus, to establish its own meaning for history. It openly rejects an astonishingly gracious divine initiative and insists on attempting to raise humanity by its own biotech bootstraps. The flogging, the humiliation, the crown of thorns, the mocking robe, the nails—all it hopes to render superfluous, superseded by technological wizardry that delivers humanity without all this pain and sacrificial love that it regards as the misconceived idea of "long-dead and pre-scientific men and women." That is the transhumanist project when seen in light of the cross. Its spirit is anti-Christ, although the antichrist prophesied in Scripture may arise out of another movement or time period. It displays the same ambition for Godlike powers, the same lawlessness in overthrowing God's order and his judgments, the same desire to outdo the splendor of Christ, his coming and his works, and to subordinate these to its own (2 Thessalonians 2:3-12).

The contest between the Son of Man's path to transcendence and the transhumanist, posthumanist technology of transcendence will be decided in the course of future events. Scripture testifies and prophesies that the Son of Man will prevail, and we believe that. This promised event, a public event, will be seen by those who expected it and those who did not, and its interpretation will be obvious to all. Contrary to postmodernism, it will not be a text with an unclear interpretation. When the Son of Man returns in glory no one will read this as his humiliating defeat. There will be no alternative, subversive, deconstructive readings.

Assessing the Worldview, Public-Policy Argument Against HGE: Part 2

Almost as an aside, we note that worldview thinking has had the positive effect of critiquing fundamentalist views that scorned intellectual thought, cast warnings of judgment on people they disliked, misused end-time prophecies to support a partisan or nationalistic position, identified every passing dictator as the antichrist, exaggerated the importance of current events and was too impatient about the pace of God's judgments or history's changes. A fundamentalist might point to HGE and say the end times are on us. The Hebrew idea of *mishpat,* of the long sifting-out judgment, has helped us to avoid the error of an overly turbulent notion of the stream of events, an overly historical view of Christianity— as if all was subject to contingency and nothing fixed. Worldview thinking corrected for this error, but it has achieved such prominence as to need critiquing.

Otherwise, its resources, leadership and institutional strength will cause it to prevail despite conceptual weaknesses.

Evans's sociological analysis helps explain its resources and institutional strength: he sees a competition between writers for resources and between professions for "jurisdiction" over HGE. This is not a cynical view that people write only what decision makers want to hear. "However, one would be naive to think that writers do not make compromises at the margins in order to obtain what is often the greatest resource—being listened to." Within the various communities (bioethical, governmental, scientific, medical), a writer or speaker must agree with its basic assumptions to gain a hearing. Each professional community tries to frame the HGE issue around terms and assumptions that lead to placing that issue in its jurisdiction.[19]

Worldview, public-policy advocates conform to these rules; we can empathize with their dilemma: conform or be ignored. At the margins, they make compromises with Christian theology by stressing creation and ignoring judgment. Here is where the idea of Christian faith as a worldview is helpful to professionals, for it can be phrased as one outlook among many, a modest language that facilitates receiving a place on the panel discussion or a grant, or being listened to. Modern societies create specialized professions for needed functions but none to specialize in warning of divine judgment. The church has pastors to preach that, but denominationalism fragments this message, and society grants secular professionals such high status as to put religious ones in the shade, as David Wells has argued. Secularism almost forces the church to use parachurch advocates or believing professionals—an evangelical knowledge class—to express its concerns about issues like HGE. They may change the case at the margins to exclude judgment and special revelation, which seem central to a Christian case against HGE. Influence is a two-way street: it would be naive not to recognize that what poses as a Christian view pushing into the secular public square can often really be a rewrite of the Christian view that is necessitated by the professional's need to gain a hearing—but in the process ends up influencing the church to minimize the concept of judgment.[20]

---

[19]Evans, *Playing God?* p. 27; see also pp. 28-29.
[20]An example is bioethicist James C. Peterson's *Genetic Turning Points,* which employs "the classic Christian tradition" (pp. 3, 15) as one possible worldview whose insights nonbelievers might find helpful; however, Peterson redefines the "tradition" to sidestep judgment and Christ's judgment-bearing atonement (pp. 71, 75); "thins" theology down to five "attitudes" roughly commensurable with the four bioethical ends (p. 43); uses Paul's resurrection discourse in 1 Corinthians 15 to support HGE's altering of our bodies, without specifying that the means to transformation (God's versus our's) are diametrically opposed (p. 280); equates cloning with identical twins despite the different means (natural, that is, God's creating, ver-

Again, that is not a conspiracy theory or a postmodern reading of ideas by their proponents' social location instead of their reasonableness. We have analyzed the worldview, public-policy advocates' ideas on their merits. Yet, realistically, the same pressures Evans sees operating on secular professionals also operate on evangelical ones. Thus, pastors and laity must join in the debate about HGE and similar moral issues. They lack experts' detailed knowledge and ought not to claim to have it if they do not. Yet they do not face the pressures professionals face; they do possess a "thick" Christian theology that includes divine judgment; their arguments may make more sense than this "thinned" bioethical discourse. Because of its professional need to gain a hearing, an evangelical knowledge class may be handicapped in presenting the full, "thick" Christian argument in the public square.

Worldview apologetics and public-policy advocacy might be examples of how the church of Christ is slow to adapt to new trends and then, when it adapts by adopting new ideas, they are already dated. These two approaches are well designed for the 1920s to the 1970s, for a time of reasoned debate over science and ideas and ideologies; they appropriately correct the fundamentalist mistakes of that era by stressing a reasoned, persuasive case with logical consistency and philosophical coherence that can motivate believers to engage in politics and help persuade nonbelievers to allow this political action; they operate on the modernist assumption that people approach issues rationally, that the soundest ideas win the debate and that governments can then use the soundest ideas in public policies that can be enforced.

Quite possibly, the twenty-first century presents a quite different situation. The defeat of communism and socialism removed much ideological debate, and the triumph of a global capitalism has made ideas into commodities that succeed or fail on their marketing appeal as much as their reasonableness. The Internet, off-shore production and other trends render nearly obsolete the notion of one government enforcing the policy that won the debate, in any restrictive sense. Promoters of outlawed or regulated ideas or products produce them in another country and still market them in the prohibiting nation. Nearly incomprehensible is the idea of winning any debate: supporters of the defeated idea spread it

---

sus our self-interested motives for cloning) and uses "genetic twinning" as a euphemism for human cloning (pp. 296-97, 301-2); and uses a therapeutic reading of the gospel to justify human cloning for therapeutic ends (pp. 344-51). The manner in which Peterson uses Christian-worldview and professional-bioethical discourse to arrive at an openness to human cloning ought to be sobering for the anti-cloning majority of evangelicals. In terms of Evans's analysis, Peterson advances an *"advisory jurisdiction"* for bioethics [over theology], which "interprets, buffers, or partially modifies actions taken by another profession [theology] within the latter's full jurisdiction"; Evans, *Playing God*, p. 32.

at will through chat rooms, websites and so on. Postmodernism and consumerism create communities of people who cannot be persuaded by one idea's superior reasonableness, since they reject the concept of one, objective truth. And, radical Islamists are America's current major enemy, one not open to contrary views however reasonably their advocates state them. Closer to home, the scientific community may not be open to reasonable concepts of limiting science. Science has acquired such momentum that it may be past the idea stage and into the stage of rapid, onrushing events, of startling new discoveries. The brainstorming is over. It is time to harvest the rich results of research. Scientists may not accept any limitations on their right of harvest.

The church may be specializing in rational ideas and in worldview thinking just when their market value, their status and impact in society, has declined significantly. We may be entering the time of decisive events, when the scriptural truth of God's judgments in human history is more relevant to current and future issues than are ideas and worldviews.

Examining one issue, HGE, cannot prove that those are the coming realities. Yet judgment is so central in Scripture that it cannot be relegated to a peripheral position in a Christian case against HGE, and that extreme project shows that it cannot be made peripheral at all. We must warn our generation that pursuing the transhumanist project will bring judgment and cannot succeed. Democratic discourse demands that we speak as if it could succeed, as if the human future is in peril. That forces us to say that the Son of Man's triumph is uncertain. It is democracy talk mandated in our public square: all debaters must speak as if the democratic process had the final word. With good intentions, worldview-public policy advocates conform to these rules. Votes are key words although not the final word. We proceed to democracy and judgment in our next chapter. Our political involvement cannot mean encouraging a democracy to believe it is exempt from the divine *mishpat* other systems face. The "objective moral order" is finally established by God's *mishpat.* The Son of Man's triumph is not negotiable. Presenting Christianity as one worldview among many may be justified in certain contexts, for limited occasions. We cannot let that be construed as a surrender of the truth of his triumph. Such surrender is not an act of humility, for the simple reason that it is someone else's hard-won triumph. It is modest for me to give up my own claims, but not those that belong to some one else. That is presumptuous.

12

What Is Our Generation's Impending Crisis?

It is time to draw this discussion to a conclusion that takes us back to our start, our survey of the left, center and right—to democracy, politics and divine judgment. We escaped our narrow, culture-bound idea of judgment to discover in the Old Testament *mishpat* a broad idea of a lengthy sifting-out process, a concept more usable in interpreting our history. We saw that Christianity is an events-based history of salvation and an interpretation of all of history, with the Son of Man's descent, ascent and return constituting history's meaning. Like Israel's Old Testament history, his trajectory involved judgment and salvation as two sides of one coin: his descent meant judgment on him and a proffered salvation for us; following his path is the one means to escape judgment (a curtain-dropping punishment, that is); his future return vindicates (saves) those who followed it and him and refutes and confutes (judges) those who rejected it and him. We applied *mishpat* and the Son of Man's triumph to the War of 1812 and the causes of the Civil War. As an interpretation of history, Christianity ought to have clues as to how to interpret U.S. history—and it does. Then we examined judgment as a concept: first in the past, when the idea became nearly incomprehensible; then in the future (so to speak), when only that idea can adequately address the biotech HGE threatening us; now, we turn to the present, to politics.

We must make an attempt at applying judgment to present politics. It is the hardest task; its difficulty causes some to shy away from the idea. Democracy demands that public speakers not warn of judgment, and Christian public-policy advocates tailor their arguments to conform to this demand. To bypass present politics would be mistakenly to conform to it, too, and to imply that judgment applies only to the distant past. As an interpretation of history, Christianity cannot be clueless about present events either—and it is not: the September 11 tragedy, its aftermath and its character as a judgment on the nation for the causes we tentatively identified. Finally, political operatives point to Election Day as a kind of Judgment Day—support us now or terrible consequences will come from our opponents' victories. A concept of a higher, divine judgment can liberate us from this dire, either-or ultimatum.

The application to present politics is not without potential pitfalls. Partisan bias in our application would condemn and end it. That is one flaw that ended Falwell's and Robertson's attempt after September 11. Warning of judgment is fraught with a potential for self-serving motives. In my home state, Minnesota, it is a gross misdemeanor to "threaten . . . temporal or spiritual injury against an individual to compel the individual to vote for or against a candidate or ballot question."[1] If narrowly applied to self-seeking candidates and injuries to individuals, that seems proper; very broadly interpreted, it could outlaw warnings of divine judgment on the nation (or Minnesota). A candidate who threatens her way into office all but disqualifies and disproves her own warnings but not the concept of divine judgment.

Even discussing the topic outside of a campaign has its dangers. We lack the advantages of hindsight, that invaluable aid to the historian. God's *mishpat* is a slow, unfolding process that is still incomplete. The unrighteous still can repent; the righteous still might fall away; the results of the sifting are not yet final. Also, we cannot be exhaustive but can consider only some tentative suggestions of how God might be judging both political parties, the nation and the church in current events. A tentative sketch can show that partisan divisions do not render the idea no longer usable. As we noted earlier, the answer to the multiple-choice question (for what offenses might God judge America?) may be "all of the above"; God is not paralyzed by the either-or false choices of our politics; he can use the Republicans to judge the Democrats and vice versa. A tentative sketch can show how this may be so.

To Warn of Judgment Is to Be Salt and Light in Our Democracy

Starting from the general and moving toward the particular, we can say that Christians who warn of judgment, paradoxically, are obeying Jeremiah's word (Jeremiah 29:7) to the exiles, to "seek the peace and prosperity of the city" we live in. As our democracy rejected the truth that it is under God's judgment, so it drifted from the truth that a democracy, too, suffers from its policies' consequences. First, it stared down prophets warning of divine judgment; second, it stared down analysts warning that certain policies will cause long-term disaster. Can we regard that as a coincidence? We cannot prove the first caused the second; the denial of judgment so gradually yet completely triumphed in our think-

---

[1]*Minnesota Statutes* (2002) 211B.07 (quoted only in part).

ing that we cannot identify a sequence of events—first this, then that. Yet Scripture teaches that God confuses human counsels after people reject him. Jeremiah also said, "The wise . . . will be dismayed and trapped. / Since they have rejected the word of the LORD, / what kind of wisdom do they have?" (Jeremiah 8:9). God is an ever-active judge; his sifting out is the norm, not the exception; a case of his judgment is not some freakish occurrence that requires strong proof before we credit it.

Here, we revisit Oliver O'Donovan's view of the United States as "a state freed from all responsibility to recognise God's self-disclosure in history" (in the Son of Man), a state that refuses to say, "He must increase, I must decrease."[2] (That is not to say that other nations make that confession.) Instead, it points to an increasing proportion of its citizens who do not believe in Christ and argues that a pluralist discourse must increase and talk of his triumph must decrease. Yet, this relativizing and pluralizing of religious truth is accompanied, for example, by candidates' and parties' relativizing of budgetary truths such as the following: decreasing taxes and increasing government spending will eventually lead to fiscal disaster. Democracy loses the capacity to forge a consensus that the latter is a truth binding on it and on all who engage in its processes. Instead, for example, centrists seeking to forge a consensus in the Penn National Commission make discourse into the absolute. That legitimates the discourse of "deficits are harmless" and marginalizes "the dogmatism" of O'Donovan's Christian view—a trend noted by Joseph Stowell at the prayer breakfast.[3]

Followers of the Son of Man's path are not revolutionaries seeking the immediate overthrow of pluralist democracy any more than he was one. His final "increase" (and theirs) will come at the Father's time. Meanwhile, they obey democracy's laws but warn of judgment on it, too, and that warning—although not seen as proper democratic discourse—can help to preserve it as salt preserves meat although *(because)* it is not meat. As Herbert Butterfield cautioned, "The processes of time have a curious way of bringing out the faultiness that is concealed in a system which at first view seems to be satisfactory."[4] So we warn that God tests

---

[2]Oliver O'Donovan, *Desire of the Nations:Rediscovering the Roots of Political Theology* (Cambridge: Cambridge University Press, 1996), pp. 219, 244, 245.

[3]Judith Rodin and Stephen P. Steinberg, eds., *Public Discourse in America: Conversation and Community in the Twenty-First Century* (Philadelphia: University of Pennsylvania Press, 2003), p. xii; see pp. xiv-xv. The "aftermath" of the September 11 tragedy is referred to on p. xiv as an example of the need for "improving public discourse" in order to create "inclusive and effective communities" whose citizens "can contribute to the collective tasks of our shared communal existence."

[4]Herbert Butterfield, *Herbert Butterfield on History*, ed. Robin Winks (New York: Garland, 1985), p. 53.

and sifts every system, including democracy, in the course of events.

Here we revisit the "fate-effecting deed," for consequences of policies appear to be only that: believers suspect God's hand is involved (for reasons given above), but as secularists doubt that, they also come to doubt the deed's efficacy to cause fate. "Democracy as creed" comes to believe that the democratically chosen deed does not bring its fate, that policies can be ingeniously designed to avoid that fate, that free markets make private vices into public fate-avoiding benefits, that "Fate!" is just the cry of opponents of the deed and that there is no Providence insuring that deeds meet their just fate. This creed is idolatry, and the Old Testament leaves us expecting a divine judgment on idolatry.[5] We find a corruption of the democratic process: Democrats and Republicans reinvent governing as the permanent campaign; spin rules; non-demagogues lose.[6] Henry Adams's book title tells it all with alliteration: *The Degradation of the Democratic Dogma* (1919). Can we believe degradation is accidental? The common element in democracy's rejection of religious prophets and concerned analysts is its self-referential self-worship—it rejects all outside voices warning of consequences.

A degradation of language also results, and it reduces prophets' and analysts' words to mere pleading, in both senses of the word—an argument for a certain position or political party, and one whose success or failure depends utterly on hearers' acceptance of it. The sovereign individual is in charge, with the remote control in his hand: if he dislikes the pleading, he presses the Off button and the pleaders disappear. Talk of judgment is seen as just talk that means only "I *really* dislike this policy." And some speakers do resort to harsh moralizing language and "moral judgments" to try to reclaim some power that the audience has seized. What we seek is neither extreme but to do our best to discern outlines in the current chain of events, of cause and effect, so as to restore the idea of God's judgments, not ours, as a real category of events—and to refute the idea that it is so impossibly unknowable that it is a waste of time to consider it. As an illustration, consider the statement "Prepare to meet your God" that appeared on road signs around rural America for many decades. A democracy sees this as a perpetual plea and may regard rust on a few existing signs and removal of countless others as indications it has successfully ignored and outlived the

---

[5]David T. Koyzis, *Political Visions and Illusions: A Survey and Christian Critique of Contemporary Ideologies* (Downers Grove, Ill.: InterVarsity Press, 2003), pp. 27-30, 124-29. Only the idea of democracy as creed comes from Koyzis; the other ideas here I take responsibility for, although they are not uniquely mine.

[6]See, e.g., Joe Klein, "The Perils of the Permanent Campaign," *Time,* November 7, 2005, pp. 44, 47.

plea. In its context in Amos 4:12, this is not a plea for repentance but God's declaration that the time for repentance is over and the time for judgment is at hand ("I will do this to you"). We seek to discern what our generation's impending crises—events and judgments—may possibly be.

A Complicated Cause-and-Effect Link Between Moral and Fiscal Bankruptcy

As an example, we turn to the complicated interactions of moral and budget politics in the past thirty years—not to replay the he said/she said political speeches that come from both parties, and not to announce a nonpartisan we said position that can resolve the dispute (impossible), but to try to discern how God is acting in and through these issues. We picture the bottom line here to be a fiscal one, partly in order to deal with hard monetary data and to stress facts over opinions, but with the moral issue of abortion being a crucial factor leading to a potential fiscal crisis. Deficits occur in budgets when outlays exceed incomes whether in a household budget, the national government's budget or the nation's exports compared to its imports. Deficits in budgets are fate-effecting deeds causing bankruptcy or dependence on foreign lenders or devaluation of our currency or another economic penalty. Deficit spending and enormous debts may involve deception: we promise to pay back sums that we are unlikely ever to be able to repay. Candidates' and parties' promises to voters, voters' inflated expectations and the promises of the "equal opportunity state" and the "choice enhancement state" have helped to push these various budgets deeply into deficit.[7]

Long before *Roe* v. *Wade* (1973) brought abortion onto the national political agenda, there was a history of deficits. During the early New Deal (1933-1937), a severe economic emergency was used to justify deficit spending; in the latter New Deal (1937-1945), it was said to be justified in times of recession, but in prosperous times the government ought to run a counterbalancing surplus. Cold War defense spending in the 1950s and during the Vietnam War caused deficits despite the prosperous times; the idea of a balanced budget gradually disappeared as a real goal; for twenty-eight years (1970-1997), under Democratic and Republican presidents, the federal government always ran a deficit, and the national debt grew to $5.4 trillion; most people still gave lip service to the idea that was a bad thing.[8] In the 1980s, many people dropped even that idea. The deficit-debtor mentality began to metastasize, beyond government to corpora-

---

[7]Koyzis, *Political Visions and Illusions*, pp. 59-61.
[8]Figures are taken from *World Almanac and Book of Facts (2005)*, p. 119.

tions and American homes: "leveraging" was a hot 1980s' term: you were underutilizing your assets if you had not mortgaged them to obtain cash, a new car, working capital or your competitor.

What caused this change in attitudes? Many factors were at work. A significant part of this deficit/debt and the accompanying mentality is a result of our political parties' wide-open bidding for voters' support, which reflects our deep divisions over social issues, particularly abortion. A policy of abortion virtually on demand, as decreed in *Roe* v. *Wade,* was a deed effecting a negative fate: national division. A political party always dislikes its opponent, but *Roe* deepened the dislike and seemed to justify ever harsher tactics to deprive opponents of victory. For Republican conservatives alarmed at the 1960s' sexual and moral revolts, at liberals' acquiescence in them, at *Roe* and at liberals' work to retain it, promising large tax cuts to voters to gain votes needed for victory was justified by the need to end the millions of abortions resulting from *Roe.* This link was not crystal clear at first, in 1978 to 1980, as the Republican party embraced the Kemp-Roth proposal for 30 percent tax cut; as it turned out, Ronald Reagan probably could have defeated Jimmy Carter in 1980 without supporting that tax cut (the Iran hostage crisis and runaway inflation were defeating Carter); during the 1980s, however, conservatives decisively broke from their previous view that spending cuts must be enacted to balance any tax cut—and abortion was part of the reason. Once tax-cut supporters made up a sizeable part of the GOP coalition, it was risky to drop this stance.[9]

History is full of unintended consequences. Conservatives expected that the economic growth triggered by tax cuts would generate enough government revenue to offset the tax cuts, and the economy did grow, but a variety of factors— an unexpectedly sharp drop in inflation, a failure to secure needed spending cuts and a bidding war in Congress to see who could offer the most tax cuts or tax breaks—produced sizeable budget deficits during the 1980s that have continued apart from a few years in the 1990s boom. Since fiscal year 1974, the national government's cumulative budget deficit while Republicans were in the White House has been $3.9 trillion. That is not to blame them only: before the 1980 campaign, Republicans often did not use a tax-cut tactic; Congress was often controlled by Democrats when a Republican was president; economic recessions produced larger deficits than any president planned, and so on. Yet the general pattern is clear. Reagan's 25 percent income tax cut, George H. W. Bush's 1988 pledge ("Read my lips. No new taxes.") despite enormous deficits, and

---

[9]See, for example, Michael Barone, *Our Country: The Shaping of America from Roosevelt to Reagan* (New York: Free Press, 1990), pp. 589, 590, 595-96, 612-16.

George W. Bush's 2000 call for a $1.6 trillion tax cut (he got a $1.3 trillion cut, over ten years, in 2001 and another cut of several hundred billion dollars in 2003) show the Republican strategy, made possible by conservatives' anger over liberals' social policies, especially abortion rights. (Others in the Republican co-alition have other reasons for tax cuts, but pro-life support is crucial to the co-alition and, thus, to its tax cuts.)[10]

This fiscal bankruptcy is thus linked to the moral bankruptcy associated with abortion. Abortion is an intensely personal and religious matter. Sexual inter-course is a deed that can be fate-effecting for a woman; marriage is meant to provide her with security and support to help her cope with her disproportion-ate role in reproduction. Father and fetus also have interests and rights. So does the Creator who is forming a life in the womb (Psalm 139:13-16). Our narrowly focused legal system abstracts the woman's individual rights from these other rights and interests; the divine *mishpat* looks at the larger picture, including our democratic system. Loren Samons argues that sex, "especially sex outside of marriage . . . constitutes a powerful expression of one's freedom" and that our democratic stress on rights and choice helps to create an out-of-control sexual economy.[11] Abortion is part of this economy of social irresponsibility, like bor-rowing more than one can ever repay. (Use of *economy* is not meant to mini-mize the moral seriousness of this matter.) In a balanced sexual economy, soci-ety limits sexual intercourse to limit the number of children to what it can raise, lovingly and adequately (leaving aside adoption). Sexual immorality causes problems. The 1960s' sexual revolution partly removed these limits and weak-ened marriage; the reproductive burden fell on women; rather than reinstate limits and strengthen marriage to protect women and children, American society provided women with a legal recourse of abortion. We sought to hide the con-sequences of our overly sexualized society—to hide our moral deficit—and to avoid the social fate our deeds would otherwise cause.

It did not work as planned. Some pregnancies did not produce babies (by 2000 abortion rates had declined but still numbered 1.3 million that year), but *Roe* produced bitter polarization in the nation.[12] Pro-life conservatives enlisted

---

[10]The cumulative deficit while Democrats occupied the Oval Office has been $190 billion. Def-icit numbers are taken from *World Almanac 2005*, p. 119. For George W. Bush's tax cuts and budget deficits, see Allen Shick, "Bush's Budget Problem," in *The George W. Bush Presidency: An Early Assessment*, ed. Fred I. Greenstein (Baltimore: Johns Hopkins University Press, 2003), pp. 78-99. The fiscal year ending in October of an inaugural year is counted as the outgoing president's responsibility; budgetary decisions were made the preceding year.

[11]Loren J. Samons II, *What's Wrong with Democracy? From Athenian Practice to American Wor-ship* (Berkeley: University of California Press, 2004), p. 179.

[12]For the number of abortions from 1992 to 2000, see *World Almanac 2005*, p. 77.

the Republican Party in a decades-long drive to appoint new Supreme Court justices who would overturn *Roe;* pro-choice liberals enlisted Democrats in a campaign to maintain *Roe;* blue-collar Catholics ("Reagan Democrats") began to vote Republican, while a lesser number of pro-choice Republicans also switched parties; as a result, Democrats lost their wide lead in voters' party identification; closer elections plus a more contentious issue contributed to the permanent campaign, in which the stakes were so high that bribing the voters with unsustainable tax cuts or higher spending were seen as acceptable tactics. The result was a national bankruptcy in the making. Can we fail to see the judging activity of God's *mishpat* in all this? Sexual immorality brings abortion brings collective judgment. Nothing in that sequence should surprise a reader of Scripture.

By 2005, investor Warren Buffet charged that the United States was becoming a "sharecropper's society" of debtors sunk so deep they might never escape (low interest rates also encouraged people to take on more debt). The fiscal 2004 federal deficit hit a record $412 billion; national debt surpassed $8 trillion; Americans' personal savings were .6 percent of disposable income; thus, foreigners' purchases of U.S. Treasury bonds finance the government's debt, with "46 percent of it now held by foreigners, especially the governments of Japan and China"; a huge trade deficit (imports exceeded American exports by about $620 billion in 2004) "means that the nation is consuming around $700 billion more than it earns each year and paying for the difference by mortgaging or selling assets"; in 2003, foreign nations' central banks financed 90 percent of America's current account deficit; foreigners—increasingly, their governments more than individuals—own about $2.5 trillion more U.S. assets than Americans own in foreign assets. The U.S. government's unfunded liabilities, "entitlements" promised to its own citizens, reached $43.3 trillion in 2004, a sum of promises that the government probably cannot fulfill.[13]

A rich nation, with the world's strongest military, tends to scorn analysts' concerns about an impending crisis as the nervous worries of Cassandras. Similar alarms were sounded about 1980s debts and deficits, and nothing happened.

---

[13]"A Sharecropper's Society," *Washington Post National Weekly Edition (WPNWE),* August 15-21, 2005, p. 25; "The Budget Boost," *WPNWE,* July 18-24, 2005, p. 25; "Anything but Reform," *WPNWE,* August 1-7, 2005, p. 10; Nouriel Roubini and Brad Setser, "Will the Bretton Woods 2 Regime Unravel Soon? The Risk of a Hard Landing in 2005-2006," pp. 2, 5, 6, 7, (February 2005), <http://www.stern.nyu.edu/globalmacro/BW2-Unraveling-Roubini-Setser.pdf>, accessed November 15, 2005; Kevin Hall [Knight Ridder Newspapers], "Debt Threatens U.S. Economy," *Duluth News Tribune,* November 4, 2005, pp. 1A, 4A (quoted). My use of the *Washington Post's* numbers should not be construed as approval of its editorial recommendations for solving these problems.

And no crisis may occur soon. Yet things do not stay the same. In the 1980s and 1990s, individual foreigners bought U.S. productive assets like stocks and companies; since 2000, foreign governments have bought nonproductive assets, U.S. Treasury bonds, that produce no goods or services but merely finance our budget deficit. An up-and-coming military power with a serious policy dispute with the United States (over Taiwan), China (its central bank) owns hundreds of billions of dollars of U.S. Treasury bonds. According to one knowledgeable observer, "Chinese officials are delighted to be funding ever larger portions of America's budget deficit. They know that if they sat out one U.S. Treasury auction, the U.S. stock markets would tumble." Here, "the borrower is servant to the lender" sounds ominous (Proverbs 22:7). Two concerned analysts, Nouriel Roubini and Brad Setser, warn that this accelerating debt financing by foreign central banks is unsustainable.[14]

Our nonchalance over our shaky situation reflects our disbelief in God's judging activity. The faultiness concealed in our system is being revealed, but we act unconcerned. "The river of time is littered with the ruins of various systems" that also felt secure.[15] Choosing such unsustainable policies, with such disastrous risks, we add to our future's hazards and cast ourselves heedlessly onto the stream of events—controlled by a divine Judge.

God's *Mishpat:* Using Each Political Party to Judge the Other to the Degree of Its Guilt

For the past thirty years, the judgment's political aspect has fallen on the Democratic party more than its rival, for it is deeply implicated in the moral deficit: raising millions from Hollywood moguls, opposing attempts to limit the sexualizing of our culture; allowing itself to be the party of choice for those who ridicule religious moralists and try to keep religion out of public schools and other public institutions. Its natural base of working-class, unionized, immigrant-descended Catholics has been deeply fragmented by abortion. Since *Roe,* it has had two successful presidential candidates: the evangelical, Jimmy Carter, who was personally anti-abortion and who won before the issue took off; and Bill Clinton, who owed his 1992 victory to Ross Perot's third-party candidacy. In presidential contests, Democrats usually lost the socially conservative South. *Roe* reawakened evangelicals who had been politically dormant. These develop-

---

[14]Ann Scott Tyson, "A Gathering Threat?" *WPNWE,* July 25-31, 2005, p. 16; James Fallows, "Countdown to a Meltdown," *The Atlantic Monthly,* July/August 2005, p. 54 n. 12; James McGregor, "Advantage, China," *WPNWE,* August 8-14, 2005, p. 22; Roubini and Setser, "Bretton Woods 2 Regime," p. 7.

[15]Butterfield, "Christianity and History," pp. 54-55.

ments hurt Democrats, who lost control of the House (1994) and the Senate (1980 and 2002), as well as the presidency for five of the eight elections since *Roe*. A Democrat might point to the razor-thin margin in 2000. Bill Clinton's economic and fiscal successes in the late 1990s, with the first budget surpluses in thirty years, put the pro-life, tax-cutting Republican strategy against the ropes. That shows the fragility of that strategy more than it hides Democrats' long, damaging slide since 1973.

Being human and adverse to the concept of divine judgment, Democrats argue that slide resulted from Democratic mistakes or nefarious Republican tactics. In the 2004 campaign, they demonized the Bush administration as a set of evil liars and warned Christians that we must vote Democrat if the poor were to be protected—all the while ignoring the fact that it was their own 1970s' decision to support abortion rights that had endangered their coalition and the political interests of the poor in the first place. Often a moral case can be made against government policies, but a given critic may have lost the moral right to make it. The 2004 election only reinforced Republican control of the White House and Congress, but the few post-election Democratic pangs of conviction did not lead to repentance.

Yet the tables will turn, and the divine sifting with its negative consequences that falls on all human systems and parties and nations will fall on the other side, too. A Democrat will return to the White House and Democratic control to Congress. The growing national insolvency will inevitably effect an electoral fate on Republicans. They have been the instruments of God for punishing our moral deficit with a fiscal one, but God does not hold his instruments guiltless. He judges them, too, as the Old Testament tells us.[16] A highly commendable goal of ending millions of abortions does not deliver a party from the consequences of an unsustainable fiscal deficit. We are not talking about moral equivalence: ending lives is far worse than wasting dollars; only a divine Judge can make the moral calculations and does. God's judgments are the norm, like a spring rain, and Republicans will not be exempt if they fail to shelter under the one umbrella, the Son of Man and his path. Being human and adverse to the idea of divine judgment, Republicans will find some other reason for their political problems, will continue to call the Democrats the deficit spenders after that charge no longer makes much sense and will refuse to see God's hand in it. It may be a rule of democracy that parties do not repent. Ironically, this election-year battling may be a vain exercise. The future of *Roe* is in the Supreme Court's hands,

---

[16]See, e.g., the Lord's use of Assyria to judge Israel and his subsequent judgment on Assyria in Isaiah 10:5-19.

and *stare decisis* may be Latin for "Supreme Courts don't repent."[17]

Other issues besides debts and deficits may be the occasion or cause of God's judgment. We have simplified matters by focusing on abortion and fiscal issues. That has allowed us to suggest how God's judgment falls on both parties (independents are not exempt either).

Does the Reality of God's Judgments Give Us Hints on What Political Stand to Take?

This look at history as the domain of a judging God is not a call to abstain from public affairs, close our doors and escape to our quiet time. An ambassador's job is not private. She does not have to accept the host government's views to make it a public one. How can the doctrine of divine judgment inform us on our proper role? We have a few hints.

First, we are freed from the largely static, philosophical, worldview approach to politics that we encountered in the biotech debate. Anachronistically, that focuses on a fixed creation system; it may add the Son of Man's redeeming work, but this is defined as merely a restoration of creation after the Fall and, thus, is shoehorned back into the system. Believers are then charged with restoring the fallen system.[18] Missing here is the dynamic historical process, in which the meaning of supposedly fixed concepts like capitalism or democracy is constantly changing. Missing is God's sifting out: he tests environmental stewardship even though its goals might be seen as noble by definition and thus exempt from his testing, in a worldview concept. The Son of Man's trajectory has already constituted history's meaning; we cannot act politically apart from it or return to a creation system that existed before it. We are naive if we engage in politics while ignoring God's ongoing *mishpat*. Our ally in the big-tent coalition may not only have a mistaken syllogism or concept that we can safely distance ourselves from but also may be under God's judgment, and that may be hazardous to us, too.

Second, it can free us from the left, center and right. As Koyzis reminds us, the ideologies of liberalism, democracy (as creed) and conservatism that drive these political movements are deeply idolatrous and thus dangerous for believers. They claim to provide a meaning to history. A focus on the Son of Man as

---

[17]The well-known *First Things* issue on "The End of Democracy? The Judicial Usurpation of Politics" (November 1996) sounded a strong, prophetic note; however, the warning was of a people rising up in an eighteenth-century type of revolution, not of divine judgment.

[18]After his fine analysis of the idolatrous ideologies and their alteration by historical processes, Koyzis turns to this ahistorical worldview approach; Koyzis, *Political Visions and Illusions*, pp. 183-93.

history's meaning pushes us quickly to confront them. A philosophical world-view approach can seem compatible with their ideas. To free ourselves from their dangerous embrace, nothing works quicker than a warning of judgment! Part of their idolatry is to make Christ a means to some other end. The left makes him a means to social justice and peace; the center, a means to help democracy function by maintaining morality despite individualism; the right, a means to conserve traditions or to maintain morality despite markets' reward for self-interest. He is the one true End, the Omega.

Third, it can free us from the democratic dogma that only we, the citizens, can avert all sorts of disasters by our political participation. The fact that God is judging in order to accomplish his purposes does not free us from our duties as citizens but from both parties' intimidating demands: support all our policies and candidates or else our opponents will win and bring disaster. Nonsense, believers can reply: to support what will bring God's judgment on us and on you makes no sense; he can cause you to triumph if you drop the objectionable policies and candidates, or your opponents' triumph may be his will to which we must submit—but, in any case, we will trust a sovereign God.

Fourth, it can free us from the tempting illusion that we, the church, are exempt from judgment. Peter warns us, "For it is time for judgment to begin with the family of God" (1 Peter 4:17). Christ's followers cannot acquiesce in making him merely a means without discovering that judgment for idolatry will begin with them. We can only briefly suggest how such judgments might look. Liberal Catholics and evangelicals participate in a movement that is becoming more toxically anti-Christian, as the left reacts against a perceived Christian right. To be opposed to the religious right becomes a key identifying mark of a liberal. If, in order to fit into this movement, they are silent on Christ's exclusive truth claims or his triumph, then they drift from orthodoxy. Anachronistically, they fix the Son of Man perpetually in the descent stage of his trajectory, always treading dusty Galilean roads and ministering to the poor, always trying to prove he is the best means to social justice and peace and never ascended, exalted or returning in triumph. True, the believer must now follow this same dusty path, but the triumph at its end cannot be surrendered. Centrist believers who conform to the stress on pluralist discourse and present the Christian tradition as one of many in the conversation may experience a similar drift, as they implicitly deny the Son of Man's triumph is ultimately political and threatens the democracy that refuses to decrease as he increases.

Theological drift is the most serious consequence. Yet it is not absent on the right either. Numerically, more Catholics and evangelicals join the Republican coalition. Judgment on it will be more widespread in the church, so we devote more attention to this position. These believers are in danger of compromising to adjust to their allies' views. Christ merely ministers to the individual's and the family's spiritual, subjective and emotional needs, while secular neo-conservatives do the heavy lifting in the important, objective realms of economics and foreign policy. We can suggest a judgment on this compromise: the church's increasing emphasis on marketing and market share, which subtly distorts its theology to meet popular demands, may result from an inability to maintain some critical distance from free-market capitalism, and that results from this alliance with a secular coalition that sees no need for critical distance.[19] To maintain a critical distance is not to be a Marxist. It is simply to assert that not every problem—certainly, not the basic human need for salvation from judgment—is a nail that the marketing hammer can solve. Paul's words about "not peddl[ing] the word of God for protest" (2 Corinthians 2:17) have become unintelligible to us, as if Paul heard some Marxist orator on a Corinth street corner. In theological terms, this is a conservative point that David Wells makes: "Christianity cannot be bought. . . . It is never God who is owned. . . . Christianity is not up for sale . . . the Church is not its retailing outlet. Its preachers are not its peddlers, and those who are Christians are not its consumers. It cannot legitimately be had as a bargain though the marketplace is full of bargain hunters."[20]

The Debate over the September 11 Tragedy: Reprise

If we take God's judgments seriously, one hopes we will never have a repeat of the post-September 11 fiasco. In Os Guinness's analysis, Falwell's and Robinson's "plain spoken, refreshingly politically incorrect, and"—given the Old Testament—"theologically plausible" claim of divine judgment was retracted "in a most unprophetic turn of events . . . with an abject apology—before its weight and possible correctness could be assessed."[21] Or, we might add, before it could be amended to accord with Scripture. Never again should we tolerate this situation: an event occurs that looks much like a judgment; yet the church is agnostic about judgment because its philosophical apologetic does not recognize that specific events can have crucial meanings; talk of judgment comes hastily on a television talk show from an evangelicalism that is market-oriented and politicized; an evangelical president silences these political allies, not for scriptural or other inaccuracies but because it is "inappropriate" to identify a divine Actor

---

[19] Os Guinness recommends a critical distance in *Prophetic Untimeliness,* pp. 65-66, 98.
[20] David F. Wells indicts this marketing frenzy in *Above All Earthly Pow'rs: Christ in a Postmodern World* (Grand Rapids: Eerdmans, 2005), pp. 308-9. See also Guinness, *Prophetic Untimeliness,* pp. 64-66.
[21] Guinness, *Prophetic Untimeliness,* p. 10.

behind the event who might be judging national sins; the would-be prophets retreat from what they see as a politically and economically (not biblically) untenable position; liberal evangelicals distance themselves from these conservatives and from Christ's exclusive truth claims in order to make common cause with their allies and with a relativistic, pluralistic, postmodern democratic sensibility.[22]

If a similar event occurs in the future, we must recognize divine judgment as a valid category of events in history; we must be cautious and accurate—not partisan or ill-informed—in assigning any event to that category; we must not back down from our diagnosis of divine judgment, certainly not for political or entrepreneurial reasons; and we must never surrender the truth and triumph of the Son of Man, which are not ours to surrender. What does it matter if the political rulers or the discourse gatekeepers find this offensive? We American Christians, of all political persuasions, are often vulnerable to a belief that America will prove an exception, vulnerable to a hope that somehow we can elect a Sanhedrin that will accept Christ, or Christ as we redefine him. That acceptance would deliver us from the Son of Man's path of obedient suffering. Scripture gives us no reason to think that will occur but encourages us to surrender our majoritarian dreams. We warn our nation that September 11 was *mishpat:* a boulder in our nation's path that forces us to choose either to humble ourselves under God's hand or to exalt ourselves by denying God could be judging us.

The Trajectory of the Son of Man: Reprise and Return

As we saw in Daniel, the series of judgments is not an endless, mindless pattern. It progresses toward a goal, "a kingdom that will never be destroyed" (Daniel 2:44). Using a similar principle, we see that the series of judgments we have suggested—Republicans used to judge Democrats, then the latter used to judge the former—is not an eternal tit-for-tat. Like all of history, A.D., these events lead toward Christ's return. Think of this as a chain of events. We do not know how many links are in the chain. Writers on prophecy and current events have consistently underestimated the chain's length and made erroneous predictions accordingly. Yet that does not mean there is no chain or that events as links are unimportant. It simply means we do not know the number of links.

Similarly, we do not know what functions the events of America's history perform in this chain or where they are located on it. Possibly the testing of our

---

[22]The events surrounding the Falwell-Robertson broadcast are most fully explored in Bruce Lincoln, *Holy Terrors: Thinking About Religion After September 11* (Chicago: University of Chicago Press, 2003), pp. 36-50; however, I do not agree with his general analysis of it.

free-market democracy (what Fukuyama called history's Last Man) must occur, and it must fail the test, before the Son of Man's return. Perhaps the Last Man must fall before the Son of Man returns. Perhaps not. Perhaps an entirely new political and economic system must arise from the residue of democracy. Perhaps democracy will repent and reform, temporarily. Our ignorance on these details does not change our fundamental message to our American democracy: it must decrease and he must increase, sooner or later. It can choose voluntarily to decrease by exalting him as history's meaning and thus secure for itself decades of humble blessings as the best current system for making mundane decisions. Or it can rebel and be forced to decrease as its self-referential, self-idolizing discourse leads it to exalt itself as history's goal and humanity's last, best hope and leads to its fiscal and moral bankruptcy. Either way, it decreases. In warning it of that truth, we are not unpatriotic, but, paradoxically, we "seek the peace and prosperity of the city" (Jeremiah 29:7). We also emphasize for individuals and the nation that the gospel of the Son of Man is not a "universal philosophical sun" that "neither rises nor sets and is without time and without history." No, it is "always shining *just for this present time*" and its present light "always carries with it (even for us!) the threat of denial and withdrawal."[23] At some point, unknown to us now, we reach the chain's end.

What guarantees that is the historical event of the Son of Man—beaten, bleeding, mocked and headed for a criminal's death on a cross, as an innocent victim obedient to God the Father—standing before a representative set of this world's rulers. The interpretation of the event is that here is God's chosen system of rule and authority, here is the one system that has passed his test, his sifting-out *mishpat,* and has been found to be righteous. All others will eventually fail that test. So will democracy. While rule by the people has many valid moral claims to make, that it is morally superior to tyranny or monarchy or aristocracy, it cannot claim that it is morally superior to rule by the heaven-descended, cross-suffering, heaven-exalted, returning Son of Man. That God chooses the very best, not second best, for his world should come as good news. Turn the coin over and see salvation on the other side.

---

[23]Hans Urs von Balthasar, *A Theology of History* (New York: Sheed and Ward, 1963), p. 69.

Epilogue

We find that Os Guinness's hope that "[a] rediscovery of the hard and the unpopular themes of the gospel" will lead to something promising is true. We are liberated. We need not be modernist, philosophical, worldview thinkers who prove nonbelievers into the kingdom while we stand safely behind our axioms and syllogisms. In fact, we offer a testimony of judgment and salvation that exposes us to risk and that cannot be proved at present but must await Christ's final triumph for its final proof. We need no longer be majoritarian public-policy campaigners who use the founders' (possible) Christian beliefs and evangelicalism's numerical success to argue that we, a Christian majority, deserve to rule the nation and to be no longer at risk due to secularizers' policies. In fact, our warnings of judgment, in obedience to our call as disciples, will deprive us of majority status if we ever have enjoyed it. We will have to risk much as faithful witnesses to the Son of Man's triumph, which is also political and, therefore, unpopular.

We need not be liberals either, who present the Son of Man as a risk-free answer to what our audience wants—a means to social justice and world peace who brings no claims or purposes of his own. In fact, he has exclusive claims, and they mean risk for us. We need not be marketers maximizing our market share, safe behind our consumer culture's tolerance of the marketing of anything that appeals to consumers' desires. In fact, testifying to judgment frees us from market share and tolerance.

We need not turn to postmodernism, with its claim that we offer only one reading of reality, to rescue faith from impersonal axioms, campaign principles or marketing plans. In fact, the testifier's role is intensely personal, but the truth of his or her testimony is crucial—the difference between honor and dishonor, righteousness and wickedness. Our relationship to the testifying Christ is intensely personal, and our risk in testifying with him leads to our deepening trust in him as his testimony proves true in the ongoing stream of historical events. That is what we offer our generation—not an impersonal but objective worldview or a personal but relativistic reading but a trustworthy Savior from judgment.

Subject and Name Index

216

Scripture Index